The Conversion Experience in America

THE
CONVERSION
EXPERIENCE
IN AMERICA

A Sourcebook on
Religious Conversion Autobiography

JAMES CRAIG HOLTE

GP

GREENWOOD PRESS
New York • Westport, Connecticut • London

Library of Congress Cataloging-in-Publication Data

Holte, James Craig.
    The conversion experience in America : a sourcebook on religious
conversion autobiography / James Craig Holte.
      p. cm.
    Includes bibliographical references and index.
    ISBN 0–313–26680–8 (alk. paper)
    1. Converts—United States—Biography.   I. Title.
BV4930.H65   1992
291.4'2—dc20   91–32173

British Library Cataloguing in Publication Data is available.

Library of Congress Catalog Card Number: 91–32173
ISBN: 0–313–26680–8

First published in 1992

Greenwood Press, 88 Post Road West, Westport, CT 06881
An imprint of Greenwood Publishing Group, Inc.

Printed in the United States of America

The paper used in this book complies with the
Permanent Paper Standard issued by the National
Information Standards Organization (Z39.48–1984).

10 9 8 7 6 5 4 3 2 1

Copyright Acknowledgment

Grateful acknowledgment is given for material appearing in chapters 3, 7, 18,
and 27 that originally appeared in different form in James Holte, *The Ethnic I: A
Sourcebook for the Study of Ethnic-American Autobiography*, Westport, Conn.:
Greenwood Press, 1988.

Contents

Preface

The Conversion Experience in America is intended as an original sourcebook for the study of American religious conversion narratives. America is rich in both conversions and autobiographies; since the first European settlers arrived, Americans have been recording their experiences in the new land, and many of these experiences involve radical transformations. Whether writing for their children, to evangelize, or to better understand their own experiences, American religious autobiographers have left an elaborate record of religious conversions in America.

No single volume could begin to document the thousands of narratives written in America over the past five centuries. This book presents biographical, bibliographic, and critical commentary on thirty significant writers of American conversion narratives. It is an introduction to the study of the subject of American conversion narratives in general and to the works of these specific writers in particular.

Although most conversion narratives follow a predictable three-part structure—early sinful life, the conversion experience, life and works after conversion—each writer adapts that pattern to the particular circumstances of his or her own experience. In writing about the transformations of their lives, these writers have left a record of the transformation of American culture as well. Thus the narratives of such colonial writers as Thomas Shepard, Jonathan Edwards, Mary Rowlandson, and John Woolman record the search for identity and order in a frontier society. The autobiographies of such nineteenth-century women writers as Rebecca Cox Jackson, Carry Nation, and Ann Eliza Young, on the other hand, demonstrate a dissatisfaction with patriarchal authority and a search for nontraditional modes of religious expression. The conversion narratives of such twentieth-century writers as Alexander Irvine, John Cogley, and Dorothy Day record the rise of the social gospel movement, whereas the autobiographies of Jim Bakker, Jerry Falwell, and Pat Robertson chronicle the rise of televangelism. Finally, the narratives of such writers as Olaudah Equiano, Frederick Douglass, Eldridge Cleaver, Black Elk, Malcolm X, and Piri Thomas provide insights into the experiences of those who lived outside the mainstream of American culture. Thus *The Conversion Experience in America* provides insights into the lives and works of thirty men and women who helped to shape the religious, social, and cultural history of the United States as well as an overview of the contexts for those lives and works. One of the basic insights that emerges from the study of these narratives is the diversity of American conversion experiences: Not all conversions are alike.

No scholarly work is created alone. I express my appreciation to my own teachers, especially Howard Schless, Bob Arner, and Wayne Miller, who taught me to try to ask intelligent questions. I also thank the department of English and the College of Arts and Sciences at East Carolina University for released time and support to work on this project. Keats Sparrow, Bertie Fearing, Carolyn Sutton, and Ruth Olrogge have been especially helpful.

Finally, this book is dedicated to my parents, who kept the faith; to Gwyn, who lives it; and to Molly, who is enough to make one believe.

Introduction: Autobiography and Conversion

And it came to pass, that, as I made my journey, and was come nigh
unto Damascus about noon, suddenly there shown from heaven a great
light round about me. And I fell unto the ground, and heard a voice
saying unto me, Saul, Saul, why persecutest thou me? And I answered,
Who art thou, Lord?—Acts 22: 6–8, King James version

Since Paul underwent his dramatic conversion on the road to Damascus,
Christians have been evangelizing in the first person, and accounts of conversion are far older than Christianity. The Genesis account of the transformation of Abram into Abraham, for example, records the conversion at
the beginning of the Judeo-Christian tradition, and the Exodus account of
the illumination of Moses at Mount Horeb chronicles the conversion at the
central point in the history of the Israelites. One could easily chart the
history of Christianity by examining conversion narratives. The New Testament descriptions of the conversions of Paul, Timothy, Nicodemus, and
Zacchaeus provide a rich variety of conversion experiences at the beginning
of the Christian era, and the autobiographies of Augustine, Ignatius of
Loyola, and Teresa of Avila illustrate the history of the Christian church
before the Reformation. The narratives of George Fox, John Bunyan, and
John Wesley record the development of a Reformed Protestant perspective.
And the works of such writers as Thomas Merton, Dorothy Day, and
Charles Colson illustrate the diversity of contemporary American Chris-
tianity.

Although conversion is a central part of the Christian experience, not all conversion experiences take place within a Christian context. In fact, many of the world's great religions were profoundly influenced by conversions. The mystery religions in the Greek and Roman world, for example, provided believers with initiation rituals that simulated and encouraged conversion behaviors. The transformation of Gautama into the Buddha is a conversion that transformed beliefs and behaviors throughout half the world, and the results of the conversion or calling of Muhammad in the Arabian peninsula are still being felt today.

These narratives record experiences that are profoundly personal, yet grounded in the particular cultures in which the writers lived. As a result, all conversion narratives are similar, yet different.

Within the past several decades, both popular and scholarly interest in the conversion experience have increased. Scholars in such fields as psychology, literature, history, and religion have undertaken a reexamination of the subject, using various methodologies. What has emerged from the study of such diverse subjects as Puritan autobiographies, evangelical sermons, cult indoctrinations, brainwashing, televangelism, faith healing, developmental psychology, and the sociology of religion is a model of the conversion process. According to Chana Ullman, in *The Transformed Self: The Psychology of Religious Conversion* (New York: Plenum, 1989); Walter Conn, in *Christian Conversion: A Developmental Interpretation of Autonomy and Surrender* (New York: Paulist, 1986); and Joe Edward Barnhart and Mary Ann Barnhart, in *The New Birth: A Naturalistic View of Religious Conversion* (Macon, Ga.: Mercer University Press, 1981), conversion often is an abrupt, intense religious experience that takes place within the context of a longer process of transformation. Early studies of conversion, drawing on the recorded experiences of converts like the apostle Paul and evangelist Charles Finney, emphasized the abruptness of the change and such physical and emotional manifestations as visions and voices. More recent scholarship has emphasized the long-term process of conversion, of which the dramatic moment is one aspect. Barnhart and Barnhart, for example, see the born-again experience as a normal psychological, sociological, and cultural maturation process; they assert that "every socialized individual has been twice-born" (p. 48). Conn, similarly, sees conversion as having moral, affective, cognitive, and religious aspects. And Ullman defines conversion as a search for stability. Writers who emphasize the larger process of conversion point to the conversions of Augustine and Thomas Merton as examples.

Perhaps one of the best examples of a thorough examination of the conversion experience using a variety of new critical approaches is Alan F. Segal's *Paul the Convert: The Apostolate and Apostasy of Saul the Pharisee* (New Haven, Conn.: Yale University Press, 1990). Segal studies Paul's conversion within the context of first-century Jewish culture and early Christian history. Using New Testament scholarship, literary criticism, and psychological, sociological, and theological approaches, Segal not only provides an understanding of the context and process of Paul's experience, but also establishes a multidisciplinary method of looking at the conversion process itself.

Conversion has become a topic of popular interest as well. The growing popularity of such groups as the Unification Church, the International Society of Krishna Consciousness, and the New Age movement has made some people see conversion as a form of psychological manipulation or brainwashing. In addition, the increasing popularity and publicity of evangelical, fundamentalist Christianity, with its emphasis on the born-again experience, has made people aware of the significance of conversion within traditional Christianity. Finally, the well-publicized conversions of such people as Charles Colson and Eldridge Cleaver have helped to create a popular interest in the subject.

Some of the most significant writing about conversions has been produced by men and women who have experienced conversion themselves, and conversion narratives are plentiful. Lewis Kaplin, in *A Bibliography of American Autobiographies* (Madison: University of Wisconsin Press, 1961), lists more than 6,000 published American autobiographies, and many of these are spiritual narratives. Perhaps the foundation for all American personal writing can be found in the spiritual narratives of the Puritans, Pilgrims, and Quakers. These writings established a tradition of recording personal religious experience that has grown more popular throughout American history. The writers of these colonial spiritual narratives did not create brand-new literary forms. Rather, as Daniel Shea has noted in his excellent study, *Spiritual Autobiography in Early America* (Princeton, N.J.: Princeton University Press, 1968):

The explicit arguments of early spiritual narratives were highly conventional. A Puritan sought to assemble the evidence for divine favoritism toward him, and many Quaker journals recount the protracted search of the narrator for truth, which he inevitably finds in the doctrine of the Society of Friends. (p. ix)

These narrative patterns were modeled after older European ones, and many contemporary spiritual narratives reflect the influence of previous writers. A number of Puritan narratives, for example, were written to establish the author's sanctification, so that he or she could be accepted as a member of the local Congregational community. These records tended to follow the steps defined by the European Reformed theologians who emphasized the depravity of man, the power of God, and the irresistible nature of grace. As a result, Puritan spiritual narratives stressed these particular elements of the conversion process, and such latter-day Protestant writers as Jerry Falwell and Charles Colson use the same pattern. Thomas Merton, on the other hand, drew on Augustine's *Confessions* as a model for his autobiography, and as a result, Merton's narrative emphasizes lengthy preparation and searching for God.

Conversion narratives, like other narratives, are controlled by conventions. A conversion is either a turning from or a turning toward, and this turning most often has a three-part structure: life before the conversion, the conversion experience itself, and life after the conversion. Conventions dictate that a writer of a conversion narrative treat all three elements, but different religious traditions emphasize different elements. The traditional Puritan narrative, for example, emphasizes the sinfulness of the person before conversion and the physical manifestations of the conversion experience itself, since the purpose of the narrative is to convince others of the legitimacy of the experience. Many Pentecostal writers, on the other hand, because of the importance they place on the gifts of the Holy Spirit, emphasize such postconversion events as spiritual healing and speaking in tongues in their autobiographies. In practice, conversion narratives are as varied as converts; some stress sin, some the dramatic moment, and some the life and work of the converted. Despite the apparent differences among narratives, as Albert E. Stone has observed in *Autobiographical Occasions and Original Acts* (Philadelphia: University of Pennsylvania Press, 1982), "spiritual autobiography in America, as in the rest of Christendom, discovers and communicates an individual's 'search for God in time and memory' " (p. 59).

All autobiography is a search. In looking back on and then re-creating their lives, autobiographers search for and identify essential times and patterns in their lives. Working within the established framework of an established literary genre, autobiographers use textual forms, functions, materials, intentions, and expectations to make meaning out of the complexity of their lives, or, as Henry Adams said of the purpose of his EDUCATION, to "run order through chaos." In *The Art of Life: Studies in American Autobiographical Literature* (Austin: University of Texas Press, 1977), M. K. Blasing notes that autobiographers create "a temporary center around which the accumulated facts of history may be organized" (p. xxiv). Different types of autobiographies present different temporary centers. Success narratives, for example, are structured around what Benjamin Franklin called a "rise from poverty and obscurity to some degree of celebrity in the world." Many ethnic autobiographies are organized around the movement of the author from outsider to insider. And in most conversion narratives, the temporary center is the experience of transformation.

Autobiography is bound by both literary choices and cultural experience. As Stephen Butterfield observed in *Black Autobiography in America* (Amherst: University of Massachusetts Press, 1974),

The genre of autobiography lives in the two worlds of history and literature, objective fact and subjective awareness.... In response to a particular historical period, the autobiographer examines, interprets, and creates the importance of his life. He may also affect history by leaving the work behind as a model for others. (p. 1)

Autobiographies, therefore, are significant social documents that reveal as much about a culture at a specific time as they do about the men and women who created them.

There also is a similarity among autobiographies. As Susanna Egan points out in *Patterns of Experience in Autobiography* (Chapel Hill: University of North Carolina Press, 1984),

The theme that any autobiographer chooses provides a shape for his narrative. It also provides a meaning. The formula of anticipation, recognition, and fulfillment is matched by the formula for separation, initiation, and return borrowed from rites of passage and described by Vladimir Propp as part of the total action of every folktale. Joseph Campbell calls the formula the "nuclear unit of the monomyth." (p. 21)

The autobiographer adapts this basic formula to his or her specific experiences, and it is easy to see the relation between the outlines of the conversion experience—preconversion sinfulness, conversion, and acts of the converted—and the basic narrative formula—anticipation, recognition, and fulfillment.

American conversion narratives in fact provide a running commentary on the development of religion in America. The autobiographies of Thomas Shepard, John Woolman, and Jonathan Edwards record the experiences and concerns of men who were influential in the establishment and preservation of Puritan and Quaker ideals. In addition, Edwards' reflections on conversion and Woolman's observations on the evolving nature of his religious ideals establish the framework for examining the dramatic moment in the process of conversion. Two other early autobiographers, Olaudah Equiano and Mary Rowlandson, provide valuable insights into the religious perceptions of colonial women and blacks.

During the nineteenth century, there were major transformations in American religions as Anglican, Presbyterian, and Congregational authority gave way to developing Baptist, Methodist, Catholic, Holiness, and other communities. In fact, a number of religious historians see much of the nineteenth-century religious experience in the United States as a reform movement grounded in millennial expectations. The autobiographies of Lyman Beecher and Charles Finney clearly establish the orthodox foundations of such a movement, and the narratives of William Miller, Daniel Alexander Payne, Rebecca Cox Jackson, Frederick Douglass, and Carry Nation trace the development of both millennialism and reform.

During the twentieth century, religion in America has continued to undergo major transformations, and as would be expected, the spiritual narratives written in this century reflect those transformations. The autobiographies of Thomas Merton and Dorothy Day, for example, describe the contemplative and social activist strands of American Catholicism, and the conversion narratives of Jerry Falwell and Pat Robertson provide insights into contemporary American fundamentalism and televangelism. The autobiographies of Piri Thomas, Malcolm X, and Charles Colson are popular examples of prison narratives, and the narratives of Alan Watts and Peter Jenkins reflect the cultural uncertainties of the 1960s and 1970s.

This book is not a history of religion in America; other scholars have undertaken that task with great diligence and success. Nor is it an anthology of the converted. To hear the voices of those who wrote these and other conversion narratives, readers need to go to the sources themselves. This work is intended as an introduction to and overview of American conversion narratives. The men and women from all races and classes who wrote of their conversion experiences have left records of the most dramatic and determinative experiences of their lives. These records also preserve the impact of these experiences on their lives and their country.

Finally, I have made no judgment as to the authenticity of the experiences described in the following autobiographies. I leave that judgment to the consciences of the autobiographers and the charitable good sense of the readers.

The
Conversion Experience
in America

1 • JIM BAKKER (1940–   )

Move That Mountain!

BIOGRAPHY

Jim Bakker was born in Muskegon, Michigan, on January 2, 1940. He grew up in a working-class family; his father, Raleigh Bakker, was a tool and die maker who provided the necessities for his family. Bakker was an indifferent student until he entered junior high school, where he developed an interest in speech, communications, and journalism. In high school, Bakker was a popular student, often serving as emcee for school dances. In 1958, Bakker ran over a three-year-old boy while driving his father's 1952 Cadillac. At first, Bakker thought that he had killed the child, but after the child recovered, Bakker dedicated his life to Jesus.

After his graduation from high school, Bakker attended North Central Bible College in Minneapolis. During his second year at North Central, Bakker married fellow Bible college student Tammy Faye LaValley. They both left school and began careers as evangelists. After working as a traveling revivalist in North Carolina for several years, Bakker was ordained an Assemblies of God minister in 1964, and the next year joined Pat Robertson at the Christian Broadcast Network (CBN) in Portsmouth, Virginia. At CBN, Bakker worked with almost every aspect of the pioneering Christian television ministry. He produced, directed, and starred in the "Jim and Tammy Show," a program for children, he helped to establish the 700 Club, and he worked both on and off camera for fund-raising and interview programming. In 1973, he left Robertson's organization to cofound the Trinity Broadcasting Network in California with Paul Crouch.

In 1974, Bakker left California and founded the PTL (Praise the Lord) Club in Charlotte, North Carolina. Bakker also became president of the Heritage Academy in Fort Mill, South Carolina, and president and chairman of the Heritage Village Church and Missionary Fellowship of Charlotte. After establishing his school and church, Bakker began developing the PTL Inspirational Network, a religious television network using the developing computer, fiber-optic, and satellite techniques. At the same time, he was building Heritage USA, a Christian theme park and amusement center.

By the mid–1980s, Bakker had become one of the most prominent tele-vangelists in the United States. In 1987, however, he was forced to resign from PTL because of a sex scandal involving former church secretary Jessica Hahn. After Bakker's departure, PTL and Heritage Ministries failed, and Bakker was indicted on twenty-four counts of fraud and conspiracy by a federal grand jury. After a sensational trial, Bakker was convicted on all counts in October 1989. Shortly thereafter he was sentenced to more than forty years in federal prison and immediately began to serve his sentence. In 1991 his sentence was reduced to fifteen years.

THE AUTOBIOGRAPHY

Jim Bakker wrote *Move That Mountain!* in 1976, just as he began to achieve success with PTL and Heritage Ministries in Charlotte. Although Bakker's autobiography contains the elements found in traditional religious narratives—life of sin, conversion experience, and life of grace and Christian deeds—the narrative owes more to Benjamin Franklin and Horatio Alger than it does to Paul or Augustine. *Move That Mountain!* is primarily a narrative of success. In describing his life and ministries, Bakker and coau-thor Robert Paul Lamb adopt the familiar narrative structure of the rise of the young man from the provinces to a position of wealth and success in society. For Bakker, writing in 1976, wealth and success seemed at hand in Heritage USA.

In the opening chapter of his autobiography, Bakker describes his life before his conversion. Although Bakker uses this section of his narrative to establish his need for conversion by listing his youthful sins—smoking and skipping Sunday school—he also begins to develop two major themes of his autobiography, his attraction to the media and his desire for success. For Bakker, the embarrassment of his family's poverty and his own success as a school photographer and disc jockey are more important than his lack of grace. Bakker writes that his life changed on a Sunday night in December 1958, when he slipped out of church to cruise around Muskegon in his father's 1952 Cadillac. While he was listening to Fats Domino sing "Blue-berry Hill" on the radio, Bakker ran over a small child. He writes,

To me, the little boy was already dead. And so was I. The fun-loving Jim Bakker, the life-of-the-party, the boy who loved the spotlight was dead.

My world had crashed on me just as I feared it would. For the first time in my life, I surrendered to God. He was my only hope now. (p. 11)

Jimmy Summerfield, the boy Bakker had hit, was, like Bakker, a member of the Central Assembly of God Church. As soon as news of the accident reached the church members, they gathered, "asking God for an outright miracle of healing." Bakker asserts that there were two miracles: Jimmy Summerfield quickly recovered and Jim Bakker turned to God. After his decision to accept Christ, Bakker felt a call to preach the gospel, and made plans to attend North Central Bible College in Minneapolis, a "good full-gospel Bible school with solid Biblical teaching" (p. 16).

Bakker attended college for less than two years, leaving to marry Tammy LaValley, a fellow Bible college student. Bakker writes that he was advised to wait and finish school before marrying, but he believed that "God had brought us together and we were destined to be married" (p. 23). After their marriage, Jim and Tammy Bakker became youth ministers at the Minneapolis Evangelistic Auditorium, where Bakker learned that the key to success as an evangelist was results; theory or theology was not essential.

Bakker describes the beginnings of his ministry in a chapter titled "On the Road for Jesus." The Bakkers left Minneapolis for a series of revivals in North Carolina. As Bakker describes the life of a traveling evangelist, he also begins to provide an account of the gifts he and his wife received. What emerges is a pattern of works for the Lord leading to gifts from the Lord's followers. One revival leads to diamond rings and another brings a mobile home, "a twenty-eight-foot Holiday Rambler with a complete bedroom, bath, kitchen and living room with full-sized furniture" (p. 43).

In writing about his move from traveling evangelist to televangelist, Bakker recalls that he asked himself late one night, "Why can't Christians have a talk show too?" (p. 51). Bakker recognized the potential of television as a tool for evangelism, and in 1965, he joined Pat Robertson's television team at CBN. The central sections of Bakker's autobiography chronicle his rise in the world of Christian television, beginning with his arrival at CBN and ending with his establishment of the PTL Club in Charlotte. Here Bakker follows the format of the narrative of success as he recounts how he and his wife began as cohosts of a children's program and prospered, both professionally and financially, to such an extent that he was able to establish his own Christian media and entertainment complex.

In the seven chapters that he devotes to his work with Pat Robertson at CBN, Bakker not only equates professional success with financial success— at one point he writes proudly that he and Tammy were able to move from an efficiency apartment to an expensive penthouse apartment—but also credits the Holy Spirit with his success. Bakker writes:

From the moment I stepped before a television camera at CBN, God began to anoint me to raise money for Christian television. I realized it the night I wept during the first "700 Club" telethon. Many times since then, God similarly anointed me. (p. 63)

In his description of his work with CBN, Bakker provides several examples of his being anointed with weepings as he successfully raised money for the network. Each time CBN is faced with a dramatic financial crisis, and each time Bakker is moved to make a dramatic and emotional television appeal for money.

In 1973, Bakker left CBN to join Paul Crouch in California in establishing a second Christian television network, TBN, or Trinity Broadcasting Network. He writes that while working in California, he was invited to Charlotte to participate in a Christian telethon. While in Charlotte, he was told by the Lord to move his ministry there, and in the final sections of his autobiography, Bakker describes the establishment of the PTL Television Network and Heritage USA. These sections are similar to those that treat CBN and TBN; Bakker describes his call, lists the obstacles he faced, and then presents testimony of how the Lord worked through him to raise money to build a television network. He ends his autobiography with a vision of the second coming, writing,

I had always believed that Christian television would be the tool to usher in the triumphant return of the Lord Jesus Christ. And with satellite communications, who knows?

God's presence seemed to descend on the center's property as the sun slowly inched down. . . . I had hope. A strong wave of hope just seemed to bathe me. . . . We would go forward until Jesus comes. (p. 183)

CRITICISM

An extraordinary amount of information about Jim Bakker is available. Most of it covers Bakker's problems with a sexual incident involving church secretary Jessica Hahn, his resignation from PTL, his attempted comeback, and, finally, his federal fraud trial and conviction. Headlines such as "God and Money; Sex Scandal, Greed, and Lust for Power Split the TV Preaching World" (*Newsweek*, 6 April 1987) and "Praise the Lord and Pass the Loot" (*The Economist*, 16 May 1987) are good indications of the nature of the media response to Bakker's moral, financial, and legal problems. The best study of Bakker and his position within the televangelism industry remains Jeffrey K. Hadden and Charles E. Swann's *Prime Time Preachers* (Reading, Mass.: Addison-Wesley, 1981). Little has been written about Bakker's own writing—*Move That Mountain!*, *Big Three Mountain Movers*, *Survival: Unite to Live*, and *You Can Make It*—or his theological and evangelical beliefs. Bakker's personality and problems were far more dramatic and exciting than his ideas.

Move That Mountain! is a significant text for anyone interested in the Bakker affair or contemporary American religion. Written more than a decade before the scandal that destroyed his popular television ministry, Jim Bakker's autobiography provides some fascinating background into the man and his attitudes. The most important is Bakker's belief in what has come to be known as "dominion theology," or the idea that if a Christian asks the Lord for something—often money—it will be given. Money and material goods become a scorecard of God's favor, and throughout his autobiography and his ministry, Bakker keeps close account of his scorecard. A related belief is Bakker's pentecostalism. Bakker saw himself as "anointed by the Lord," and as such he viewed his actions as divinely inspired. The third fundamental assumption seen in the autobiography is Bakker's assertion that "results are all that counts." For Bakker, theological positions, traditions, and rituals were irrelevant. What emerges from *Move That Mountain!* is a picture of a man with no constraints. Bakker describes himself as a man called and led by the Holy Spirit to be financially successful and popular, for success and popularity are signs of the Lord's favor.

Read with hindsight, *Move That Mountain!* is a prophetic book. Bakker himself describes the seeds of his own undoing. In chronicling his success, Bakker portrays a set of values that would lead to his undoing.

BIBLIOGRAPHY

Applebome, Peter. "PTL Founder's Fraud Trial Opens as Jury Is Selected." *New York Times*, 22 August 1989, A19, col. 3.

Bakker, Jim. *Move That Mountain!* Charlotte, N.C.: PTL, 1976.

———. *Big Three Mountain Movers*. Charlotte, N.C.: PTL, 1977.

———. *Survival: Unite to Live*. Charlotte, N.C.: PTL, 1981.

———. *You Can Make It*. Charlotte, N.C.: PTL, 1983.

———. "But Disgrace Does Pay." *Washington Post*, 28 February 1988, C3, col. 5.

"Bakker and Ex-Aide Are Ordered to Pay $7.7 Million to PTL." *New York Times*, 11 November 1988, A27, col. 6.

"Bakker and Hahn Trade Charges." *New York Times*, 28 March 1987, 6L, col. 4.

Barnhart, Joe E. *Jim and Tammy: Charismatic Intrigue Inside PTL*. In collaboration with Stephen Winzenburg. Buffalo: Prometheus, 1988.

Clapp, Rodney. "Give Me That Old-Time Pragmatism." *Wall Street Journal*, 1 May 1987, 20W, col. 4.

Corry, John. "Preaching on Screen." *New York Times*, 2 April 1987, 23N, col. 1.

Dart, John. "Park That PTL Built Rides Roller-Coaster of Success, Scandal." *Los Angeles Times*, 30 March 1987, sec. 1, p. 3, col. 4.

Dowling, Claudia Glenn. "God's Green Acres: At Home with the Televangelists." *Life*, June 1987, 54–61.

"Evangelist Says He Was Misled in Giving Up PTL." *New York Times*, 27 May 1987, A19, col. 2.

Fay, Martha. "God's Country: Despite the Bakkers' Fall from Grace, Heritage USA Flourishes." *Life*, August 1987, 84–88.

Freedman, Samuel G. "How Bakker Widened the Eye of the Needle." *New York Times*, 14 June 1987, sec. 4, p. E26, col. 1.

Gardner, Martin. "Giving God a Hand." *New York Review of Books*, 34 (1987): 17–23. [13 August]

Gilliam, Dorothy. "A TV Morality Play." *Washington Post*, 30 March 1987, D3, col. 5.

Hammond, Phillip E. "For Many, PTL Stands for Truth, Beauty, Not Scandal." *Los Angeles Times*, 4 June 1987, sec. 11, p. 5, col. 1.

Harris, Art, and Michail Isikoff. "The Good Life at PTL: A Litany of Excess." *Washington Post*, 24 May 1987, A3, col. 1.

Hevesi, Dennis. "Hand of Devil Is Seen in Bakker's Fall." *New York Times*, 13 April 1987, 11N, col. 4.

Hume, Ellen, "Bakker Scandal Hurts Robertson's Bid to Attract More Than Faithful to His Race for Presidency." *Wall Street Journal*, 3 July 1987, 28W, col. 1.

Hunter, James Davidson. "Flap Will Not Doom Evangelicalism: Strength Is in Movement's Vision, Not Its Personalities." *Los Angeles Times*, 27 March 1987, sec. 11, p. 5, col. 3.

Isikoff, Michail. "Luxury Items of Bakkers Auctioned Off; $200,000 Raised for PTL Ministry." *Washington Post*, 24 May 1987, A3, col. 1.

"Jim Bakker Pleads Not Guilty to PTL Fraud." *New York Times*, 18 January 1989, A11, col. 3.

Johnson, Haynes. "The Bakkers: Faith and Betrayal." *Washington Post*, 25 March 1987, A2, col. 5.

King, Wayne. "Bakker, Evangelist, Resigns His Ministry over Sexual Incident." *New York Times*, 21 March 1987, 1N, col. 1.

Kopkind, Andrew. "Jim Bakker's Lost America." *Esquire*, December 1987, 174–79.

Lauter, David. "Early Return Would 'Doom Ministry,' Falwell Warns Bakker." *Los Angeles Times*, 27 April 1987, sec. 1, p. 3, col. 2.

Mann, Judy. "Soap in the Bible Belt." *Washington Post*, 24 February 1988, B3, col. 5.

Martz, Larry. "God and Money; Sex Scandal, Greed, and Lust for Power Split the TV Preaching World." *Newsweek*, 6 April 1987, 16–23.

Martz, Larry, and Ginny Carroll. *Ministry of Greed: The Inside Story of the Televangelists and Their Holy Wars*. New York: Weidenfeld, Nicholson, 1988.

McLendon, Mary Adams. "Jim Bakker: Seen by Millions, Known by Few." *Saturday Evening Post*, April 1981, 50–54.

Ostling, Richard, and Jon D. Hull. "Of God and Greed; Bakker and Falwell Trade Charges in Televangelism's Unholy Row." *Time*, 8 June 1987, 70–74.

"Praise the Lord and Pass the Loot." *The Economist*, 16 May 1987, L 23–27.

Rosenfeld, Megan. "Bakker Says His Ministry Is at an End; Claims He Is Owed Millions in Royalties." *Washington Post*, 2 May 1987, A1, col. 1.

Sahagun, Louis. "Bakker Pleads for Support, Considers a New Ministry." *Los Angeles Times*, 28 May 1987, sec. 1, p. 1, col. 1.

Stepp, Laura Sessions. "Evangelicals: Ecstasy and Temptation; Bakker, Swaggart Falls Spur Discussion of Sex." *Washington Post*, 11 April 1988, A3, col. 1.

Sweet, Leonard I. "Pearlygate Satires Are Weak on Substance." *The Christian Century*, 29 July 1987, 644–46.

"The Televangelist Fiasco: Top '87 Religion Story." *The Christian Century*, 23 December 1987, 1163–66.

Toner, Robin. "Bakker's Troubles Test Faith at Religious Resort." *New York Times*, 29 March 1987, sec. 1, p. 19, col. 1.

Treadwell, David. "Bakker Charged with Bilking PTL Followers; Indictment Accuses Evangelist, Aide of Fraud in Selling 'Partnerships' for Vacations at Hotel." *Los Angeles Times*, 6 December 1988, sec. 1, p. 1, col. 2.

Wadler, Joyce. "Breaking Faith, Two TV Idols Fall; They Preached to Millions, but Their Sins Brought Jim and Tammy Bakker to Ruin." *People Weekly*, 18 May 1987, 27:80–82.

Watson, Russell. "Heaven Can Wait." *Newsweek*, 8 June 1987, 58–64.

Wicker, Tom. "A Ministry of Loot." *New York Times*, 30 May 1987, 15N, col. 6.

Willimon, William H. "Suffering for Jesus." *The Christian Century*, 31 October 1984, 1005–2.

2 • LYMAN BEECHER (1775–1863)

The Autobiography of Lyman Beecher

BIOGRAPHY

Lyman Beecher was born in New Haven, Connecticut, in 1775. His mother died at his birth, and although his father was a prosperous blacksmith and remarried, Beecher was raised by his aunt and uncle. He grew up trained in the Federalism and Calvinism of postrevolutionary Connecticut, and in 1793, he entered Yale College. At Yale, he studied under Timothy Dwight, the new college president, and was influenced by Dwight's "campaign to save the nation from atheistic iniquity and Jeffersonian democracy" (p. xvi). Beecher excelled in all his studies, with the exception of mathematics, and after graduation, he remained at Yale to study theology. In 1779, he was called as pastor to the Presbyterian Church of East Hampton, Long Island. In that same year, he married Roxana Foote.

In 1801, the Presbyterian and Congregational Churches had formed an association, recognizing the ordination of each denomination's ministers, and in 1810, Beecher accepted the position of pastor of the Congregational Church in Litchfield, Connecticut. At this time, Connecticut was one of three states to have an established (official) state church. Beecher led the fight to retain the established Congregational Church in Connecticut, but lost when the Democratic party captured the state in 1818. In 1813, Beecher helped to organize the Connecticut Society for the Suppression of Vice and the Promotion of Good Morals; he also became active in the American Education Society and the American Bible Society, both voluntary associations dedicated to promote the intellectual and moral culture of the nation through the inculcation of Christian values. Beecher became well known for his work, and in 1818, he was awarded a doctor of divinity degree by Middlebury College.

In 1816, his first wife died, and Beecher married Harriet Porter. In 1826, he left Litchfield for the Hanover Street Church in Boston. By this time, Beecher was one of the most famous clergymen of his age. In addition to his pastorship and voluntary associations, Beecher had been preaching temperance sermons and conducting successful revivals. In 1827, he met with New York revivalist Charles Grandison Finney, to avoid a split in the evangelical community. In 1831, Beecher preached a series of anti-Catholic sermons, and in 1832, he published his famous *A Plea for the West*, which advocated education, Christianity, and reform for the frontier. Shortly after, he was named president of Lane Seminary in Cincinnati and ordained as pastor of the Second Presbyterian Church in Cincinnati.

In 1835, Beecher's second wife died, and the next year he married Lydia Jackson. During this time, the issue of slavery divided Lane Seminary. In 1834, while Beecher was in the East, Lane students engaged in a debate that resulted in a call for the immediate abolition of slavery. Seminary trustees stepped in and expelled a number of students, and community reaction in Cincinnati, which was, in general, against abolition, forced a number of students to move. On his return, Beecher attempted to strike a compromise between the students and the trustees, but he failed. A number of the students moved to the new Oberlin College, where Charles Grandison Finney taught.

In 1843, Beecher resigned from the Second Presbyterian Church, and in 1850, he resigned from Lane Seminary. In 1851, he returned to Boston, where he worked on collected works. In 1856, he moved in with his son, Henry Ward Beecher, and with the help of his children, he put together his *Autobiography*. Beecher died in 1863.

THE AUTOBIOGRAPHY

Lyman Beecher was one of the most influential churchmen in the early decades of the nineteenth century. His two-volume autobiography provides readers with a significant amount of information about American Protestantism from the Revolution to just before the Civil War. The *Autobiography* itself is unusual. Beecher began composing it late in his life with the assistance of his family. It includes excerpts from sermons, letters to and from Beecher, and comments by friends and family. As a result, the autobiography is not a carefully crafted narrative, but rather an encyclopedia of information about Beecher. Many of the sections, however, are told by Beecher himself, and these do provide a personal account of the youth, education, conversion, and works of an important American.

Lyman Beecher begins his autobiography with a description of his ancestors. He writes that his family came to New England in 1638 and that most members were honest and hardworking. He recalls his early days living with his uncle Lot Benton, a substantial farmer. He also begins to establish one of the major themes of his autobiography, the need for order in society, when he mentions the hard times that came with the Whiskey Insurrection and Shays' Rebellion that followed the Revolution. He introduces a second theme shortly thereafter when he observes, "They say that every body knows about God naturally. A lie. All such ideas are by teaching" (p. 19). Throughout his life, Beecher would distrust such "dangerous" ideas as democracy, innate goodness, and individual inspiration. The only way a person could come to a proper understanding of the nature of man, God, and society was through education, and Beecher records, happily, that he "had a good orthodox education; was serious minded, conscientious, and had a settled fear of God and terror of the day of judgement" (p. 19). These attributes were proper Puritan virtues, and as Beecher describes his continued education and conversion at Yale, he provides an insightful picture of the postrevolutionary Puritan revival led by Timothy Dwight.

Beecher writes that the Yale he attended was caught up in the "infidelity of the Tom Paine school." He records that "most of the class before me were infidels, and called each other Voltaire, Rousseau, D'Alembert, etc., etc." (p. 27). When Dwight took over the presidency, this attitude changed. Dwight's topic for class disputation was "Is the Bible the word of God?" Dwight's leadership moved Yale away from infidelity and provided the framework for Beecher's conversion. Beecher remembers that in the middle of his junior year at Yale, he was fully awakened. He writes:

One day, as we were sitting at home, mother looked out of the window, and saw a drunkard passing. "Poor man," said she, "I hope he'll receive all his punishment in this life. He was under conviction once, and thought he had religion; but he's nothing but a poor drunkard now." (p. 28)

His mother's observation made Beecher think, and he soon began to pray and became convinced of his own sinfulness. He remembers falling into despair, realizing that he was "under the law, was stumbling in the doctrines, and had no views of Christ" (p. 29). The only help he received was in the sermons of Dwight. These led him to a close reading of the Bible. Looking back on the experience Beecher remembers:

It was many months that I suffered; and, finally, the light did not come in a sudden blaze, but by degrees. I began to see more into the doctrines of the Bible. Election and decrees were less stumbling-blocks. I came in by that door. I felt reconciled and resigned, yet with alterations of darkness and discouragement, and a severe conflict whether it would be right for me to preach, which extended even into my Divinity year. (p. 30)

Beecher's recollections indicate that not only were the traditional steps present—conviction of sin, doubt and despair, Bible reading, and assurance—but also that the conversion was a process that took place over an extended period. The fact that Dwight's sermons and presence at Yale provided Beecher with a framework for his conversion is crucial. In his own work as a revivalist, Beecher, unlike such other famous evangelists as George Whitefield and Charles Grandison Finney, would always work within the institutional framework of the local church so that the converts would have proper spiritual guidance throughout their conversion experience.

Throughout his ministry, Beecher linked reform with conversion. Soon after his arrival at Litchfield, he became a leading member of the Connecticut temperance movement, arguing against the "undue consumption of ardent spirits." He soon joined with others in the state in a general reform movement that called for prohibition and strict enforcement of the sabbath laws. Beecher led the fight for enforcement of these laws, arguing that the moral decline of the citizenry was a cause of the rising tide of Jeffersonianism, which he saw as atheistic anarchy. Between 1810 and 1820, the battle between the forces of God and the forces of Satan centered on the issue of establishment. Congregationalism (since 1801 aligned with Presbyterianism) was the established or state-supported religion of Connecticut. Beecher supported this system as the best way to promote virtue and order in the state. He recalls, however, that

the ambitious minority early began to make use of the minor sects on the ground of invidious distinctions, thus making them restive. So the democracy, as it rose, included nearly all the minor sects, besides the Sabbath-breakers, rum-selling tipling folk, infidels, and ruff-scuff generally, and made a dead set against us of the standing order. (p. 251)

The infidels eventually won, and the Congregational Church in Connecticut was disestablished. Beecher writes:

It was as dark a day as ever I saw. The odium thrown upon the ministry was inconceivable. The injury done to the cause of Christ, as we then supposed, was irreparable. For several days I suffered what no tongue can tell FOR THE BEST THING THAT EVER HAPPENED TO THE STATE OF CONNECTICUT. It cut the churches loose from dependence on state support. It threw them wholly on their own resources and on God. (pp. 252–53)

Beecher came to realize that once the church was no longer part of the state, it gained influence, and that by voluntary associations, societies, missions, and revivals, it could exert a deeper influence on society. During the rest of his career, Beecher would use those tools effectively.

Beecher gained his national reputation as a revivalist, and in his autobiography, he presents his method. Unlike the itinerant evangelists who toured frontier communities, Beecher worked with established churches and ministers, preaching regeneration and offering supportive services for those who felt moved. His presentations were not overly emotional, and he would offer classes in the Bible to follow up his sermons. His method in fact was modeled on his own experience at Yale, and was successful throughout New England, where Congregational and Presbyterian Churches existed to provide support. During the 1820s, Beecher's influence grew, and he eventually was called in to settle a dispute between Charles Grandison Finney, whose emotional revivals were sweeping through western New York, and Dr. Asahel Nettleton, an influential minister who believed in the more structured New England method. A compromise eventually was reached, with each side respecting the work of the other, but in the process, Beecher came to believe that the future of the country would be determined by the work of the church in the West, and when he was invited to head the Lane Seminary in Cincinnati, Beecher was elated.

During the 1830s and 1840s, Beecher's life and works were bound up with Lane Seminary and bringing Christianity to the West. Lane had been established to provide trained ministers for the western territories, and Beecher realized that without a seminary-trained ministry, there would be no established support system for the thousands of converts being made by the Baptist, Methodist, and Presbyterian circuit riders traveling throughout the territories. He also believed that a trained clergy was necessary to combat what he feared was the potential for Catholic influence west of the Appalachian Mountains.

In the second volume of his autobiography, Beecher provides a great deal of information about his term as president of Lane Seminary. He writes fondly of his journey from the East to Cincinnati and of his establishment of his family in Walnut Hills. The account of the antislavery imbroglio, which caused a rift in Cincinnati and the seminary, is told with less fondness. Beecher writes that the initial seminary class was "a noble class of young men, uncommonly strong, a little uncivilized, entirely radical, and terribly in earnest" (pp. 2, 241). This class was led by Theodore D. Weld, who drew on the radicalism of the class members during Beecher's absence to declare support for the abolition of slavery. At this time, the most popular antislavery position called for colonization, or sending to Africa already-freed slaves, rather than for abolition of the institution itself. This position was advocated by most Northern churchmen, and throughout his ministry, Beecher relied on the formal structures of the church to provide checks on the radical ideas and enthusiasms that developed in local churches. Even though he personally was opposed to slavery, Beecher argued against the radical position taken by Weld and his class, and attempted to find a compromise between the students and the more conservative members of the seminary's board. He failed, and the students left Lane, many going to the more radical seminary at Oberlin, Ohio, where Charles Finney taught and preached.

The final chapters of his autobiography chronicle Beecher's tenure at Lane, advocacy of education, including his work with the famous *McGuffey Readers*, and retirement to Boston. In these final sections, the autobiography draws more heavily on Beecher's earlier letters, sermons, and notes, as well as observations by friends and family members. This material, much of it collected and edited by Beecher's famous children, changes the tone of the text, and as a result, *The Autobiography of Lyman Beecher* ends as a biography of Lyman Beecher.

CRITICISM

In his study of Lyman Beecher, *Pedagogue for God's Kingdom: Lyman Beecher and the Second Great Awakening* (Boston: University Press of America, 1985), James W. Fraser sees Lyman Beecher as representative of an entire generation of American churchmen who grew up after the Revolution and who lived through the second great awakening and used their energies in an attempt to "mold an entire configuration of institutions to preserve the thrust of that movement and thus bring in the millennium— God's kingdom in America" (p. 3). The history of Christianity in the United States from the Revolution to the Civil War can indeed be seen as an attempt to establish the millennial kingdom, and Lyman Beecher was one of the most influential men of the period. His work, first in revivals and then in education, reflects the main interests of the Protestant community, and his move from New England to the frontier of Ohio parallels the development of the country. Beecher's autobiography is a significant document in that it captures the reformist concerns of mainstream Protestantism during the crucial decades of the first part of the nineteenth century.

BIBLIOGRAPHY

Beecher, Lyman. *A Plea for the West*. Cincinnati: Truman and Smith, 1825.
———. *A Plea for Colleges*. Cincinnati: Truman and Smith, 1836.
———. *Beecher's Works*. 3 vols. Boston: John P. Jewett, 1852–53.
———. *The Autobiography of Lyman Beecher*. 2 vols. 1864. Cambridge, Mass.: Harvard University Press, 1961.
Bols, John B. *The Great Revival 1787–1805*. Lexington: University Press of Kentucky, 1972.
Foster, Charles I. *An Errand of Mercy: The Evangelical United Front, 1790–1837*. Chapel Hill: University of North Carolina Press, 1960.
Fraser, James W. *Pedagogue for God's Kingdom: Lyman Beecher and the Second Great Awakening*. Boston: University Press of America, 1985.

Griffen, Clifford S. *Their Brothers' Keepers: Moral Stewardship in the United States, 1860–1865*. New Brunswick, N.J.: Rutgers University Press, 1960.

Harding Vincent. "Lyman Beecher and the Transformation of American Protestantism, 1775–1863." Thesis, Chicago, 1965.

Niebuhr, H. Richard. *The Kingdom of God in America*. New York: Harper & Brothers, 1937.

Tuveson, Earnest Lee. *Redeemer Nation, the Idea of America's Millennial Role*. Chicago: University of Chicago Press, 1968.

3 • BLACK ELK (1863–1950)

Black Elk Speaks

BIOGRAPHY

In August 1930, poet John Neihardt, gathering material for his narrative poem *Cycle of the West*, met Black Elk, an Oglala Sioux *wichasa wakon*, or holy man. Neihardt asked Black Elk to speak to him about the old times, and the result of those conversations is *Black Elk Speaks*, one of the most popular autobiographies of an American Indian.

Black Elk lived during the crucial decades of American Indian history, and the story of his life has influenced several generations of readers, native and nonnative American alike. Black Elk was born in 1863 near the Little Powder River in the Dakota Territory. The early part of his life reflects prereservation Sioux culture, whereas his adulthood was spent on government reservations. Black Elk was a witness to some of the events that marked the end of a way of life for the Plains Indians. Black Elk was present at both the Battle of the Little Big Horn and the massacre at Wounded Knee; in addition, he performed in Buffalo Bill's Wild West Show in both the United States and Europe. After living as a "wild Indian," fighting government troops, participating in the Ghost Dance movement, and enduring life on a reservation, Black Elk provided readers with a native American perspective on more than seventy years of American history. He died on August 19, 1950.

AUTOBIOGRAPHY

Black Elk Speaks is a work deserving attention. The narrative that Neihardt recorded is more than a story of the adventures of a man who witnessed the passing of a way of life; *Black Elk Speaks* is "the story of a mighty vision" Black Elk received when he was nine. This vision provided meaning and coherence for Black Elk, and in telling the story of his vision to Neihardt, he ensured the transmission of the wisdom he attained, a wisdom as much concerned with community and a way of life as with an individual.

In telling his life story, Black Elk, like many other ethnic-American writers, speaks with a representative voice. He begins his narrative with a statement of his purpose:

My friend, I am going to tell you the story of my life, as you wish; and if it were only the story of my life I would not tell it; for what is one man that he should make much of his winters, even when they bend him like a heavy snow? So many other men have lived and shall live that story, to be grass upon the hills.

It is the story of all life that is holy and is good to tell, and of us two-leggeds sharing in it with four-leggeds and the wings of the air and all green things; for these are children of one mother and their father is one spirit. (p. 1)

Unlike most mainstream American autobiographies, *Black Elk Speaks* is not a celebration of the self; on the contrary, Black Elk sees its significance in its universality, which was the measure of a story's worth in traditional native American cultures.

The conflict between native American and white cultures is a central theme in Black Elk's narrative, and he begins to develop it at the outset of his work, describing how his people were happy in their own country before the whites (Wasichus) came and there was fighting because white men were driven crazy by the gold they discovered in the Indian lands and demanded to build a road through the Sioux territory. Throughout the early sections of his narrative, Black Elk develops the building tension between the cultures. He describes tribal life and buffalo hunting in nostalgic terms, always set against continual encroachments of white civilization and the resulting battles. Black Elk successfully captures a culture in conflict, and he uses this conflict to establish the urgency of his great vision, which becomes the crucial event in his life and the controlling idea of his autobiography.

When Black Elk was nine years old, he heard a voice calling to him saying, "It is time; now they are calling you" (p. 21). He immediately fell unconscious and remained so, unmoving, for twelve days in the grip of his vision. Black Elk describes his vision in twenty-two detailed pages. In this mystical experience, Black Elk was addressed by the powers of the world—six grandfathers representing the powers of the North, South, East, West, Earth, and Sky—and taken to the center of the earth to see the future. In the vision, he was given the task of restoring the sacred hoop of the Sioux nation and making the whole tree of life bloom again. If he were to succeed in this task, one of the grandfathers promised him that he would see "a good nation walking in a sacred manner in a good land!" (p. 36). If he were successful, he would stop the invasion of the white man and return the land and the people to their original states.

In addition to giving Black Elk wisdom and power, the vision compelled him to act. To function as a holy man, Black Elk needed to act out in a ritual manner portions of his vision, to relive parts of the dream for those he was attempting to help. The vision became a psychological imperative for Black Elk, and his autobiography, which tells for the first time his entire vision, is another kind of ritual reenactment.

Black Elk's autobiography is concerned with history as well as mysticism. Black Elk sets the need to restore his land and his people within the framework of the Indian wars. He presents the Sioux attitude succinctly: "We were in our own country all the time and we only wanted to be left alone. The soldiers came there to kill us, and many got rubbed out. It was our country and we did not want to have trouble" (p. 105). Black Elk provides a detailed description of the Battle of the Little Big Horn as a turning point in the life of the Sioux. The trouble began in 1874, when General Custer led his troops into the Black Hills. Black Elk's position is clear: He recalls the treaty of 1869 that gave the land to the Sioux forever. He also writes that the cause for all the troubles was General Custer's discovery of gold.

Although the Sioux won the battle with Custer, they lost the war. Despite heroic resistance and numerous acts of personal bravery, the Sioux nation was decimated by soldiers, hunger, and disease. Black Elk's account of the aftermath of the battle with Custer is told with resignation, as if in looking back at that period of his life, he realizes that the outcome was inevitable. In contrast to his wisdom of a good people in a good land, the end of the hostilities left the Sioux scattered on reservations and depending on the white man for food.

Black Elk did not exercise his power during the wars, but in 1882, when he was nineteen, he performed his first cure. Black Elk's success as a healer is ironic; his vision commanded him to heal his land and people, to restore the sacred circle of the Sioux nation, but he began to heal sick people only after the entire nation had been broken.

Once Black Elk begins to describe his experiences as a healer, the nature of the autobiography changes. The early sections can be seen as a narrative of native American life before the coming of the reservations. In the second section of his autobiography, Black Elk moves from a story of a man to a story about the environment. In these passages, *Black Elk Speaks* becomes the story of "all that is holy," a story of the relation between the good earth and a good people. In telling of the powers of the bison and the elk, Black Elk places himself in a symbiotic relationship to the land, the animals, and his people. As a holy man becoming aware of his powers and the responsibilities of his vision, he is compelled to understand the "powers" of all creation so that he can call on them successfully. Black Elk provides an example and an explanation of the elk ceremony, which he performed as part of his growth in wisdom. After finishing his description, he explains that the ceremony was so significant that it gave meaning to his life and put him in harmony with the Power of the World. The Power of the World was changing, however, and the same year that Black Elk performed his ceremony, the last of the bison herds was slaughtered. The environment itself had been transformed by the white man, and Black Elk prepared himself to learn another lesson.

The next section of *Black Elk Speaks* is called "Across the Big Water," and in it, Black Elk describes the fate of the Sioux. "The nation's hoop was broken, and there was no center any longer for the flowering tree. The people were in despair" (p. 214). Black Elk continued to heal for three years, but in 1881, he joined a band of Sioux to perform in Buffalo Bill's Wild West Show. He remembers thinking that he should go to learn the white man's secret so that he could use it to help his people.

Black Elk's journey with Buffalo Bill becomes an empty pilgrimage. He learns that there is no "secret," and he grown continually more alienated as he moves farther from his homeland. Black Elk describes performing in New York, England, France, and Germany. He even provides an account of a special performance before Grandmother England (Queen Victoria) and remembers both her warm welcome for the performing Indians and the sanctuary her land (Canada) provided many Sioux after the Dakota wars.

Black Elk returned to the Sioux in 1889 and discovered that his "people were pitiful and in despair" (p. 231). He seemed to have lost his vision, and at first, he refused to heal. But the people were weak from hunger, and the outbreaks of measles and whooping cough were severe. He again began to work cures. At that time, the Ghost Dance revival reached the Sioux.

The Ghost Dance originated among the far western tribes and quickly spread throughout the native American communities. It was a messianic faith, taught by Wovoka, also called Jack Wilson. Known as the Wanekia (One Who Makes Live), Wovoka, who was considered to be the son of the Ghost Spirit, had a vision of another world about to come that would save the Indian people, make the whites disappear, and return all the bison to a richly reborn earth. The attraction of such a faith is obvious. To a people facing cultural extinction, it offered a possibility of a return to the old days and an eradication of the hated enemy. At first, Black Elk was skeptical, but the more he learned about the Ghost Dance, the more he saw in it a re-creation of the nation's hoop similar to that of his own vision. He eventually decided to add his energies to the growing movement and began to participate in the dances. He soon had another vision, this one compelling him to make Ghost Shirts for the dancers.

The dancing spread throughout the Dakota reservations during the spring and summer of 1890. Watching the ritual, government officials saw the beginnings of a potential uprising and condemned it. Nevertheless, the dancing continued until the confrontation of Wounded Knee on December 19, 1890.

At Wounded Knee, more than 500 soldiers supported by artillery and rapid-fire wagon guns attacked the Sioux at the Pine Ridge Reservation. Black Elk was there and took part in the battle, which quickly became a massacre. His account of the famous slaughter is moving, but his recollection of the aftermath of Wounded Knee is even more powerful:

Men and women and children were heaped and scattered all over the flat at the bottom of the hill where the soldiers had their wagon guns, and westward up the dry gulch all the way to the high ridge, the dead women and children and babies were scattered. When I saw this I wished that I had died too, but I was not sorry for the women and the children. It was better for them to be happy in the other world, and I wanted to be there too. (p. 260)

Both the Ghost Dance movement and the Indian resistance died at Wounded Knee. In the final chapter of his autobiography, "The End of the Dream," Black Elk recounts the wanderings of the Wounded Knee survivors through the Dakotas until they returned, starving and freezing, to the Pine Ridge Reservation to lay down their arms in front of waiting soldiers. In his final paragraph, Black Elk depicts himself as a "pitiful old man who has done nothing, for the nation's hoop is broken and scattered. There is no center any longer, and the sacred tree is dead" (p. 270).

CRITICISM

Black Elk Speaks is a powerful lament. In combining the history of the Indian wars, the training and practice of a holy man, and a vision of a nation lost, Black Elk has given his readers an invaluable insight into native American culture and religion. This, as well as the firsthand accounts of the battles at the Little Big Horn and Wounded Knee, helps to explain the autobiography's continued popularity.

Janet Varner Gunn, writing in her excellent study of personal narratives, *Autobiography: Toward a Poetics of Experience*, asserts that *Black Elk Speaks* is more than a mere lament over a lost culture and an appeal to the yearning for simpler times. She sees the autobiography as an outstanding example of a contemporary religious narrative, a non-Augustinian journey of selfhood that moves "from a world shared and coherent values to fragmentation, a valley of dried bones which even the most powerful of spirits cannot infuse again with their former life" (p. 140).

This genre itself is significant, as William Bloodworth observed in "Varieties of American Indian Autobiography":

Indian autobiographies deserve our attention not only because they are truly and indisputably American or because, as Luther Standing Bear has said about his own story, "No one is able to understand the Indian race like an Indian." They also represent a diverse and complex literary genre, one that obliges us to consider the nature of autobiographical expression in traditional Indian cultures, the role of outside white influence in the recording of personal experience, and the ultimate aesthetic as well as documentary value of the work. (p. 67)

Several important considerations remain for the student of Black Elk Speaks. First, Black Elk's life is filtered through the consciousness of John Neihardt, and even the most faithful recorder alters the information he transcribes. Although the words are those of Black Elk, does the structure of the narrative, emphasizing the loss of innocence and the deterioration of the environment because of the onslaught of the white man, belong to Black Elk, or has it been imposed by Neihardt? In addition, as William Bloodworth has noted in "Varieties of American Indian Autobiography," Black Elk converted to Catholicism before his meeting with Neihardt, and his recollections of both his visions and his life may be colored by Christian theology or New Testament apocalyptic thought. Does some of the imagery in Black Elk's vision, for example, come from a native tradition, or from the Book of Revelation?

Despite these potential problems, Black Elk Speaks is a significant American autobiography. It is more than a personal chronicle of an eyewitness to great battles. Black Elk Speaks is an articulate and moving personal history of an Indian holy man, and in combining communal history with individual vision, Black Elk speaks eloquently for the Sioux nation.

BIBLIOGRAPHY

Black Elk, as told to John G. Neihardt. Black Elk Speaks. New York: William Morrow, 1932. Reprint. Lincoln: University of Nebraska Press, 1979.

Bloodworth, William. "Varieties of American Indian Autobiography." MELUS 5, 3(1978): 67–81.

———. "Neihardt, Momaday, and the Art of American Indian Autobiography." Teaching English in the Two-Year College 4 (1978): 137–43.

Gunn, Janet Varner. Autobiography: Toward a Poetics of Experience. Philadelphia: University of Pennsylvania Press, 1982.

Holte, James. The Ethnic I: A Sourcebook for Ethnic-American Autobiography. Westport, Conn.: Greenwood Press, 1988.

Lee, A. Robert. First Person Singular: Studies in American Autobiography. New York: St. Martin's Press, 1988.

McKluskey, Sally. "Black Elk Speaks and So Does John Neihardt." Western American Literature 6 (1972): 238.

Neihardt, John G. The Sixth Grandfather: Black Elk's Teachings Given to John G. Neihardt. Lincoln: University of Nebraska Press, 1984.

O'Brian, Lynn Woods. *Plains Indians Autobiography*. Boise: Boise State University Press, 1973.

Sayre, Robert. "Visions and Experience in *Black Elk Speaks*." *College English* 32 (1971): 509–35.

4 • ELDRIDGE CLEAVER (1935–   )

Soul on Fire

BIOGRAPHY

Eldridge Cleaver was born in Little Rock, Arkansas, on August 31, 1935. His family moved to Phoenix, Arizona, and later to Los Angeles. In 1954, Cleaver began serving a series of jail terms at Soledad, Folsom, and San Quentin prisons for marijuana possession and rape. In prison, Cleaver developed an interest in reading, and became a Black Muslim and a supporter of Malcolm X. In addition, he began writing and produced a series of essays and letters that appeared in 1968 as *Soul on Ice*, a powerful and popular intellectual and spiritual autobiography.

In 1968, Cleaver was paroled from prison and joined the Black Panther organization, founded by Huey Newton and Bobby Seal. He also became a staff writer for *Ramparts* and a popular college lecturer. Soon Cleaver was named minister of information for the Black Panthers, and in that position, he helped to develop strategies for black-power organization. In 1969, Cleaver fled the United States after he was sentenced to prison for a parole violation. He lived for a time in Cuba before moving to North Korea, Algeria, and, finally, France. In 1975, Cleaver returned to the United States and pleaded guilty to assaulting a police officer ten years earlier. He received probation, and was ordered to perform 2,000 hours of community service. At the time of his return to the country, Cleaver announced that he had become a born-again Christian. In 1978, he published his second autobiographical work, *Soul on Fire*. In 1982, Cleaver became a member of the Church of Jesus Christ of Latter-Day Saints and a supporter of conservative Republican politics.

THE AUTOBIOGRAPHY

Eldridge Cleaver's life has been full of dramatic transformations, and in his two autobiographical narratives, *Soul on Ice* and *Soul on Fire*, he charts the transformations that led him from juvenile delinquency to prison, intellectualism, militancy, the Black Muslims, the Black Panthers, communism, exile, and, finally, Christianity. In his famous book, *Soul on Ice*, Cleaver described his own development as a black man in a white world, outlined his life in prison and his religious experiences that led him to become a follower of Malcolm X, and provided a criticism of American culture, especially the impact of capitalism and racism on members of the black community in the United States. *Soul on Ice* was one of the most articulate and intelligent works to come out of the political activity of the 1960s, and in it, Cleaver established his reputation as an intelligent thinker and a powerful writer.

Soul on Fire, published in 1978, after Cleaver's return to the United States, covers some of the same material but from a different perspective. Between the publication of his first and second autobiographies, Cleaver had been the Peace and Freedom party candidate for president of the United States, a fugitive from the law, a political exile, and a converted Christian. These later experiences changed the way he writes about his life, and in *Soul on Fire*, Cleaver returns to his youth, prison experience, and radical politics to again provide a critique of American society, but this time a critique from a Christian perspective.

Cleaver begins *Soul on Fire* with a description of his return to the United States to face outstanding federal and state warrants. He writes that as the plane flew from Paris to New York, he began to recall the events that led up to his flight from the law, and to a large extent, *Soul on Fire* is a meditation on those events.

In the early sections of his autobiography, Cleaver presents his childhood, prison experiences, and career as a revolutionary. In his first book, Cleaver used these experiences to construct a sermon against the sins of white, capitalist America; in his second book, he does not deny the sinfulness of society, but he extends it to all of society, himself included. In describing his childhood, for example, Cleaver includes not only examples of the discrimination he, his family, and other blacks faced, but also examples of his mother's Christian faith. The result is a more balanced, if less dramatic, portrait than Cleaver provided in *Soul on Ice*.

Cleaver's prison experiences—physical, intellectual, and spiritual—were the center of *Soul on Ice*. In *Soul on Fire*, Cleaver summarized that crucial period in his life:

The nine years I spent in prison (San Quentin, Folsom, California Men's Colony East, and Soledad, again) were the transition days that took me from marijuana-

peddling rapist to revolutionary. I would go the whole route of being enamored
with Marxism, initiated in the Black Muslim religion, and of reading the Great
Books. Frankly, the study of the Great Books did more for me intellectually than
the other two. The Black Panther Party, which I joined upon my release from prison,
was to become the political and social vehicle for the ideas that captured my attention. (p. 65)

One of the most significant elements of *Soul on Fire* is Cleaver's refusal
to dismiss or apologize for parts of his life that might, at first, appear to be
at odds with his Christian conversion. Although he ultimately does reject
Black Muslim and Marxist doctrine, he writes that both ideologies provided
him with important ideas and directions at crucial times in his life, and
when he describes his involvement with the Black Panther party and the
civil rights and antiwar movements of the 1960s, Cleaver asserts that the
confrontations that took place were both necessary and just.

Cleaver's argument in support of the black power movement of the 1960s
is grounded in the context of national racism and violence. He introduces
the political section of his narrative with references to the murder of Martin
Luther King, the death of Elijah Muhammad, and the assassination of Malcolm X. In addition, Cleaver argues that by 1967, nonviolence had failed,
and the Black Panther party was a natural development necessary to change
the hearts and minds of both black and white Americans. His portrait of
the Panthers is perhaps the most dramatic section of his narrative. He writes,
for example, that

the only way to deal with the violence which was shedding its grace all over the
United States—and rather thoroughly in Vietnam—was to pack some ourselves. I
was very much at home with this, and my swift rise in the Panther leadership circle
came from two sources: my celebrity status as the best-selling author of *Soul on Ice*
and my ghetto background which never choked at the sight or sound of a gun.
(p. 90)

Cleaver follows this comment with a description of the development of the
Black Panther party, its goals and strategy, the armed confrontations with
the police, and the eventual arrests, imprisonments, or exile of the leadership.

In April 1968, there was a shoot-out in Oakland between the Black
Panthers and police authorities, and in November 1968, with Huey Newton
in prison, Cleaver fled the United States for Cuba. In his autobiography,
Cleaver writes that this was one of the turning points in his life. Having
the opportunity to live in Cuba, China, and Algeria enabled him to experience communist societies firsthand, and as a result, he was forced to
reexamine his attitudes about the United States.

Cleaver describes his pilgrimage through the Third World as a journey
of discovery. At each stop—Cuba, Algeria, North Korea, China—his expectations are shattered. In Cuba, Cleaver found that the police were as

suspicious of the Black Panthers as American police had been; in Algeria, Cleaver was exiled to a small, run-down house; and in both North Korea and China, Cleaver discovered racism and militarism. Cleaver writes that the Marxist ideology that he had adopted in prison seemed nowhere in practice in the communist countries he visited. He and his family eventually settled in France.

Cleaver's reputation as a writer and political exile had preceded him to France, and he was well received there. Cleaver soon realized, however, that he was no longer politically active: Black American activists paid him little attention, and he no longer had influence with either European or Third World political leaders. In addition, he discovered that his children were more European than American. Cleaver grew despondent, even contemplating suicide. He recalls that he thought his life was going nowhere. He remembers one particular evening sitting on the balcony of his apartment on the Mediterranean coast and staring at the moon. First he saw himself in the moon, and then, he writes,

as I stared at the image, it changed, and I saw my former heroes paraded before my eyes. Here were Fidel Castro, Mao Tse-tung, Karl Marx, Frederick Engels, passing in review—each one appearing for a moment of time, and then dropping out of sight, like fallen heroes. Finally, at the end of the procession, in dazzling, shimmering light, the image of Jesus Christ appeared. (p. 211)

Cleaver recalls that he immediately fell to his knees and began to cry. After he gained control of himself, he found a Bible in his bookcase and began to read the Lord's Prayer and Psalm 23. He then fell asleep.

In the final pages of *Soul on Fire*, Cleaver describes how he decided to return to the United States. He writes that although his life had been radically changed the night of his conversion, "renewal is an unfolding process," and he followed the guidance of the Holy Spirit in approaching American government representatives in Paris about returning to the United States. He recalls that he felt no fear or confusion, for he believed that God was leading him somewhere to do something. Cleaver served nine months in the Alameda County Jail in San Francisco, and while there, he studied the Bible and was befriended by a number of Christians, including George Stevens, an ex-black militant who had become a Christian minister, and Arthur De Moss, president of the National Liberty Corporation. After his release from jail, Cleaver met with Billy Graham and Chuck Colson, and shortly after began a speaking tour of the country. He ends his narrative by answering those who asked him if he is being used. "I am here to be used until I am used up," he writes. "I praise the Lord" (p. 233).

CRITICISM

The enthusiasm that greeted the publication of *Soul on Ice* in 1968 was matched with the skepticism that greeted the publication of *Soul on Fire* ten years later. More than a few readers wondered if Cleaver had claimed religious conversion as a way of avoiding a long prison sentence, or if he had been used by members of the religious right. In addition, some critics who were willing to accept a prison conversion to the Black Muslim faith were unwilling to accept a French conversion to fundamentalist Christianity.

An understanding of the conversion process can help to answer this question. As Barnhart and Barnhart point out in *The New Birth: A Naturalistic View of Religious Conversion*, most people undergo a series of transformational events in their lives that can be called conversions. In fact, whereas some religious traditions isolate a conversion to a particular place and time, others emphasize the ongoing process of change. Because a reader accepts the validity of Cleaver's first conversion, there is no reason he must deny the validity of the second.

In fact, one of the most interesting aspects of Cleaver's autobiographies is his emphasis on continual change. In both *Soul on Ice* and *Soul on Fire*, Eldridge Cleaver depicts himself as a man who is willing to change his way of life when his beliefs are transformed. Cleaver's autobiographies record the life of a man who has had the opportunity to make himself over more than once.

BIBLIOGRAPHY

Barnhart, Joe Edward, and Mary Ann Barnhart. *The New Birth: A Naturalistic View of Religious Conversion*. Macon, Ga.: Mercer University Press, 1981.
Butterfield, Stephen. *Black Autobiography in America*. Amherst: University of Massachusetts Press, 1974.
Cleaver, Eldridge. *Soul on Ice*. New York: Dell, 1968.
———. *Soul on Fire*. Waco, Tex.: Word, 1978.
Stepto, Robert B. *Behind the Veil: A Study of Afro-American Narrative*. Urbana: University of Illinois Press, 1979.
Stone, Albert E. *Autobiographical Occasions and Original Acts: Versions of American Identity from Henry Adams to Nate Shaw*. Philadelphia: University of Pennsylvania Press, 1982.

5 • JOHN COGLEY (1917–1976)

A Canterbury Tale: Experiences and Reflections: 1916–1976

BIOGRAPHY

John Cogley was born in Chicago in 1916. He grew up in a Catholic environment, attending Catholic grade school and receiving a scholarship to St. Philip High School. He began to study for the priesthood and attended a special Chicago preparatory school. He soon decided not to continue those studies and began taking college courses at Loyola University and Rosary College. During this time, Cogley became acquainted with the Catholic Worker movement. Established by Dorothy Day, the Catholic Worker movement provided houses for the homeless in several American cities and advocated integration, workers' rights, and support for the poor. Cogley helped to establish the Chicago chapter, and later went to live at the Mott Street house in New York, which served as the national headquarters for the movement.

During World War II, Cogley was trained as a radio operator and was stationed in the United States. After the war, he returned to Loyola University, and after graduation, he, along with his wife and children, moved to Switzerland, where Cogley studied Thomistic philosophy at the University of Fribourg.

On his return to the United States, Cogley was offered a position as editor at *Commonweal*, the liberal Catholic journal. At *Commonweal*, Cogley became a spokesman for the progressive wing of the American Catholic Church. In his writings and public speaking, he argued for ecumenical relations among churches and civil rights and against McCarthyism. In addition, he became an advocate of more lay control of the Catholic Church. In 1954, Cogley left *Commonweal* to take a position at the Fund for the Republic, an institute sponsored by the Ford Foundation and headed by Robert Hutchins, former president of the University of Chicago. In that position, Cogley worked on such major projects as blacklisting in Hollywood and religion in America. In 1960, he served as an advisor on the presidential campaign of John F. Kennedy.

In 1963, Cogley went to Rome as religion correspondent for the *New York Times* to cover the Second Vatican Council. Cogley was pleased with many of the changes that took place during the Council, but at the same time, he was experiencing personal dissatisfaction with Catholicism. Unhappy over the continuing clerical control over the church, the doctrine of infallibility, the rigidity of Catholic teachings on birth control, Cogley began moving toward the Episcopal Church. In 1973, he became an Episcopalian and began to study for holy orders. He died in 1976.

THE AUTOBIOGRAPHY

John Cogley's autobiography, *A Canterbury Tale*, is a brief and insightful portrait of American Catholicism in the middle decades of the twentieth century. It also is the story of a conversion—although Cogley himself denies that he actually converted to or from anything—that took place over thirty years. Most conversion narratives depict a dramatic moment of change, but recent studies have suggested that the actual process of conversion may take place slowly over a long period. Cogley's conversion from Catholicism to the Episcopal Church was not dramatic, and his narrative of his religious life documents the countless small events of his life that led him to realize late in his life that he was "more Anglican than Catholic." Cogley's attitude toward this transformation can be seen in his dedication of his book:

To the two Churches in my life:
The Roman Catholic Church, which first imparted to me the Christian vision of faith, hope, and charity;
The Episcopal Church, where that faith was purified, that hope strengthened, and that charity, perhaps, expanded. (p. v)

Rather than depicting his movement from Rome to Canterbury as a break, Cogley describes a long pilgrimage from one communion to another. For Cogley, as for a number of other writers of spiritual narratives, conversion primarily is another term for spiritual growth.

Cogley begins his narrative by announcing that his memoir is written by a practicing Episcopalian but is about the Catholic community in the United States. Specifically, it is about the Catholic community in the United States from the 1930s through the 1960s, a period of dramatic change in American

Catholicism, and Cogley, first as a member of the Catholic Worker movement and then as a religious writer for *Commonweal* and the *New York
Times,* was in a perfect position to observe and chronicle the changes taking
place.

Cogley's recollections of his early life include elements of both major
factions of the American Catholic Church: conservative and activist. Cogley
writes that he grew up living with his grandmother, and after attending a
Catholic grade school, he received a scholarship to St. Philip High School,
run by the Servite Fathers, a religious order founded in 1233 that was "highly
baroque in its liturgical usages, pious practices, and preachments. The special behavior of the order—its particular devotions—were extremely sentimental: they were focused on devotion to the sorrows of the Mother of
Christ" (p. 4). This description begins to establish Cogley's picture of the
conservative wing of the Catholic Church. Beginning here with his account
of his early education and continuing throughout his narrative, Cogley
develops a portrait of traditional American Catholicism emphasizing political conservativism, clerical control, sentimentality, and patriarchal authoritarianism. Cogley balances this with his portrait of the Catholic Worker
movement and the development of the activist wing of the Catholic Church,
which stressed social action, experimentation in ritual, and democratic decision making. After describing his high school education and youthful
studies for the priesthood, Cogley moves to one of the main themes of his
narrative, his involvement with the Catholic Worker movement before
World War II.

The Catholic Worker movement was founded by Dorothy Day as an
organized attempt to apply Catholic principles to such social ills as poverty
and discrimination. The movement took its name from its newspaper, *The
Catholic Worker,* and began with the establishment of a shelter in New
York for the homeless that provided beds, food, and clothing, as well as
education and religious devotions. In addition, the shelter was the home of
Day, her mentor, Peter Maurin, and the young volunteers who ran the
program. The New York shelter, or Mott Street House of Hospitality,
provided a model for similar houses throughout the United States. In his
autobiography, Cogley describes Dorothy Day's visit to Chicago, her establishment of a shelter there, and his early involvement with the plans. He
also describes his move to New York and the Mott Street House, where he
lived and worked as a member of the community until he was asked to
return to Chicago to take over the hospitality house there.

Cogley writes that St. Joseph's House of Hospitality on Blue Island Avenue
in Chicago served as an important resource for the poor in Chicago during
the Depression. Cogley notes that he and other resident workers raised
funds, gave talks to local schools and parishes, coordinated services with
city relief organizations and the police, and eventually established a Chicago
Catholic Worker to broadcast the plight of the homeless and unemployed

in Chicago. Cogley became editor of the paper, and while running the shelter, he began to gain the experience that would make him one of the most influential religious writers of his time. Looking back at what he calls the "*Catholic Worker* phase" of his live, Cogley reflects that his work with the movement was crucial; it taught him practical judgment and journalism, but more important, it taught him high moral ideals and to "combine my indignation of structural social evil with compassion for my fellow man" (p. 34). Not everyone shared these feelings about the Catholic Worker movement. Cogley also recalls that many of the traditional Catholics saw Day and her followers as subversives, communists, and kooks. This stage in Cogley's life ended when he was drafted in 1942.

Cogley writes that his military service was "thoroughly undistinguished and undangerous" (p. 36). After his training as a radio operator, Cogley spent the duration of the war based in the United States in what he refers to as "utter safety and comparative comfort" (p. 36). He recalls that when he was released from military service, he was nearly thirty, married, and the father of two children, and eager to get on with some kind of civilian life. Cogley accepted a position as editor of *Today*, a Catholic magazine aimed at high school and college students, and began attending Loyola University in Chicago full time. He graduated from Loyola in 1947 and enrolled at the University of Fribourg in Switzerland to begin graduate studies in Thomistic philosophy.

Cogley's depiction of his studies at the University of Fribourg captures traditional Catholicism before the Second Vatican Council and illustrates Cogley's attraction to and problems with his church. Cogley writes that the university and the surrounding area was quiet and peaceful, that the classes—all taught in Latin—were small and exciting, and that the atmosphere had not changed much since the Middle Ages. His studies, based on the *Summa Theologica* of Thomas Aquinas, required immersion in the rigid rationalism of Catholic theology, but Cogley recalls that he was intrigued by just such study. On the other hand, he remembers a professor lecturing his class, in which Cogley was the only student not preparing for the priesthood, on the services the students could provide for the church. Cogley recalls:

Clearly for my sake, the lone layman, he suggested that the laity, too, had an important role to play in the world and that they might be found doing almost anything. I, too, could serve the cause of the Church if I wished to, despite my vocational handicap, by assisting my clerical betters and upholding the true position when no priest was around to state Catholic teaching. (p. 42)

After receiving his graduate degree, Cogley returned to the United States and accepted the position of columnist and executive editor of *Commonweal*, the most influential progressive American Catholic periodical of the time. This was one of the most productive periods of Cogley's life. He established his family in New York, wrote and lectured, and soon became known as one of the most prominent Catholic journalists in America. Reflecting on his experiences at *Commonweal*, Cogley asserts that because of such editorial positions as *Commonweal*'s attacks on Senator Joseph McCarthy, criticism of the Legion of Decency, and questions about miracles, he and other "Commonweal Catholics" were considered by many to be "not Catholic enough" (p. 51). Cogley writes that confrontations within the American Catholic community indicated the breakup of what he calls the "self-imposed ghettoization" of American Catholics. Before World War II, American Catholicism was primarily an urban faith, with its members sharing habits of speech, habits of thought, and habits of behavior. Cogley notes that after the war, American Catholics moved to the suburbs along with the rest of the new middle class, and as a result, many developed new attitudes and perceptions. Cogley observes that although this ghetto mentality did help millions of first- and second-generation Catholic Americans adapt to a new land, by the 1950s, it had hardened into a reactionary veneration for ritual and authority. Cogley's response to the reaction he received from traditional Catholics was to begin to lose faith in the Catholic Church as an institution.

In 1956, Cogley was named a member of the executive staff of the Ford Foundation's Fund for the Republic, and in that position, he helped to compile and edit the two-volume *Report on Blacklisting*, which exposed the Hollywood practice of denying employment in the movie industry to anyone who was accused of being sympathetic to communism, socialism or other "un-American" ideology. Cogley worked for the Fund for the Republic from 1956 until 1964, and in his autobiography, he writes that during these years, while continuing to write for *Commonweal* and *The New Republic*, he began to seriously question the relation of the institutional Catholic Church to politics in the United States and his own place in that church. He consistently found himself taking positions opposed by the Catholic hierarchy, and he also found himself being drawn to the Episcopal Church. He remembers, however, making a conscious decision not to change churches.

In 1963, Cogley went to Rome to cover the Second Vatican Council. First as a correspondent for the Religious News Service and later as religious news correspondent and religious editor for the *New York Times*, Cogley wrote about the changes taking place in the Catholic Church. In *A Canterbury Tale*, he summarizes the work of the Council as an opening up of the church to the outside world. He especially praises the new freedoms implicit in the ecumenical relations established between the Catholic Church and other religious bodies. He recalls, however, that the winds of change blowing through the church did not transform Catholicism entirely. Cogley continued to struggle with papal authority, clerical celibacy, and the Catholic position on birth control. Nevertheless, he writes that he was no longer a Catholic in the "old understanding of the term," but many other Catholics who thought as he did believed that they were still members in good standing, since the church seemed not to demand full agreement on all issues of faith. Again he decided to stay.

In the final sections of his autobiography, Cogley describes his decision to leave the Catholic Church and become an Episcopalian. He recalls that although the mid–1960s were a special time for American Catholics, with new freedoms emerging and old rules changing, he felt himself again drawn to the Episcopal Church. He writes:

I turned more and more to Anglicanism. It enjoyed antiquity, it claimed apostolic succession, it avoided nonbiblical superstitions, it admitted historic errors, it did not propose outmoded explanations (substantiation) for the mysteries of the faith, and it allowed for real weight in the authority of all its members, lay or clerical. Moreover, contemporary Anglicanism provided for a theological pluralism that ranged from the profound conservatism of E. M. Mascall to the progressive excesses of a bishop Pike. (p. 101)

Cogley found in the Episcopal Church Catholicism without superstition and with democracy and pluralism. It provided him a religious framework with a familiar ritual and dogma, but without the authoritarian structure he always found distasteful. In September 1973, Cogley formally became a member of the Episcopal Church. He died, a deacon of the church, in 1976.

CRITICISM

Despite John Cogley's statement that he did not believe he underwent a conversion, his account of his long journey from Catholicism to Anglicanism is a conversion narrative. Contemporary studies of the conversion process stress that conversion need not be dramatic or sudden; rather, conversion often is a long-term process during which a person changes fundamental beliefs, perceptions, and behaviors. Cogley himself refers to two famous conversions in his autobiography, Augustine's and Cardinal Newman's, and both of these involved long deliberations over time.

In fact, Newman's account of his movement from Anglicanism to Catholicism, Apologia Pro Vita Sua, provides the model for Cogley's movement from Catholicism to Anglicanism. Both autobiographies are narratives of intellectual, emotional, and spiritual quests. Newman, born and trained in the Anglican faith, found in Catholicism the security he found lacking in nineteenth-century Anglicanism. Cogley, on the other hand, found in the Episcopal Church the intellectual freedom and absence of what he called "peasant piety" that he found in twentieth-century American Catholicism.

BIBLIOGRAPHY

Cogley, John. *Report on Blacklisting*. 2 vols. New York: Fund for the Republic, 1956.

———, ed. *Religion in America*. New York: Meridian, 1958.

———. *Religion in a Secular Age: The Search for Final Meaning*. New York: Praeger, 1967.

———. *Catholic America*. New York: Dial, 1973.

———. *A Canterbury Tale: Experiences and Reflections: 1916–1976*. New York: Seabury, 1976.

Fiske, John. "John Cogley Dies at 60; Expert on Catholicism." *New York Times*, 30 March 1976, 34L.

Newman, John H. *Apologia Pro Vita Sua*. New York: W. W. Norton, 1968.

6 • CHARLES W. COLSON (1931–)

Born Again

BIOGRAPHY

Charles Colson was born in Boston on October 16, 1931. His father, who left school at sixteen to help support his family, became an attorney and eventually worked for the Securities and Exchange Commission. In 1949, Colson turned down a scholarship from Harvard because he thought the university was too radical and instead enrolled at Brown, where he graduated in 1953. After graduation, Colson served in the Marine Corps. In 1959, he graduated from Georgetown University Law School, and during the 1960s, he developed a successful law practice in Washington, D.C.

Colson developed an interest in politics early in his career. He was Republican senator Leverett Saltonstall's campaign manager in 1960 and later his administrative assistant; he campaigned for Republican presidential candidate Barry Goldwater in 1964; and in 1968, he joined Richard Nixon's presidential campaign. In 1969, Colson began to work at the White House, first as a political strategist under H. R. Haldeman and then, after the 1970 elections, as a special assistant to President Nixon. In 1971, he supervised, with John Erlichman, a White House special investigations unit, the Plumbers, which was established to identify people suspected of leaking information to the press. In addition, he had the White House staff draw up a list of political and media enemies and became involved in several covert, illegal activities.

Preparing for President Nixon's reelection campaign, Colson, Erlichman, and Haldeman established the Committee to Re-Elect the President

(CREEP). Under that organization's supervision, G. Gordon Liddy developed the project for the electronic surveillance of Democratic party committee chairman Lawrence O'Brien's office at the Watergate Hotel, and the Watergate affair, which would lead to the resignation of President Nixon and the conviction of many of his top aides, including Charles Colson, began.

In 1972, after Nixon's reelection, Colson submitted his resignation and returned to private law practice. In March 1972, Colson was indicted by the Watergate grand jury, and in June, facing a possible fifteen-year prison sentence, he pleaded guilty to a charge of obstructing justice and was sentenced to one to three years in federal prison.

Before Colson's indictment but while he was under investigation, news of Colson's dramatic conversion became public, and many people believed that it was a ploy to avoid prosecution and imprisonment. Colson's subsequent activities, however, have convinced many of his sincerity. After serving seven months in federal prison, he returned to Washington, where he works to help minister to prison inmates.

THE AUTOBIOGRAPHY

Chuck Colson began writing *Born Again* while in federal prison in Alabama. The narrative grew out of two activities: an examination of his actions as part of the Watergate conspiracy in a search for the "deeper meaning" of what had happened to him and others, and an attempt to tell his old friends in Washington how real God was to him and others in prison. Colson believed that he needed to explain himself, his actions, and his conversions; and he believed that God was urging him to use his own life story as a vehicle to reach others. In writing his autobiography, Colson came to see Watergate as part of a healthy cleansing of the nation. In answering the question "how could we who had the trust of the nation have strayed so far afield" (p. 9), Colson began to see Watergate as part of a national spiritual rebirth, a disillusionment that would call forth a revival of religious faith, and his autobiography is both a confession of his part in Watergate and a call for moral and religious revival.

Born Again is a book about both religion and politics, and Colson begins his narrative by describing what should have been the high point of his political career, the celebration of Richard Nixon's reelection. Colson's description, however, is far from celebratory:

I stood there thinking that, unlike any celebration I had attended in twenty years of politics, there was no air of triumph here. The faces before us were unsmiling, looking, in fact, disappointed and even imposed upon. Around the big boards where the continuing returns were posting record-breaking returns for Nixon, there was scarcely a ripple of excitement. (p. 13)

At the outset of his narrative, Colson presents the Nixon White House as a place of both frantic activity and emptiness. In the early chapters of his autobiography, as he describes his work as a special assistant to the president, which earned him the reputation as "Nixon's Hatchet Man," Colson juxtaposes his political chronology with references to this growing sense that something was wrong in his life.

In the first third of his autobiography, Colson gives an insider's view of the workings of the White House from 1970, when he became special assistant to Richard Nixon, until 1973, when his resignation was accepted. These were significant years in American history, and Colson's descriptions of the administration's attempts to end the Vietnam War, responses to antiwar demonstrations, concerns and maneuvers over Daniel Ellsberg and the release of the Pentagon Papers, and plans to reelect the president make interesting reading. As Colson records the events leading up to the election, he shows an administration convinced of its own righteousness, an administration assured that it could do whatever it had to because it was right. Looking back to the days after the break-in at Watergate and before the election, Colson writes:

Hubris became the mark of the Nixon man because *hubris* was the quality Nixon admired most.... Maybe it was bald stupidity to expect to get away with breaking into one of the most heavily guarded office buildings in Washington, but it sure was *hubris*.... We had set in motion forces that would sooner or later make Watergate, or something like it, inevitable. (p. 72)

The specter of Watergate hangs over Colson's entire narrative. It was the pivotal public event in his life. Because of the break-in and what followed, the entire direction of a presidency, and the lives of those who worked for the president, changed. Put in terms of classical drama, it was the hubris of Nixon and his associates that brought forth the tragedy. Although aware of tragic elements in his narrative, Colson's perspective is different because it is his conversion that transforms his life in a much more radical way than Watergate. The dramatic transformation in *Born Again* is not from special assistant to the president to prisoner, but rather from sinner to saint. In the central chapters of his narrative, Colson describes his growing awareness of his own need for something more in his life and his eventual turning to God.

In the summer of 1973, while Watergate was in the news daily, Colson began to reexamine his life. At this time, he met Thomas L. Phillips, chairman of the board of Raytheon Company, and Phillips told Colson the account of his own conversion and offered him hope and a book, C. S. Lewis' *Mere Christianity*. Colson took the book with him on a vacation to the Maine coast, and after spending a week reading and thinking, he accepted Christ.

All conversions are dramatic, but some appear more suddenly than others. Paul's blinding experience on the road to Damascus is perhaps the best-known example of the dramatic conversion, whereas Augustine's years of wrestling with his conscience is a classic example of the developmental conversion. Colson presents his own as part of a natural process. Although the actual accepting of Jesus was a sudden event that occurred on a Friday morning on the coast of Maine, Colson sets that moment in a sequence of events involving self-examination, preparation, study, and, finally, an education of the consequences of his decision. As he charts his personal growth in faith, he records the growing revelations about the White House's involvement in Watergate. The personal and political finally intersect as Colson found himself drawn to Paul's Letter to the Philippians:

I look upon everything as loss compared with the overwhelming gain of knowing Christ Jesus my Lord. For his sake I did in fact suffer the loss of everything, but considered it mere garbage compared with being able to win Christ. (Phil. 3:8, 9, The New Testament in Modern English [revised ed.])

During the same period, Colson's conversion became public knowledge, much to the delight of the press, which covered the news of "the White House Tough Guy's" conversion with skepticism and sarcasm. Editorial writers and political cartoonists made much of the conversion, and Colson includes some of the best cartoons in his book.

Charles Colson found himself facing a moral dilemma in 1973; he was, as Mike Wallace acidly observed on "60 Minutes," caught between his prior faith in Richard Nixon and his new faith in Christ. Additionally, he was under criminal investigation while his conversion urged him to public confession. Finally, after much soul-searching, Colson decided to plead guilty to one count of obstruction of justice and serve whatever sentence he received. He recalls deciding that his call to Christ cut him off from his previous life and required him to make a complete break. On June 3, Colson pleaded guilty, and on July 8, he left for prison.

Captivity narratives are a standard form of Christian discourse, and like John Bunyan, Mary Rowlandson, and Paul himself, Colson writes of his prison experiences to demonstrate the goodness of God. For many converts, prison becomes an incubator for the faith, and as Colson describes his prison life, first at Fort Holabird near Baltimore and then at Maxwell Prison in Alabama, he concentrates not on the deprivations of prison life, but on the growing Christian community he discovered behind bars.

Colson describes his seven-month incarceration as a training period. Although he does describe the solitude, the intimidation, and the fear of being in jail, he stresses what he learned from the experience. Shortly after he was imprisoned, he began to wonder if his imprisonment was God's plan for him, and after praying, he thought to himself, "Of course, of course, of course.... There is a purpose to my being here, perhaps a mission the Lord has called me to" (p. 284). Once he had decided that he could serve the Lord in prison as well as out, Colson accepts his confinement and helps to minister to other prisoners and grows in his own faith to the point that he can say at the end of a prison prayer meeting, "Praise the Lord that I am in prison and have this chance to be a witness for Jesus Christ" (p. 309). In addition to becoming a witness, Colson describes his charismatic experience, first speaking in tongues and then faith healing. By the time he is released, Colson is convinced not only of the direction of his life—to minister to the spiritual needs of prison inmates—but also of this growth as a spirit-filled, charismatic Christian.

CRITICISM

Born Again is an unusual conversion narrative for a number of reasons. First, it provides an inside look at the Nixon administration during the months leading up to and immediately after the Watergate break-in. Charles Colson's comments about the events and the characters that made up that particular part of American history offer readers a unique perspective. Second, Colson's discussion of the impact of his religious conversion on his political convictions is interesting. Early in *Born Again*, Colson asserts that the Nixon presidency was no different from those that preceded it, and throughout his autobiography, Colson never questions the goals of the administration. In a sense, politically he remains a Nixonian in spite of being born again. What conversion seems to have taught Colson is not that some political actions are immoral, but rather that politics itself is essentially immoral. One is either part of the world or out of the world. Colson's personal response, in both his autobiography and his postprison ministry, is to remove himself from the world.

Almost all the criticism about Charles Colson is concerned with his role in Watergate. As one of the central actors in that political drama, Colson is an important figure in both the popular and the scholarly examinations of the end of the Nixon administration. At times, articles about Colson continue to appear in the media in connection with his prison ministry.

BIBLIOGRAPHY

Buckley, W. F., Jr. "Colson, Nixon, and the CIA." *National Review*, 2 August 1974, 884–85.
———. "Prison Reform." *National Review*, 14 May 1982, 585.
———. "Breaching Church-State at Taconic." *National Review*, 19 October 1984, 62.
Colson, Charles. *Born Again*. Old Tappan, N.J.: F. H. Revell, 1976.
"Colson: From Tough Politics to Religion?" *U.S. News & World Report*, 17 June 1974, 27.

"Colson's Motivation." *National Review*, 21 June 1974, 686–87.

"Colson's Weird Scenario." *Time*, 8 July 1974, 16.

"A Convert's Convictions." *Newsweek*, 19 October 1987, 10.

Doane, D. P. "How Time Has Treated the Watergate Crew." *U.S. News & World Report*, 14 June 1982, 52.

Esty, F. R., Jr. "Evidence of God's Power." *Christianity Today*, 6 April 1984, 48–49.

Fields, H. "PW Interviews." *Publishers Weekly*, 30 September 1983, 117–18.

"Four Walls Close in on Nixon." *Time*, 17 June 1974, 13–14 +.

Goldman, P., and C. Wiley. "Haldeman Speaks Out." *Newsweek*, 27 February 1978, 29–31.

Hallett, D. "Low-level Memoir of the Nixon White House." *New York Times Magazine*, 20 October 1974, 39–42 +.

Hefley, J. C. "Colson, Cons, and Christ." *Christianity Today*, 4 July 1975, 57.

Horrock, N. "Whispers About Colson." *Newsweek*, 5 March 1973, 21.

"Humbled Hatchet Man." *Time*, 2 February 1976, 20.

Lindsay, J. L. "Colson: Beat the Devil." *Newsweek*, 17 June 1974, 19–20 +.

Mack, J. "God and Man in Jail." *The Progressive*, April 1985, 50.

Magnuson, E. "Aftermath of a Burglary." *Time*, 14 June 1982, 30.

"Man Who Converted to Softball." *Time*, 17 June 1974, 15–16.

"Nation: Sentencing by Judge Gerhard Gesell." *Time*, 1 July 1974, 11–12.

"New Beginning for Charles Colson." *The Christian Century*, 3 July 1974, 691.

"Nixon: Fly Now—Pay Later?" *Newsweek*, 1 July 1974, 16–18.

Osborne, J. "Kicking Sand." *New Republic*, 16 December 1972, 9–10.

Sheils, M. "Chuck Colson's Leveler." *Newsweek*, 9 September 1974, 72–73.

Spring, B. "Slain Philippine Leader Aquino Is a Christian Martyr, Says Colson." *Christianity Today*, 7 October 1983, 54–55.

"Where They Are Now: The Nixon-Ford Media Team." *Broadcasting*, 8 August 1977, 27.

"Why Charles Colson's Heart Is Still in Prison." [Interview] *Christianity Today*, 16 September 1983, 12–16.

Wills, G. "Born Again Politics." *New York Times*, 1 August 1976, 8–9 +.

Woodward, K. L., and S. Monroe. "Colson Goes Back to Jail." *Newsweek*, 7 September 1981, 41.

7 • NICKY CRUZ (1938–)

Run, Baby, Run

BIOGRAPHY

Nicky Cruz was born in Puerto Rico in 1938. In 1955, his parents sent him to New York to live with his older brother. On the island, Cruz had been brought up by spiritual parents who practiced a form of witchcraft, and in New York, he quickly found school and work boring. He joined a street gang, the Mau Maus, and by 1956, he had become a gang leader. In 1958, Cruz met evangelist David Wilkerson, who was working with ghetto children in New York, and became a Christian. In the early 1960s, Cruz attended Bible school in California, and by 1965, he had begun preaching and working with Outreach for Youth. Cruz remains a popular Christian evangelist. His autobiography, *Run, Baby, Run*, has sold more than two million copies since 1968, and the fictionalized story of his conversion, *The Cross and the Switchblade*, is a popular novel and a popular film.

THE AUTOBIOGRAPHY

Run, Baby, Run is a religious narrative. Cruz and coauthor Jamie Buckingham use a specific model to organize the material in the text. Cruz sees his experiences as religious, and structures them around his conversion in much the same way as Augustine did with his *Confessions* and John Bunyan did in *Grace Abounding to the Chief of Sinners*. These and other conversion narratives are built around the dramatic conversion experience and emphasize the qualitative difference in the life of the autobiographer before and after that conversion. Cruz's intent is didactic; he is less interested in revealing himself as a person than in presenting his life as an example. Ultimately the center of the narrative is less Nicky Cruz and more the "power of the Holy Spirit" that infuses and transforms him. Daniel Shea, writing in *Spiritual Autobiography in Early America*, points out that "since Paul and Augustine, indeed since Pentecost, Christians have been evangelizing in the first person" (p. 88). In using a conversion experience to evangelize, a writer forms an argument in which he presents evidence from his personal experience in a pattern that details the conversion process and gives witness to a life changed by that conversion. In *Run, Baby, Run*, Cruz is not primarily interested in the conversion itself; rather, he presents himself in his autobiography as a witness to the power of Jesus Christ and the effect of that power on his life.

Run, Baby, Run also is part of another tradition, a tradition begun in colonial New England and carried throughout the development of American literature. Like William Bradford's *History of Plymouth Plantation*, John Winthrop's *History of New England*, and even Cotton Mather's *Magnalia Christi Americana*, Cruz's narrative can be seen as a personal history celebrating God's workings in the new land, workings full of mystery, purpose, and power. Like these writers, Cruz sees God working actively on individuals to lead a chosen people to salvation, and he presents his own life as but one more example of God's remarkable providences.

Cruz constructs his narrative of dramatic conversion around certain obvious contrasts: his character before his conversion and his character after, the grim setting of the early part of the narrative and the religiously infused setting after, and his criminal activities before his conversion and his Christian action after. Also, because Cruz intends to make his conversion as dramatic as possible, the narrative is tightly structured; dramatic incident follows dramatic incident, and action is more important than motivation, at least until the moment of the conversion. To further heighten the contrast between the old Cruz and the spiritually reborn Cruz, the autobiography emphasizes the worst aspects of Cruz's life before his conversion and the best after. Cruz develops the two-part structure of the narrative by placing the conversion itself at the center of the narrative. Thus part one presents Cruz's swift descent into the world of crime and sin, and part two chronicles his struggle to make use of his gift and live the life of a born-again Christian.

Because *Run, Baby, Run* is a religious narrative, Cruz is less concerned with the specific problems caused by his being a Puerto Rican in New York than he is with the more universal and representative aspects of his life. His crimes, drug experiences, gang leadership, and sexual exploits could have been those of any urban street tough, and his description of his behavior after his conversion serves as an example of how a born-again Christian should act in a contemporary urban environment. Although his concerns are not primarily Puerto Rican, it would be a mistake to assume that the narrative of his life throws no light on the Puerto Rican experience in America. He is successful in his re-creation of the prejudice faced by Puerto Ricans in the new land, of the street culture of New York City, of the problems caused by the inability to speak English, of the effects of poverty, and of the shock of the movement from rural Puerto Rico to the streets of New York. Also, Cruz's narrative does demonstrate that some Puerto Ricans do survive and prosper in this country, and that evangelical Christianity, an old and powerful force in American history, has reached America's most recent newcomers.

Cruz opens his narrative with his first American experience. As with many Puerto Ricans and earlier immigrants, the introduction is harsh. The first words that Cruz hears from an American are "pig" and "filthy spic." Cruz then uses the weather to develop a contrast between New York City and Puerto Rico. He first describes the cold streets filled with dirty melting snow and then shifts to a memory of his warm home on the island. The contrast is effective.

Although Cruz is careful to build a striking contrast between the island and the city to emphasize the shock of the arrival, he does not sentimentalize the island; he calls it a "land of witchcraft and voodoo, of religious superstition and great ignorance" (p. 1). His father in fact was a leading spiritualist on the island who sent his son away to New York because he could not control him. As in many ethnic-American autobiographies, the impact of the city on the newcomer is totally unsettling. Because he speaks no English, Cruz cannot get around the city and is a victim of unfair treatment without even being aware of it. A restaurant owner charges him ten dollars for two hamburgers, leaving him penniless. Cruz then describes how he wanders around the city for a week eating what he can steal and sleeping in doorways and in abandoned buildings until he meets a kindly old man who speaks Spanish and helps him to get in contact with Cruz's older brother, who lives in the city. In the opening chapter of his autobiography, Cruz skillfully re-creates the first impressions of a stranger in New York; the cold, rudeness, hunger, confusion, and constant sense of motion. Cruz sets the loneliness and the helplessness of the newcomer against the massiveness and indifference of the urban landscape.

Much has been written about the fate of Puerto Rican children in the New York public schools, and Cruz's depiction of his school experiences in illustrative of much of that material. Cruz describes his black and Puerto Rican school as more like a jail than a school. He chronicles fights and intimidations, drawing a picture of an institution in which the teachers and administrators spend their time in a futile attempt to impose discipline and students spend theirs trying to win or stay out of fights. Cruz decides that school is useless and that his brother is trying to be a father to him, so he leaves both for a life on the streets. There he quickly begins to learn more about urban life. Like other immigrant autobiographers, Cruz comments on the contrast between his expectations and the reality he discovers in New York. The promise of America, which attracts millions, is set against the actual circumstances that the immigrants find on their arrival. In this passage, Cruz is both personal and representative:

After two months I still wasn't accustomed to life in New York. Back in Puerto Rico I had seen pictures of the Statue of Liberty and the United Nations Building. But here, in the ghetto, as far as the eye could see there was nothing but apartments, filled with human flesh. Each window symbolized a family, eking out a miserable existence. I thought of the zoo in San Juan with the pacing bears and the chattering monkeys behind bars. They wallow in their own filth. They eat stale meat or wilted lettuce. They fight among themselves and the only time they get together is when they are attacking an intruder. Animals aren't meant to live this way, with only a painted jungle scene on the rear of a cage to remind them of what they are supposed to be. And neither are people. But here, in the ghetto, do. (p. 30)

Cruz uses this same analogy through the first half of his narrative, effectively creating a sense of the city as a "concrete jungle." In this jungle, survival is the only real priority, and to survive on the street, Cruz turns to robbery to get money for his rent and food. Finally, he joins a street gang, the Mau Maus, to have protection and be part of an effective social unit.

The depictions of his gang activity are the most graphic part of the autobiography and, from the standpoint of the conversion motif, the most important section of the first part of the narrative, for they show the depths of the degradation into which he sinks before his conversion. The gang quickly becomes Cruz's family, his reason for living, and the only social structure for which he has any respect—the one social unit fit to exist and survive in the urban jungle. It provides protection, community, sex, money, drugs, and an escape from the ugly reality of the ghetto for its members. Cruz presents New York as a city of warring gangs, each controlling an area of the city, defending its territory against all outsiders, whether the outsiders are members of rival gangs or the police. Without membership in a gang, a person cannot survive, and Cruz provides several examples of what happens to people who do not belong. The luckiest get off with a severe beating; the unlucky ones are killed or maimed. Although the gang structure provides much for its members, it also demands much: absolute courage, absolute loyalty, and the ability to undergo a vicious initiation. The depiction of the initiation is of central importance to the narrative because it concretizes the violence that infuses the first part of the autobiography and demonstrates the lengths to which Cruz was willing to go in search of a way to deal with his position as an outsider. Cruz describes the initiation of the new members by Carlos, the leader of the Mau Maus:

"I'm gonna turn and walk twenty steps to the other wall," he said, "you stand right where you are. You say you're a tough kid. Well, we're gonna find out just how tough. When I get to twenty, I'm gonna turn and throw this knife. If you flinch or duck you're chicken. If you don't, even if the knife sticks in you, you're a tough kid and can join the Mau Maus. Got it?" (p. 45)

Cruz effectively combines language and action to create the ever-present threat of violence. When the initiate falters, he is stabbed in both armpits and thrown out into the streets. Rather than being repelled by this violence, Cruz is fascinated by the blood; when it is his turn, he chooses a second method of initiation, fighting five gang members at once. He loses, of course, but he proves himself. When he regains consciousness, he is given a pistol and is welcomed into the family.

Once he is a member of the family, Cruz quickly rises within it; in less than one year he becomes president of the gang and is its most violent and proficient fighter. Under his leadership, the gang engages in mass street wars, numerous robberies, attacks on neighborhood churches, and a suicidal open war against the police. After this reign of terror, he is finally taken to the police station where he is told, "The only way to handle these S.O.B.'s is to beat the hell out of them. They're all a bunch of filthy, stinking pigs. We got a jail full of niggers, wops, and spics. You're just like all the rest, and if you get out of line, we'll make you wish you were dead" (p. 89). Cruz responds to this threat with a threat of his own: "Go ahead and hit me, but one day I'm gonna come to your house and kill your wife and children" (p. 90). Cruz includes this response to indicate how far his alienation has gone; he has declared total war on society and does not care about the consequences of his actions. At the age of eighteen, he has a record of twenty-one arrests, ranging from robbery to assault with intent to kill. This section of the narrative depicts how life in the jungle has taken its toll; when he is brought before the juvenile judge, he is told that he "lives like an animal and acts like an animal." Instead of sending him to prison, the judge recommends psychiatric care. It fails, and Cruz returns to the streets.

Cruz places his arrest and the failure of psychiatric care directly before the conversion in his narrative. His comments to the police and his psychiatrist's despair at this behavior mark the limits of his descent. At this point in the narrative, he describes himself as barely human, cut off from all people and activities outside the gang. It appears he has only two options: prison or death on the streets.

The transformation of Cruz's life is presented in the next chapter, titled "The Encounter." Here Cruz dramatically describes his confrontation with the Reverend David Wilkerson, love, and the power of God. Wilkerson is a Pentecostal minister who specializes in teen crusades in East Coast cities. He has canvassed the Puerto Rican community, advertising a youth crusade directed at Puerto Rican gang members. The Mau Maus are challenged by Wilkerson to attend, and they go, planning to disrupt the meeting. However, in the middle of Wilkerson's sermon on repentance and the power of prayer,

Cruz is strangely moved. He describes looking into himself for the first time in years and being repulsed by what he sees. For the first time since he was a child, Cruz cries, and under Wilkerson's direction, he pours himself out to God. Cruz's comments on his conversion are quite simple:

I opened my mouth, but the words that came out were not mine. "O God, if You love me, come into my life. I'm tired of running. Come into my life and change me. Please change me."
    That's all it was. But I felt myself being picked up and swept heavenward. (p. 121)

Although some readers might find such a sudden and complete conversion too dramatic or too startling to be realistic, it must be remembered that Cruz is describing a religious and emotional experience, not an intellectual one, and he is describing it within an accepted religious context. In addition, many writers of conversion narratives have used the convention of a moment of illumination and transformation to describe their conversion experiences. Paul's confrontation on the road to Damascus is the best-known example, but Cruz's conversion is part of that tradition. His narrative is an illustration of just this point. He presents himself before his conversion as the product of years of neglect, dissipation, and the influence of the ghetto, yet in one dramatic instant, he is changed by the power of God. Cruz does not explain his conversion; he presents it to his audience to take as a matter of faith.

A dramatic change in tone and pace takes place at this point in the narrative. The new direction is established in a conversation that Cruz has with Wilkerson shortly after the conversion. Wilkerson tells Cruz that he will be filled with power and the gifts of the Holy Spirit, and when Cruz asks about the gifts, Wilkerson responds with a catechismal definition of Pentecostalism. Cruz, like a good student, asks questions, and Wilkerson provides the correct doctrinal answers. In this passage, Wilkerson tells Cruz that he must tarry until he receives his gifts.

The second half of the narrative recounts this tarrying and baptism. Less dramatic and less expressive of elements of the Puerto Rican experience in the United States, it presents Cruz's preparation, baptism, and work for the Lord as a kind of initiation, but in this case, the initiation is not into the culture at large, but into a special part of American subculture—Pentecostal Christianity. These events help to strengthen the contrast between the first and second parts of the narrative and place Cruz's actions within the pattern established by earlier ethnic writers by moving him out of the city, providing him with an education, and enabling him to return to the city with a new perspective. Wilkerson sends Cruz to the Bible Institute at La Puente, California, where he studies English and the Bible, practices self-discipline, and, finally, while assisting at a Pentecostal mission in Los Angeles, is filled with the Holy Spirit and baptized. With his heart and mind transformed, Cruz returns to New York to establish a ministry within the ghetto from which he came. Like a number of conversions, *Run, Baby, Run* ends pointing toward the future, with Cruz leaving New York with his ministry established, about to perform the Lord's work across the nation.

CRITICISM

Writing in *The Nuyorican Experience: Literature of the Puerto Rican Minority*, Eugene Mohr remarks that Cruz's autobiography has enjoyed a long popularity because, aside from its church sponsorship, "there is an additional appeal in the book's being a double success story: Nicky escapes both a life of sin and life in El Barrio. And one life is an objective correlative of the other" (p. 68). Almost every commentary about Cruz's work places it within a religious context. Billy Graham, for example, calls the book remarkable because "it has all the elements of a tragedy, violence and intrigue—plus the greatest of all ingredients: the power of the gospel of Jesus Christ" (*Run, Baby, Run*, p. vii).

Run, Baby, Run also is a work for nonevangelicals. Cruz's autobiography, although an excellent example of the traditional conversion story, provides a stark instance of the impact of New York City and, by extension, urban American culture on a newcomer. It documents the poverty, hostility, and racism that many Spanish-speaking Americans confront. In addition, Cruz shows how a traditional narrative form can be used effectively by a contemporary writer.

Run, Baby, Run also is of interest because it provides an excellent example of how the traditional conversion narrative can be adapted by a nontraditional writer. The conversion experience appears to be a central part of American culture, and American writers from Jonathan Edwards to Nicky Cruz have used the conventions of that genre to describe their spiritual life in America.

BIBLIOGRAPHY

Cordasco, Francesco, Eugene Bucchioni, and Diego Castellanos. *Puerto Ricans on the United States Mainland: A Bibliography of Reports, Texts, Critical Studies, and Related Materials.* Totowa, N.J.: Rowan & Littlefield, 1972.

Cruz, Nicky, with Jamie Buckingham. *Run, Baby, Run.* 1968 (1st ed.). New York: Jove, 1978.

Holte, James. *The Ethnic I: A Sourcebook for Ethnic-American Autobiography.* Westport, Conn.: Greenwood Press, 1988.

Mohr, Eugene. *The Nuyorican Experience: Literature of the Puerto Rican Minority.* Westport, Conn.: Greenwood Press, 1982.

Shea, Daniel. *Spiritual Autobiography in Early America*. Princeton, N.J.: Princeton
    University Press, 1968.
Wakefield, Dan. *Island in the City: The World of Spanish Harlem*. Boston: Houghton
    Mifflin, 1959.

8 • MARY FRANCIS CLARE CUSACK (1830–1899)

The Nun of Kenmare

BIOGRAPHY

Margaret Anna Cusack was born in Dublin in 1830 and raised in a wealthy Anglican family in Ireland and later in Exeter, England. She received an outstanding education, and after coming in contact with the Oxford movement, she joined an Anglican religious order. In 1858, she left the Anglican Church and became a Catholic, joining the Irish Poor Clares in Newry, Ireland, the next year, taking the name Sister Mary Francis Clare.

From 1859 to 1879, Sister Mary Francis Clare Cusack devoted herself to writing. She published poetry, histories, and biographies, and even some sacred music. In 1874, she published *Woman's Work in Modern Society*, which addressed some of the problems facing women in the late nineteenth century. During the time Clare was in Newry, and later in Kenmare, the people of Ireland were suffering from the effects of British colonial rule, famine, and the Industrial Revolution. Few cash crops were being produced, many of the working men had been forced to emigrate to either the United States or the industrial cities of England, there was no local industry, and as a result, those who remained, primarily women and children, suffered. In addition, in 1879, a major famine destroyed what crops remained from the earlier famine years. In that year, Clare became internationally known as the Nun of Kenmare when she raised more than 20,000 pounds to help feed and shelter the destitute in County Mayo.

In 1884, Cusack sought dispensation from her vows as an Irish Poor Clare and approval from Rome to establish a new religious community, dedicated to teaching industrial skills to poor Irish girls. Cusack believed that religious education and training for jobs would make Irish girls employable, breaking the cycle of poverty that had existed in Ireland for generations. Although she founded her community, the St. Joseph Sisters of Peace, she was unable to establish a home in Ireland for her order. In November 1884, she arrived in New York City with Pope Leo XIII's approval to establish a home and employment bureau for immigrant girls. She was unable to get permission from the bishop of New York for her endeavor, but in March 1885, she established her community in Newark, New Jersey.

During the next several years, Cusack battled with the American Catholic hierarchy as she attempted to establish schools in a number of cities. In 1887, she wrote a 176-page pamphlet, "The Question of Today: Anti-Poverty and Progress, Labor and Capital," which was interpreted by American bishops as an attack on the church's position on issues of economic justice. Cusack lost what support she had in the church hierarchy, and in July 1888, she left the order she established and later left the Catholic Church. She died on June 6, 1899, in Leamington, England.

THE AUTOBIOGRAPHY

Sister Mary Francis Clare Cusack published her autobiography, *The Nun of Kenmare*, in 1888, after she left the St. Joseph Sisters of Peace, the religious order she established. Cusack was aware of the seriousness of her decision to renounce her vows, and in the beginning of her autobiography, she writes:

The writing of this book has been a subject of long and serious consideration. I am not ignorant of the very grave issues which it involves; they are serious to myself, and they are serious to men of very high position, whose actions are herein detailed.

I have written this work because I know that I owe an explanation to the many thousands who have contributed not out of their wealth, but out of their poverty, to the good work which I tried to establish in Kenmare, Knock, and America. (p. 1)

Her autobiography is a defense, and as she records the events of her life that brought her to Catholicism and the convent and then away from both, she articulates the frustrations of an intelligent, progressive woman forced to battle a conservative, male hierarchy on both sides of the Atlantic in the late nineteenth century.

Like many other well-educated English and Anglo-Irish, Cusack was drawn to the high-church revival in the Church of England during the nineteenth century. Before becoming a Catholic, she entered an Anglican convent. Influenced by the writings of Cardinal Newman and other members of the Oxford movement, Cusack entered the Roman Catholic Church in 1858, joining the Irish Order of Poor Clares and moving to their convent in Newry, Ireland, in 1859. For the first twenty years of sisterhood, Cusack devoted her time and energy to writing, and in her autobiography, she recalls her pleasure at being a writer, listing the titles of her books and favorable comments from her readers.

After describing her literary work, Cusack provides a chronicle of the Irish troubles. In a short chapter titled "The Famine Year in Ireland," she describes the famine year of 1879 in the context of Irish political and economic history. Confronting the effects of the famine in Kenmare accelerated Cusack's movement from purely literary interests to social, and later political, ones. Earlier, in 1874, Cusack had written about the position of working women in contemporary society, but when she began to see the amount of personal and social devastation caused by the famine, she moved to direct action. In her autobiography, she describes how she established The Nun of Kenmare's Distress Fund and how she raised and distributed the money that came in from around the world. In addition, she includes letters of appeals and thanks, giving her readers a sense of what her work was like during that year.

From 1879 to 1884, Cusack worked to establish a convent and industrial school for girls in the village of Knock, famous at the time for a reputed appearance of the Virgin Mary. Thousands of young women, most without any skills or means of supporting themselves, were forced by the famine and lack of economic development in Ireland to emigrate to the United States and England. Cusack saw the need for a new religious order, a group of women dedicated to the education and training of poor women. Her idea was a radical one, and she ran into opposition from within her own order and from Irish priests and bishops. Finally, in 1884, she went to Rome, and after meeting with Pope Leo XIII, she received a dispensation from her vows as an Irish Poor Clare and founded the St. Joseph Sisters of Peace. Cusack's depiction of her work during these years makes up the major part of her autobiography. As she describes how she attempted to establish a community that would incorporate her ideas about the social and economic position of women in the late nineteenth century, Cusack develops one of the central themes of her narrative, the opposition of the male hierarchy to any structural changes. Although she had the support of the pope, Cusack was unable to receive permission from the Irish bishops. Angered at being unable to help poor Irish women in Ireland, she moved to the United States to establish her community to assist Irish immigrants.

In the United States, Cusack discovered the same hostility to change she found in Ireland. She was refused permission to establish her order in New York and Baltimore, and she finally set up a small convent in Newark, New Jersey. In a chapter called "Good Works That Have Not Been Accomplished," Cusack argues that the mission of the church, "the duty of the hierarchy," had constantly been thwarted by institutional church. She provides historical examples from church history and then cites examples from her own life in the church. For Cusack, this conflict reached a crisis in 1887, when she wrote her controversial pamphlet called "The Question of Today: Anti-Poverty and Progress, Labor and Capital." In this work, Cusack defended the radical priest, Father Edward McGlynn, who had been excommunicated for supporting social reformer Henry George in the New York City mayoral election of 1886. Archbishop Corrigan of New York accused Cusack of attacking the authority of the church and demanded she apologize and withdraw her publication. Cusack attempted to stop the publication, but after her work appeared, she resigned as mother superior of her order and returned to England, where she died in 1899.

CRITICISM

The Nun of Kenmare is a fascinating autobiography. It provides a detailed account of both the United States and the Catholic Church in transition as well as the spiritual journey of a progressive woman in the late nineteenth century. Cusack's observations about the economic and social situation of Ireland and her descriptions of urban life among the Irish immigrants in the United States give an overview of the immigration experience on both sides of the Atlantic. In addition, Cusack's presentation of her belief in the charitable role of the church, what would become known as the social gospel, and the hostility to that emphasis by many in ecclesiastical authority provide early examples of a conflict that exists within the Christian community to this day. Cusack's autobiography also is important because it clearly demonstrates the hostility Cusack discovered within the patriarchal structure of the Catholic Church. Cusack asserts that much of the opposition she faced, both in Ireland and in the United States, came about not because her ideas were radical, but because her male superiors believed that it was not a woman's place to question their authority.

Mary Francis Clare Cusack left the Catholic Church after she left the St. Joseph Sisters of Peace, and was, for a time, forgotten. Little scholarship exists about her. This situation is beginning to change. Rosalie McQuaide, writing in *America* in 1984, noted that after the Second Vatican Council, the Sisters of Peace began to show a renewed interest in their founder, and two major works have appeared, Irene French Eager's *Margaret Anna Cusack: One Woman's Campaign for Woman's Rights* (Dublin: Arlen, 1980) and Dorothy Vidulich's *Peace Pays the Price: A Study of Margaret Anna Cusack, the Nun of Kenmare, Founder of the Sisters of St. Joseph of Peace* (Englewood Cliffs, N.J.: Center for Peace and Justice, 1975). Her life, her work, and her controversies remain significant areas of study.

BIBLIOGRAPHY

Cusack, Mary Francis. *Saint Clare, Saint Colette, and the Poor Clares.* Dublin: Fowler, 1864.

———. *A Few Words on the Present Crisis in Ireland as It Affects the Whole Catholic Church*. Dublin: DublinSteam, 1865.

———. *The Life and Revelations of Saint Gertrude, Virgin and Abbess, of the Order of the St. Benedict by a Religious of the Order of Poor Clares*. London: Burns, Lambert, 1865.

———. *An Illustrated History of Ireland:: From the Earliest Period*. With Historical Illustrations by Henry Doyle. London: Longmans, Green, 1868.

———. *The Patriot's History of Ireland*. Ireland: National Publication Office, 1869.

———. *The Student's Manual of Irish History*. London: Longmans, Green, 1870.

———. *A Compendium of Irish History*. Boston: Donahoe, 1871.

———. *A History of the Kingdom of Kerry*. London: Longmans, Green, 1871.

———. *Jesus and Jerusalem; or The Way Home*. Boston: Donahoe, 1871.

———. *Advice to Irish Girls in America, by Nun of Kenmare (Sister Mary Francis Clare)*. New York: McGee, 1872.

———. *Hornehurst Rectory*. New York: Sadlier, 1872.

———. *The Liberator: His Life and Times, Political and Social*. Kenmare, Ireland: Kenmare, 1872. [Daniel O'Connell]

———. *The Life of Father Matthew, the People's Soggarth Aroon*. New York: Sadlier, 1872.

———. *St. Patrick's Manual; or, The Manual of St. Patrick, Being a Guide to Catholic Devotion*. New York: Sadlier, 1874.

———. *Woman's Work in Modern Society*. London: Kenmare, 1874.

———. *A History of the City and County of Cork*. Dublin: McGlashan, Gill, 1875.

———. *The Trias Thaumaturga; or, Three Wonder-Working Saints of Ireland, St. Patrick, St. Bridget, and St. Columbia*. Edinburgh: Ballantyne, Hanson, 1875?

———. *In Memoriam Mary O'Hagan Abbess and Foundress of the Convent of Poor Clares, Kenmare*. London: Burns, 1876.

———. *A History of the Irish Nation, Social, Ecclesiastical, Biographical, Industrial and Antiquarian*. London: Murdoch, 1877.

———. *The Lives of Saint Columbia and Saint Brigit*. London: Burns, 1877.

———. *The Life of the Most Rev. Joseph Dixon, D.D., Primate of All Ireland*. London: Burns, 1878.

———. *The Apparition at Knock, with the Depositions of the Witnesses . . . and the Conversion for a Young Protestant Lady by a Vision of the Blessed Virgin*. London: Burns, Oates, 1880.

———. *The Case of Ireland Stated: A Plea for My People and My Race*. Dublin: Gill, 1880.

———. *The Famine in Ireland: Thanks and Appeal to Munificent America*. Kenmare, Ireland: Kenmare, 1880.

———. *The Pilgrim's Way to Heaven*. 4th ed. London: Burns, Oates, 1880.

———. *The Apparition of the Blessed Virgin, St. Joseph, and St. John the Evangelist, at Knock, Co. Mayo, Ireland. Taken from the Account Written by Sister Mary Francis Clare, "The Nun of Kenmare." To Which Is Added an Account of the Apparition of Our Lady at Lourdes, from Approved Sources*. New York: Gay, 1881.

———. *Cloister Songs and Hymns for Children*. London: Burns, 1881.

———. *The Present Case of Ireland Plainly Stated: A Plea for My People and My Race*. New York: Kennedy, 1881.

————. *Three Visits to Knock with the Medical Certificates of Cures and Authentic Accounts of Different Apparitions.* New York: Kennedy, 1882.

————. *M. F. Cusack's History of Ireland.* Condensed, Revised, and Continued by J. H. Beale. New Haven, Conn.: Gay, 1883.

————. *From Killarney to New York; or, How Thade Became a Banker.* Boston: O'Loughlin, 1886.

————. *Tim Carty's Trial; or, Whistling at Landlords: A Play for the Times.* New York: Mears, 1886.

————. "The Question of Today: Anti-Poverty and Progress, Labor and Capital." Chicago: Belford, Clarke, 1887.

————. *The Nun of Kenmare: An Autobiography.* Boston: Tickner, 1888.

————. *Life Inside the Church of Rome.* London: Hazell, 1889.

————. *What Rome Teaches.* New York: Baker, Taylor, 1891.

————. *The Black Pope: A History of the Jesuits.* London: Marshall, 1896.

————. ["Vigilant," pseud.]. *Revolution and War; or, Britain's Peril and Her Secret Foes.* New and revised ed. London: Paul, 1913.

————. *Franciscan Rhymes Culled from the Little Flowers of Saint Francis.* Dublin: Gill, 1931.

"Deaconess Movement." *North American Review,* August 1892, 245–48.

Eager, Irene French. *The Nun of Kenmare.* Cork: Mercier, 1970.

————. *Margaret Anna Cusack: One Woman's Campaign for Women's Rights: A Biography.* Revised ed. Dublin: Arlen, 1980.

McQuaide, Rosalie. "The Nun of Kenmare." *America,* 29 September 1984, 169–71.

Vidulich, Dorothy. *Peace Pays a Price: A Study of Margaret Anna Cusack, the Nun of Kenmare, Foundress of the Sisters of St. Joseph of Peace.* Photos by Ray Gora. Englewood Cliffs, N.J.: Center for Peace and Justice, 1975.

9 · DOROTHY DAY (1897–1980)

The Long Loneliness

BIOGRAPHY

Dorothy Day was born on November 8, 1897, in Brooklyn, New York. Her father, John I. Day, was a sportswriter who eventually became the racing editor of the *New York Morning Telegraph*. Day grew up in Berkeley, Oakland, Chicago, and New York as her family moved around the country following her father from newspaper to newspaper. Day grew up in a nominally Protestant family; she was baptized and confirmed an Episcopalian, but neither she nor the other members of her family expressed much interest in religion. When Day was sixteen, she entered the University of Illinois and joined the Socialist party.

In 1916, she moved to New York City with her family and joined the Industrial Workers of the World (IWW). She worked as a writer for the Socialist paper *The Call* and the radical leftist magazine *The Masses*. In November 1917, she took part in a demonstration in front of the White House to protest the United States' entry into World War I. She was arrested, and along with sixty other women, she was jailed in the Occoquan Work House, where she participated in a ten-day hunger strike. After her release, she returned to New York, where she served as a probationary nurse in the Kings County Hospital in Brooklyn.

During the 1920s, Day lived in France, where she wrote *The Eleventh Virgin*, a novel; in New Orleans, where she was a feature writer for *The New Orleans Item*; in Hollywood, where she was a scriptwriter for Pathé films; and in Staten Island, New York, where she lived in a common-law marriage with Forster Batterham. In 1927, her daughter, Tamar Teresa, was born, and Day, concerned how her life would affect her daughter, converted to Catholicism.

Conversion did not dampen Day's radicalism. In 1933, she and Peter Maurin began publishing *The Catholic Worker* out of her apartment. *The Catholic Worker* became one of the most influential political papers of the period. Day and Maurin advocated the establishment of urban houses of hospitality for the homeless poor and farming and craft communes for "workers to become scholars and scholars to become workers." In addition to articulating the concerns of the Catholic social action movement in the 1930s, Day and *The Catholic Worker* opposed Francisco Franco in the Spanish Civil War, opposed military conscription during World War II, and encouraged passive resistance to nuclear war preparations during the 1950s and 1960s. In 1973, she was arrested with Cesar Chavez and the striking United Farm Workers union members in Fresno, California.

In 1972, Day was awarded the University of Notre Dame's Laetare Medal for her work in the Catholic social action movement. She died on November 29, 1980, in Mary House, *The Catholic Worker*'s hospice, on the Lower East Side of New York City.

THE AUTOBIOGRAPHY

Dorothy Day's autobiography, *The Long Loneliness*, was published in 1952, during a period when many of the positions taken by Day and *The Catholic Worker* were not popular. Day had written about herself previously. *From Union Square to Rome* was an apologia for her conversion to Catholicism published by a Catholic press, but in her autobiography, she describes her beliefs, acts, and conversion in the context of her personal life and social beliefs. In the introduction to *The Long Loneliness*, she compares writing autobiography to confession:

Going to confession is hard. Writing a book is hard, because you are "giving yourself away." But if you love, you want to give yourself. You write as you are impelled to write, about man and his problems, his relation to God and his fellows. You write about yourself because in the long run all of man's problems are the same, his human need of sustenance and love. (p. 10)

Like many religious autobiographers, Day sees the value of her writing not in her specific achievements as a person, but in the universal elements of her experience. For Day, as for Paul and John Bunyan, autobiography is an act of service to God and community rather than an act of self-gratification.

Although Day begins her autobiography by describing her childhood and adolescence, the real story of her life began when she entered the University of Illinois. She remarks that even as a child, she searched for what she calls "the abundant life," a life in which everyone was kind and lived fully for others, and she made the first step toward that life when she joined the Socialist party at the University of Illinois.

Day describes her life as a college student and radical activist with enthusiasm. She remembers that she was conscious of the class war in the United States but unconcerned with the war going on in Europe. She recalls her enthusiasm for reading Karl Marx, Upton Sinclair, Jack London, Fedor Dostoevski, and Leo Tolstoi. She writes that at the time, she was "in love with the masses" and that she believed that "the poor and oppressed were going to rise up, they were collectively the new Messiah, and they would release the captives" (p. 46). Day's reference to the Messiah is deliberate here, for although at the time she thought that religion would interfere with her work with the oppressed, after her conversion, she would learn that it was possible to combine religion and radicalism. Her two years at college gave Day the opportunity to read, write, and begin to make connections within the American socialist community. These activities would prove valuable when she moved with her family to New York and immersed herself in the radical activities there.

Working as a writer for the *Call*, Day became attracted to the anarchist theories of the IWW, and throughout her life, the idea of free association of decentralized groups, one of the foundations of IWW theory, would remain important to her. Day depicts life in the radical movement as a many-sided struggle; at the *Call*, for example, socialists fought with those sympathetic to the American Federation of Labor, who mistrusted the direct action advocated by the Wobblies (members of the IWW), who, in turn, were impatient with the dialect of the orthodox Marxists. This factionalism ended with the American entry into World War I and the development of a peace movement supported by most of the Left.

Day left the *Call* for *The Masses*, a more radical paper, which eventually was shut down for opposing conscription. Day then moved from reporting to direct political action, and going to Washington to take part in a demonstration on behalf of political prisoners and against the war. It was there that she first experienced prison and began her slow process of religious conversion.

Arrested outside the White House, Day was sentenced to thirty days in prison. She and her fellow protestors immediately began a hunger strike. Day writes that in jail, she had no sense of radicalism; she lost all consciousness of any cause and all feeling of her own identity. The hunger strike lasted for ten days, during which time Day read the Bible and began to find comfort in the Psalms. Later she would see this as her first step toward religion, but after her release, she stopped thinking about God and returned to activism. She continued to write, and worked as a nurse for a year. She wrote a novel and later sold the movie rights for $5,000. In the 1920s, she lived in a common-law marriage on Staten Island with Forster Batterham and lived the life of a bohemian intellectual, complete with friendships and literary discussions with Malcolm Cowley, Allen Tate, and Hart Crane.

Day calls the second part of her narrative "Natural Happiness," and in it, she describes her bohemian life as a pastoral retreat. Living in a small cottage on the coast of Staten Island, Day had the benefit of living in the country with access to the city. It was, she writes, an ideal place. It also was a place where she began to develop many of the ideas she would later articulate as editor of *The Catholic Worker*. Growing some of her own food and living in a community of artists, intellectuals, and radicals, Day began to see self-sufficiency and communal life as ways to live virtuously in a capitalistic system. At the same time, Day became interested in religion, and began to visit Catholic churches and read Catholic literature. In 1927, she discovered that she was pregnant, and her interest in religion increased. When her daughter was born, she broke off her relation with Batterham, had her daughter baptized a Catholic, and became one herself.

Day's conversion was not dramatic, and her description of the experience emphasizes the almost inevitable process by which she was drawn to the Catholic Church. She uses the analogy of planting seeds and germination, and she refers explicitly to Francis Thompson's famous poem, "The Hound of Heaven," in which God patiently stalks a fleeing prodigal son. Day describes a season of reading, praying, and agonizing, balancing her growing faith against her love for Batterham, who remains an atheist and disapproves of marriage. The birth of her daughter makes her decision easy, and she describes the peace and joy that comes with her decision.

Unlike many writers of conversion narratives, Day does not use the conversion experience to mark the transformation of sinner to saint. Day recanted none of her radicalism; she remained as committed to the masses after her conversion as she was before. Conversion in fact intensified her devotion to the poor and the oppressed. The only difference was that she began to work with a Christian framework, finding an outlet for both her talent and her energy in the creation of a radical Catholic journal with Peter Maurin. On May 1, 1933, Day and Maurin published the first issue of *The Catholic Worker*, which called for a Christian social order to replace capitalism.

Day saw no contradiction between her Catholicism and her radical activity; in fact, she saw political action as an expression of her faith. As a result, the description of her work after her conversion is similar to that of her activity before the conversion. She recognized, however, that some people might see her as "going over to the opposition because the Church was lined up with property, with the wealthy, with the state, with capitalism, with all the forces of reaction. 'Too often,' Cardinal Mundelein said 'has the Church lined up on the wrong side' " (p. 149). Yet she was determined that she could follow Christ and be a poor, chaste, and obedient Catholic while serving the poor, whom she called the Church of Christ made visible.

Day is most widely known for her work as editor of *The Catholic Worker*, and she describes her involvement with the paper in a chapter called "Paper, People and Work." From a first issue of 2,500 copies in 1933, *The Catholic Worker* grew to a paper with a circulation of 150,000 by 1936. In describing her work, Day stresses the cooperative nature of *The Catholic Worker* and its adherence to principles. Editors Day and Maurin advocated a long-term solution to the problems of unemployment and poverty. Observing an unemployed population in the United States of more than thirteen million in 1933, Day and Maurin argued for a green revolution of voluntary associations—urban hospices for the city poor and farming communes to provide food and land for the rural poor. In addition, they argued that the state should enter into the realm of charity only in times of great crisis—famine, earthquake, drought. The only solutions to poverty that would work were personal and structural: all people must be made to see their responsibility for poverty in society and become involved in its eradication and all people must be given access to the means of production and security—land and shelter. *The Catholic Worker* argued for a transformation of both the individual and society, and during the 1930s, the gospel according to Day and Maurin was well received.

At the outbreak of World War II, *The Catholic Worker*'s policy of pacifism resulted in a loss of influence and subscribers, and in a chapter titled "War Is the Health of the State," Day defends her unpopular revolutionary pacifism by arguing that the Sermon on the Mount compelled her to be a pacifist, and *The Catholic Worker* had been "pacifist in class war, race war, in the Ethiopian war, the Spanish Civil War, all through World War II, as we are now during the Korean War" (p. 264). In answering her critics, she argued from the early position of the church that those who had been baptized should not join the army. For Day, war, like poverty or racism, was an evil that must be confronted.

Day concludes her autobiography with a description of Peter Maurin's death and uses it to summarize their mutually held beliefs:

"We need to make the kind of society," Peter had said, "where it is easier for people to be good." . . . And because the love of God made him love his neighbor, he wanted to cry out against the evils of the day—the state, war, usury, the degradation of man, the lack of a philosophy of work. He sang the delights of poverty (he was not talking of destitution) as a means of making a step to the land, of getting back to the dear natural things of earth and sky, home and children. (p. 280)

Many of the same things could be said about Day herself.

CRITICISM

Dorothy Day lived a long and fruitful life. After she published her autobiography in 1952, she continued to write, edit *The Catholic Worker*, and organize against the evils she saw in the modern American state. She was a major force in the development of the American Catholic social movement, and during her later years, she inspired a new generation of Catholic activists. Among those who were directly influenced by her own work were Thomas Merton, Daniel and Phillip Berrigan, Michael Harrington, and Ivan Illich, and as noted in *American Reformers: An H. W. Wilson Biographical Dictionary*:

Dorothy Day was instrumental in rousing the social conscience of American Catholicism in the twentieth century. With its emphasis on active engagement in works of mercy and peace, from feeding the hungry to nonviolently resisting "the warfare state," *The Catholic Worker* was a seminal and enduring force in raising the consciousness of American Catholics above parochialism and in the formation of the American Catholic "new left." (p. 218)

Interest in her life and work grew after her death in 1980, and a number of useful sources are available for students of Day and *The Catholic Worker*. Perhaps the best comment on her life remains the University of Notre Dame's comment on awarding her the Laetare Medal in 1972 for "comforting the afflicted and afflicting the comforted virtually all of her life."

BIBLIOGRAPHY

American Dissent from Thomas Jefferson to Cesar Chavez. Melbourne, Fla.: Krieger, 1981, 123–37.

Berrigan, D. "Day to Remember." *U.S. Catholic*, May 1981, 30–32.

Cameron, J. M. "Dorothy Day (1897–1980)." *New York Review of Books*, 22 January 1981, 8.

Campbell, D. "The Catholic Earth Mother: Dorothy Day and Women's Power in the Church." *Cross Currents*, Fall 1984, 270–82.

Coles, Robert. "Dorothy Day." *New Republic*, 6 June 1981, 28–32.

———. *Dorothy Day: A Radical Devotion.* Reading, Mass.: Addison-Wesley, 1987.

Cort, J. C. "In a Time of Gigantic Evil." *Commonweal*, 24 September 1982, 500–502.

———. "My Life at the *Catholic Worker*." *Commonweal*, 20 June 1980, 361–67.

Cunneen, S. "Dorothy Day: The Storyteller as Human Model." *Cross Currents*, Fall 1984, 283–93.

Day, Dorothy. *The Eleventh Virgin.* New York: Boni, 1924.

———. *From Union Square to Rome.* Silver Spring, Md.: The Preservation of the Faith Press, 1938.

———. *House of Hospitality.* New York: Sheed & Ward, 1939.

———. *On Pilgrimage.* New York: Catholic Worker Books, 1948.

———. *The Long Loneliness: The Autobiography of Dorothy Day.* New York: Harper & Brothers, 1952.

———. *I Remember Peter Maurin.* Cambridge, Mass.: American Friends Service Committee, 1958.

————. *Therese*. Notre Dame, Ind.: Fides, 1960.

————. *Loaves and Fishes*. New York: Harper & Row, 1963.

————. *Meditations*. Selected and arranged by Stanley Vishnewski. New York: Newman, 1970.

————. *On Pilgrimage: The Sixties*. New York: Curtis, 1972.

————. *By Little and By Little: The Selected Writings of Dorothy Day*. Edited by Robert Ellsberg. New York: Alfred A. Knopf, 1983.

"Dorothy Day." *U.S. Catholic*, May 1985, 38.

Egan, E. "Final Word Is Love." *Cross Currents*, Winter 1980, 377–84.

Fehren, H. I. "I Was Going to Write a Letter." *U.S. Catholic*, Fall 1988, 38–40.

Forest, James. *Love Is the Measure: A Biography of Dorothy Day*. New York: Paulist Press, 1986.

Gregory, J. "Remembering Dorothy Day." *America*, 25 April 1981, 344–47.

Harrington, M. "Existential Saint." *New York Times Book Review*, 13 June 1982, 3+.

Jordan, P. "Dorothy Day: Still a Radical." *Commonweal*, 29 November 1985, 665–69.

Klejment, Anne. *Dorothy Day and* The Catholic Worker: *A Bibliography and Index*. New York: Garland, 1986.

MacDonald, D. "Dorothy Day." In *Thirteen for Christ*. Edited by Melville Harcourt. New York: Sheed & Ward, 1963, 233–53, 258–59.

Mayer, M. "God's Panhandler." *Progressive*, February 1981, 14–15.

————. *Harsh and Dreadful Love: Dorothy Day and the Catholic Worker Movement*. Garden City, N.Y.: Doubleday, 1974.

Miller, William D. "Dorothy Day, 1897–1980: All Was Grace." *America*, 13 December 1980, 382–86.

————. *All Is Grace: The Spirituality of Dorothy Day*. Garden City, N.Y.: Doubleday, 1987.

Nevins, Albert J. *Builders of Catholic America*. Huntington, Ind.: Our Sunday Visitor, 1985, 237–50.

Piehl, Mel. *Breaking Bread:* The Catholic Worker *and the Origin of Catholic Radicalism in America*. Philadelphia: Temple University Press, 1982.

————. "An Enduring Voice and Vocation." *Commonweal*, 13 May 1985, 285–86.

"Radical Prophet." *Time*, 20 August 1973, 8.

Roberts, Nancy. "Building a New Earth: Dorothy Day and *The Catholic Worker*." *The Christian Century*, 10 December 1980, 1217–21.

————. "Journalism for Justice: Dorothy Day and *The Catholic Worker*." *Journalism History*, Spring/Summer, 1983, 2–9.

————. *Dorothy Day and* The Catholic Worker. Albany: State University of New York Press, 1984.

Sweeney, Terrance A. *God & . . . Thirty Interviews*. Minneapolis: Winston Press, 1985, 28–30.

Vishnewski, S. "Dorothy Day: A Sign of Contradiction." *Catholic World*, August 1969, 203–6.

Vree, D. "Radical Holiness." *Commonweal*, 6 May 1983, 266–69.

Whitman, Alden, ed. *American Reformers: An H. W. Wilson Biographical Dictionary*. New York: Wilson, 1985.

Wills, Gary. "Dorothy Day at the Barricades." In *Fifty Who Made a Difference*. Edited by Lee Eisenberg. New York: Villard Books, 1984, 164–70. [Also in *Esquire*, December 1983, 228–30 + .]

Woodward, K. L. "Two Paradoxical Saints." *New York Times Book Review*, 6 September 1987, 10.

10 • FREDERICK DOUGLASS (1817–1895)

Narrative of the Life of Frederick Douglass, an American Slave: Written by Himself

BIOGRAPHY

Frederick Augustus Washington Bailey was born at Holly Hill Farm on Tuckahoe Creek in Talbot County, Maryland, in 1817. His mother was a slave, and his father, whom he never met, is presumed to have been white and may have been his mother's master. He was reared by his grandparents and only occasionally saw his mother, who came to visit from a neighboring plantation. In 1824, he was moved to the Lloyd Plantation. Within a year of that move, his mother died. In 1826, he was sent to Baltimore with the Hugh Auld family. He became the companion of young Tommy Auld. Mrs. Auld began to teach Douglass to read, but her husband made her stop, saying, "If you give a nigger an inch, he will take an ell. Learning will *spoil* the best nigger in the world. If you teach that nigger ... how to read, there will be no keeping him" (p. 58). Douglass continued to read in secret, learning from the *Columbian Orator* and the *Baltimore American*. In 1831, Douglass experienced a religious conversion and joined the Bethel African Methodist Episcopal Church.

In 1833, Douglass was moved from Baltimore to St. Michaels, Maryland, and put to work for Thomas Auld. He was placed under the supervision of Edward Covey, a notorious "slave breaker," and put to work as a field hand. In 1836, after an attempted escape and imprisonment, Douglass was returned to Baltimore, where he worked as an apprentice caulker. In 1838, with the help of freedwoman Anna Murray, Douglass escaped to New

Bedford, where he was joined by Murray and took the name Douglass from a character in Sir Walter Scott's *Lady of the Lake*.

In 1841, Douglass began to speak at antislavery meetings, becoming an agent for the Massachusetts Anti-Slavery Society. In 1845, his autobiography, *Narrative of the Life of Frederick Douglass*, was published. The *Narrative* was a success, and Douglass toured the United States, Scotland, and England speaking at abolitionist meetings. For the next two decades, Douglass was an influential figure in radical American politics. In 1848, he attended the famous Women's Rights Convention at Seneca Falls, New York, where he helped to form an alliance between the abolitionists and the women's rights advocates. He founded an abolitionist paper, *North Star*. In 1851, he broke with William Lloyd Garrison, the national leader of the abolitionist movement, arguing that political action was necessary for the abolition of slavery. In 1855, his second autobiography, *My Bondage and Freedom*, was published. In 1856, he endorsed Republican John C. Freemont Smith for president, and over the next several years began working with John Brown to develop ways of encouraging slaves to revolt. When Brown was arrested after his attack on the military arsenal at Harpers Ferry, Douglass traveled to Canada and then England to avoid arrest as an accomplice, since some members of the government believed that he had taken part in the planning of the raid.

On his return to the United States, Douglass argued for the abolition of slavery, and after 1863 traveled throughout the North urging blacks to enlist in the Union Army. In 1864, he supported Lincoln for reelection, and in 1868 campaigned for Ulysses S. Grant. By this time, Frederick Douglass had become the most influential black in America, and he received a number of political appointments after the Civil War, serving as United States Marshal for the District of Columbia, Recorder of Deeds for the District of Columbia, and Consul General to Haiti. In 1881, his third autobiography, *Life and Times of Frederick Douglass*, was published. Douglass died on February 20, 1895.

THE AUTOBIOGRAPHY

Frederick Douglass wrote three autobiographies during his lifetime, and each reflects the author's concerns at the time of composition. The *Narrative of the Life of Frederick Douglass* has been called by Ann Kibbey "an incendiary polemic written more to fuel the abolitionist cause than to convey the nature of the slave experience" (Bloom, p. 131). Although a much more complicated work than a mere polemic, the *Narrative* was intended to arouse the passions of its readers, and contemporary comment and successful sales indicate that Douglass had judged his audience correctly. In the *Narrative*, Douglass describes his pursuit of freedom that coincides with his discovery of self. The focus of the work is on Douglass' conversion from slave to freeman; all else is omitted, and as a result, the *Narrative* is short and dramatic. Douglass' second autobiography, *My Bondage and Freedom,* was published in 1855. It is three times the length of the *Narrative,* and includes a description of Douglass' life as a freeman and extracts from his anti-slavery speeches. His final autobiographical work, the *Life and Times of Frederick Douglass,* was published in 1881, and in it, Douglass shifted the focus away from his life as a slave to his Civil War and postwar work. The *Life and Times* was the least successful of the autobiographies.

The *Narrative of the Life of Frederick Douglass* is a remarkable document. The title itself emphasizes the unique nature of the autobiography. Other slave narratives had appeared in print earlier, and in fact, the genre was a popular form in the nineteenth century. Almost all of them, however, had been ghostwritten or heavily edited by whites. Douglass' autobiography was something new, and its success made Douglass the most famous and influential black in the American reform movement. The *Narrative* also is remarkable for its success as both a political and a literary text. As a political work, the *Narrative* was incendiary. In both the North and in England, Douglass and his autobiography created a sensation. As a literary work, the *Narrative* also is a success. In describing his quest for freedom and selfhood, Douglass combines description of his life with arguments against slavery to create a call to action that reads like a passionate sermon. As Robert O'Meally has noted, "this is a text meant to be preached" (Bloom, p. 78).

One of the standard features of the nineteenth-century slave narrative is prefatory material attesting to the truth of the tale that followed. Douglass follows the tradition in his narrative, including a preface written by William Lloyd Garrison, editor of the *Liberator* and the leading abolitionist in the country, and a letter from Wendell Philips, one of the most important New England abolitionists. The preface and the letter attest to Douglass' work in the abolitionist movement and to his power as a speaker, and urge Northern readers to work for the abolition of slavery.

The narrative itself begins in sharp contrast to the introductory material. Garrison's preface and Philips' letter establish the place Douglass has reached after his escape—a free man with influential friends speaking out passionately against slavery. Chapter One opens with the opposite image of Douglass:

I was born in Tuckahoe, near Hillsborough, and about twelve miles from Easton, in Talbot county, Maryland. I have no accurate knowledge of my age, never having seen an authentic record of it. By far the larger part of the slaves know as little of their age as horses know of theirs, and it is the wish of most masters of my knowledge to keep their slaves thus ignorant. . . . My mother was Harriet Bailey. She was the daughter of Isaac and Betsey Bailey, both colored and quite dark. . . . My father was a white man. . . . I never saw my mother, to know her as such, more than four or five times in my life. (pp. 23–24)

With this beginning, Douglass positions himself as far from his privileged status in New England as possible; he is ignorant, an orphan, and a piece of property. As he continues to describe his early life, Douglass emphasizes the emotional as well as physical deprivations faced by slaves. In addition to his descriptions of inadequate food, shelter, and clothing, standard features of the slave narrative, Douglass includes vivid examples of the destruction of family life and the constant threat of violence that were part of the slave system. He is careful to argue that slavery destroyed white as well as black family life, pointing out that the seduction and rape of women slaves by white masters created an entire class of people, unrecognized children of the slavemasters, that created anger and jealousy in white families as well as fear in black families. Having complete control over their slave property enabled slaveowners not only to break up existing black families or forbid marriage, but also to force themselves on their slaves. When Douglass describes how his master, who was not known as a man of pure morals and who had forbidden Douglass' Aunt Hester, an attractive young woman, to go out in the evening or keep company with any men, discovered her in the company of a young slave named Ned Roberts and then whipped her in a frenzy, he captures the destructive core at the center of the slave system.

In the early chapters of the *Narrative*, Douglass establishes a rhetorical pattern of description and exhortation that he will use throughout his narrative. His depiction of Aunt Hester's whipping leads to general comments on violence of the system. His description of how a plantation works leads to comments on slave songs and the need for divine deliverance. His account of the yearly clothing ration for slaves leads to observations of how poverty and powerlessness destroy families as ruthlessly as a wicked master. He uses this same pattern as he describes his new life in Baltimore, where he found religion, literacy, and then the desire to be free.

Writing of his move to Baltimore, Douglass observes:

Going to live in Baltimore laid the foundation, and opened the gateway, to all my subsequent prosperity. I have ever regarded it as the first plain manifestation of that kind of providence which has ever since attended me, and marked my life with so many favors. (p. 56)

This statement links the *Narrative* with two American autobiographical traditions: the first, the success narrative with the reference to prosperity, and the second, the conversion narrative with the reference to providence. In the pages that follow, Douglass develops both elements of his life as he describes how he began to discover who he was and what he wanted to become.

In Baltimore, Mrs. Auld, Douglass' new mistress, began to teach him to read, but she was forbidden to continue by her husband when he discovered the lessons. Douglass recalls how Mr. Auld told his wife that reading made a slave "unmanageable and of no use to his master...discontented and unhappy" (p. 58). Douglass writes how this confrontation had set him on the pathway to freedom. He decided to continue learning to read. His motivation now came as much from his opposition to his master as from the initial kindness of his mistress. Douglass records that his master's opposition to his reading taught him a valuable lesson: to despise what his master loved and desire what his master dreaded. In a very real sense, he continued to read and began to define who he was in an act of defiance against his master and the slave system. When he confronted oppression, Douglass began to create himself.

As he provides examples of his reading, Douglass continues to link his learning with his growing sense of self. He remembers when he was twelve he read dialogues between slaves and their masters and speeches on Catholic emancipation in the *Columbian Orator*. Douglass immediately identified with both issues, and he writes:

The more I read the more I was led to abhor and detest my enslavers. I could regard them in no other light than a band of successful robbers, who had left their homes, and gone to Africa, and stolen us from our homes, and in a strange land reduced us to slavery. (p. 67)

His master's comments were prophetic. Reading enabled Douglass to put himself and his position as a slave in a larger context, and the discovery of that context and his response to it began the conversion of slave to freeman.

Douglass' stay in Baltimore was relatively short, and on his return to the country, his situation changed. He suffered because he had known what it was to be treated kindly, and back on the plantation, he soon discovered nothing had changed. His master decided that city life had made Douglass unsuitable for his purposes and sent him to work for Edward Covey, a farm-renter and notorious slave-breaker. Douglass went to work for Edward Covey on January 11, 1833, and the one year he remained with Covey marks the turning point of his life. In the first six months of his stay, Douglass was regularly beaten. He recalls that he was broken in body and spirit, and his desire to read had disappeared. Here, facing constant brutality, "the dark night of slavery closed in upon me; and behold a man transformed into a brute" (p. 95).

In response, Douglass prayed for deliverance. In a famous passage, Douglass recalls sitting by the Chesapeake Bay watching the white-sailed ships moving freely out toward the sea. He equates the ships with angels, flying freely while he is bound to the hell of slavery. This extended metaphor captures Douglass' feelings at the depth of his suffering. He follows this passage with the comment, "You have seen how a man was made a slave; you shall see how a slave was made a man" (p. 97).

Douglass writes that he finally decided he could no longer take Covey's abuse. One Monday Covey ordered Douglass to go to the barn and feed his horses. Covey followed Douglass into the barn, planning to whip him. Douglass decided to fight back, and he writes that they fought for two hours. After the fight, Douglass expected to be taken to a public whipping post, but instead, Covey did nothing. Douglass writes that Covey did not punish him because he was afraid that he would lose his reputation as a slave-breaker and overseer if it became known that a sixteen-year-old slave had successfully defied him. Douglass also writes that this was the turning point in his life as a slave.

I felt as I never felt before. It was a glorious resurrection, from the tomb of slavery, to the heaven of freedom. My long-crushed spirit rose, cowardice departed, bold defiance took its place; and I now resolved that, however long I remained a slave in form, the day had passed forever when I could remain a slave in fact. (p. 105)

As he had earlier, Douglass uses traditional religious imagery to describe his transformation; slavery is death, freedom is heaven, and the change is a resurrection. Whereas in most conversion narratives the transformation from sinner to saved is the main point, Douglass uses the language of conversion to describe a different transformation, the change from slavery to freedom. This change, like the change that occurred when his master had forbidden him to read, came about through an act of defiance. Again Douglass asserts that transformation and selfhood come about through opposition to the slave system.

In the final chapters of the *Narrative*, Douglass comments on the Christianity of slaveowners as he describes his life on the plantation and in Baltimore while planning to escape. Throughout the debate over slavery, slaveowners and abolitionists had used the Bible to justify their positions, and Douglass, whose *Narrative* was intended as a polemic against slavery, uses depictions of Christian slavemasters as a powerful argument against slavery. He writes, for example, how one master became more vicious toward his slaves after his conversion, finding sanction for his slaveholding and believing in the righteousness of his actions. Douglass writes that another converted master routinely forbade his slaves to hold Sunday services or read from the Bible, believing both activities dangerous. Finally, in his appendix to the *Narrative*, Douglass argues that the slaveholding religion is not Christianity, that no man who owns slaves and wields a whip can be a follower of Christ, and that often revivals of religion and revivals of the slave trade go hand in hand. Having been converted to Christianity and converted to freedom, Douglass finds the latter, given the state of Christianity in America, a more meaningful transformation.

Although explicit in his criticism of slaveholding religion, Douglass is more reticent about his actual escape. He writes that he will not provide exact details because if his movements were known, it would be more difficult for other slaves to escape and put those who assisted him in danger. Instead, he provides a general picture of how he obtained papers that said he was a free sailor and reached Philadelphia and then New York by train. He ends his story with a description of how, while attending an antislavery meeting in Nantucket, on August 11, 1841, he felt moved to speak. In a sense, the *Narrative* is a continuation of that speech.

CRITICISM

The *Narrative of the Life of Frederick Douglass* is one of the major autobiographical works in the American literary canon. On its publication in 1845, it became an immediate success in England as well as the United States and was quickly translated into French and German. More than 5,000 copies were sold in the first four months after publication, and by 1850, a total of more than 30,000 copies had been published. Initial critical response was favorable as well. The *New York Tribune*, for example, called it "simple, true, coherent," and "an excellent piece of writing."

Recent critics have suggested that the *Narrative* is far from simple. Most critics agree that Douglass' autobiography grew out of the fugitive-slave genre popular in the antebellum North and that Douglass' success at juxtaposing incident and argument made the *Narrative* effective as both a literary text and a vehicle for social reform.

The excellent collection of essays, *Modern Critical Interpretations of the Narrative of the Life of Frederick Douglass*, edited by Harold Bloom, demonstrates the range of critical opinions of and approaches to Douglass' autobiography. Albert Stone sees the *Narrative* as a prototype for such later successful black autobiographies as *Black Boy* and *I Know Why the Caged Bird Sings*; Roger G. O'Meally defines the text as a black sermon; William J. Andrews sees the autobiography as a black jeremiad; and Bloom himself focuses on Douglass' treatment of "Southern erotic sadism in the psychic economy of slaveholding" (p. vii).

In an equally important critical work, *The Mind of Frederick Douglass*, Waldo E. Martin places Douglass and his work within the social, intellectual, and political framework of nineteenth-century America. He notes, for example, that intellectual activism was one of the motivating factors behind all of Douglass' writing, and that

in his three autobiographies—*Narrative of the Life of Frederick Douglass, An American Slave: Written by Himself* (1845); *My Bondage and Freedom* (1855); and *Life and Times of Frederick Douglass* (1881 and 1892 revised edition)—Douglass carefully delineated his self image. It betrayed a conscious and unconscious elaboration of his idealized self—a self conscious hero complex. Not withstanding the differences among these autobiographies, each reveals his strong compulsion to play a determinative role in the design and construction of history's heroic vision of himself. (p. 272)

The autobiographical Douglass is, then, a heroic figure, either a self-made man or a convert, not only for his actual deeds, but also for the needs of the autobiographer's readers.

There is critical debate over whether the autobiography is a conversion narrative. Some scholars point to Douglass' critique of slaveholding Christianity and the lack of an examination of his actual religious conversion to argue against conversion. On the other hand, the overall pattern of the text clearly suggests a reading emphasizing conversion. As Benjamin Franklin secularized the conversion narrative in the eighteenth century, Douglass transformed a record of religious transformation into a political document. In his *Narrative*, Douglass records how he was converted from slave to literate, Christian, activist abolitionist, and the autobiography itself is indeed a sermon.

BIBLIOGRAPHY

Andrews, W. L. "Frederick Douglass, Preacher." *American Literature*, 54 (1982): 592–97.

Baker, Houston A., Jr. *Long Black Song: Essays in Black American Literature and Culture.* Charlottesville: University of Virginia Press, 1972.

———. "The Problem of Being: Some Reflections on Black Autobiography." *Obsidian*, 1, no. 1 (1974): 18–30.

———. *The Journey Back: Issues in Black Literature and Criticism.* Chicago: University of Chicago Press, 1980.

———. *Blues, Ideology, and Afro-American Literature.* Chicago: University of Chicago Press, 1984.

Bloom, Harold, ed. *Modern Critical Interpretations of* The Narrative of the Life of Frederick Douglass. New York: Chelsea, 1988.

Bontemps, Arna. *Great Slave Narratives.* Boston: Beacon Press, 1969.

———. *Free at Last: Frederick Douglass' Narrative of the Life of Frederick Douglass.* New York: Dodd, Mead, 1971.

Brawley, Benjamin, ed. *Early Negro American Writers.* Chapel Hill: University of North Carolina Press, 1969.

Brignano, Russell C. *Black Americans in Autobiography: An Annotated Bibliography of Autobiographies and Autobiographical Books Written Since the Civil War.* Rev. and exp. ed. Durham, N.C.: Duke University Press, 1984.

Butterfield, Stephen. *Black Autobiography in America.* Amherst: University of Massachusetts Press, 1974.

Chesnutt, Charles W. *Frederick Douglass.* Boston: Small, Maynard, 1899.

Clasby, Nancy T. "Frederick Douglass's 'Narrative': A Content Analysis." *CLA Journal*, 14 (1971): 242–50.

Couser, G. Thomas. *American Autobiography: The Prophetic Mode.* Amherst: University of Massachusetts Press, 1979.

De Pietro, Thomas. "Vision and Revision in the Autobiographies of Frederick Douglass." *CLA Journal*, 26 (1983): 384–96.

Douglass, Frederick. *Narrative of the Life of Frederick Douglass, An American Slave: Written by Himself*. 1845. Reprint. Cambridge, Mass.: Harvard University Press, Belknap Press, 1967.

———. *My Bondage and Freedom*. 1855. Reprint. New York: Dover, 1969.

———. *Life and Times of Frederick Douglass*. 1881. Reprint. New York: Macmillan, 1962.

———. *Frederick Douglass: Selections from His Writings*. New York: International, 1945.

———. *The Frederick Douglass Papers: Series One: Speeches, Debates, and Interviews*. Volume 1: 1841–1846. Edited by John W. Blassingame. New Haven, Conn.: Yale University Press, 1979.

Felgar, Robert. "The Rediscovery of Frederick Douglass." *Mississippi Quarterly: The Journal of Southern Culture*, 35 (1982): 427–38.

Foner, Philip S. *The Life and Writings of Frederick Douglass*. 4 vols. New York: International Publishers, 1950–55.

———. *Frederick Douglass: A Biography*. New York: Citadel, 1964.

Gibson, Donald B. "Reconciling Public and Private in Frederick Douglass's 'Narrative.'" *American Literature*, 57 (1985): 549–69.

Graham, Shirley. *There Was Once a Slave*. New York: Julian Messner, 1947.

Haskett, Norman D. "Afro-American Images of Africa: Four Antebellum Black Authors." *Ufahamu*, 3, no. 1 (1972): 29–40.

Holland, Frederic May. *Frederick Douglass: The Colored Orator*. New York: Funk & Wagnalls, 1985.

Jugurtha, Lillie Butler. "Point of View in the Afro-American Slave Narratives: A Study of Narratives by Douglass and Pennington." In *The Art of the Slave Narrative: Original Essays in Criticism and Theory*. Edited by John Sekora and Darwin T. Turner. Macomb: Western Illinois University Press: Essays in Literature Books, 1982.

Loggins, Veron. *The Negro Author: His Development in America*. New York: Columbia University Press, 1931.

MacKethan, Lucinda H. "Metaphors of Mastery in the Slave Narratives." In *The Art of the Slave Narrative: Original Essays in Criticism and Theory*. Edited by John Sekora and Darwin T. Turner. Macomb: Western Illinois University Press, 1982.

Martin, Waldo E. *The Mind of Frederick Douglass*. Chapel Hill: University of North Carolina Press, 1984.

Matlock, James. "The Autobiography of Frederick Douglass." *Phylon*, 40 (March 1979): 15–28.

Nichols, Charles Harold. *Many Thousands Gone: The Ex-Slaves' Account of Their Bondage and Freedom*. Leiden: Brill, 1963.

Olney, James. " 'I Was Born': Slave Narratives, Their Status as Autobiography and as Literature." In *The Slave Narrative*. Edited by Charles T. Davis and Henry Louis Gates, Jr. New York: Oxford University Press, 1985.

Ostendorf, Bernd. "Violence and Freedom: The Covey Episode in Frederick Douglass's Autobiography." In *Mythos und Aulklarung in der americanischen Literatur/Myth and Enlightenment in American Literature*. Edited by Dieter

Meindl and Friedrich W. Horlacher. Erlangen: Universitatsbund Erlangen-Nurberg, 1985.

Piper, Henry Dan. "The Place of Frederick Douglass's Narrative of the Life of an American Slave in the Development of a Native American Prose Style." *Journal of Afro-American Issues*, 5, no. 2 (1977): 183–91.

Pitre, M. "Frederick Douglass: The Politician vs. the Social Reformer." *Phylon*, 40 (1979): 270–77.

———. "Frederick Douglass and American Diplomacy in The Caribbean." *Journal of Black Studies*, 13 (1983): 457–75.

Preston, Dickson J. *Young Frederick Douglass: The Maryland Years*. Baltimore: Johns Hopkins University Press, 1980.

Quarles, Benjamin. Introduction to John Harvard Library edition of the *Narrative of the Life of Frederick Douglass*. Cambridge, Mass.: Harvard University Press, 1960.

———. *Frederick Douglass*. Washington, D.C.: Associated Publishers, 1968.

———. "Narrative of the Life of Frederick Douglass." In *Landmarks of American Writing*. Edited by Hennig Cohen. New York: Basic Books, 1969.

———. "Frederick Douglass: Black Imperishable." *Quarterly Journal of the Library of Congress*, 28 (1972): 159–69.

Ripley, Peter. "The Autobiographical Writings of Frederick Douglass." *Southern Studies*, 24 (1985): 5–29.

Sekora, John. "The Dilemma of Frederick Douglass: The Slave Narrative as Literary Institution." *Essays in Literature*, 10, no. 2 (Fall 1983): 219–26.

Stepto, Robert B. *Behind the Veil: A Study of Afro-American Narrative*. Urbana: University of Illinois Press, 1979.

Sundquist, Eric J. "Frederick Douglass: Literacy and Paternalism." *Raritan*, 6, no. 2 (Fall 1986): 108–24.

Terry, Eugene. "Black Autobiography: Discernible Forms." *Okike*, 19 (September 1981): 6–10.

Walker, Peter F. *Moral Choices: Memory, Desire, and Imagination in Nineteenth Century American Abolition*. Baton Rouge: Louisiana State University Press, 1978.

Washington, Booker T. *Frederick Douglass*. New York: Haskell House, 1968.

Vellin, Jean Fagan. *The Intricate Knot: Black Figures in American Literature, 1776–1863*. New York: New York University Press, 1972.

Zeitz, Lisa Margaret. "Biblical Allusion and Imagery in Frederick Douglass's 'Narrative.' " *CLA Journal*, 25 (1981): 56–64.

11 • JONATHAN EDWARDS (1703–1758)

Personal Narrative

BIOGRAPHY

Jonathan Edwards was born in East Windsor, Connecticut, on October 5, 1703. His father, Timothy, was a graduate of Harvard and a Puritan minister. His mother, Esther Stoddard, was the daughter of the famous Puritan clergyman Solomon Stoddard. Edwards' early education was directed by his parents, who had access to most of the books then in circulation in New England. As a result, by the time he was thirteen, Edwards had been trained in Latin, basic mathematics, composition, and theology. In addition, he had developed an interest in observing nature and had, at the age of twelve, composed a short essay, "Of Insects."

In 1716, at the age of thirteen, Edwards entered Yale College, where he had the opportunity to read the "new" science in the works of Isaac Newton and John Locke. The works of these and other contemporary scientific writers had a profound impact on Edwards, and much of his later speculative writing is a sustained attempt to use the new insights to develop a scientific and philosophical theology to support the fundamental beliefs of Puritanism. Edwards graduated from Yale in September 1720 but remained in New Haven for two years studying theology. In 1722, he accepted the position of minister of a Presbyterian church in New York. In 1724, he was offered the position of tutor at Yale. In 1726, he resigned that position to become assistant minister to Solomon Stoddard at Northampton, Massachusetts. In 1729, Stoddard, who was the most influential minister in the entire Connecticut Valley and western Massachusetts, died, and Edwards took his place. He remained as minister in Northampton until 1750, when he was dismissed by his congregation after an extended battle over admission to church membership.

In many ways, Edwards was seen by his contemporaries as a conservative throwback to the strict Puritanism of an earlier time. He argued against the liberal changes in theology made by some of the Puritan ministers in Boston, and he preached the strict Calvinism he inherited: innate depravity, irresistible grace, absolute election, limited atonement, and the preservation of the saints. To this basic theology Edwards added the radical idea that conversion was a sensory experience, one that was felt by the emotions and could be encouraged by proper preaching. The impact of this can be seen in the Great Awakening, an enthusiastic movement that swept through the colonies during the 1730s and 1740s.

During the early 1730s, Edwards began preaching revival with an emphasis on the unworthiness of man. By 1734, church membership had increased and town bitterness had decreased in Northampton, and soon revival was spreading throughout the Connecticut Valley. In 1740, the second stage of the revival began with the arrival of English evangelist George Whitefield, who spoke at mass meetings, drawing 4,000 persons one Sunday and 15,000 the next. Edwards toured with Whitefield throughout western Massachusetts and Connecticut, and by the time Whitefield left for the middle and southern colonies, revival was again at its height. It was at this time that Edwards preached his most famous sermon at Enfield, "Sinners in the Hands of an Angry God." This sermon, which captures the essential elements of the revival—God's awesome power and justice, man's sinfulness, the need to repent—is perhaps the most famous piece of Puritan prose and found in almost every anthology of American literature. It is, however, not representative of Edwards' writing, which is, in general, far more intellectual and controlled than this affective sermon.

By 1742, the effects of the Awakening were beginning to wear off, and many of the Puritan ministers began to criticize what they were now calling the emotional enthusiasms of the revival. In response, Edwards wrote *Some Thoughts Concerning the Present State of Revival of Religion in New England*, which defended the revival and examined the characteristics of true conversion and revival. In 1744, Edwards discovered some young people in his congregation reading "obscene" material, *Midwifery Rightly Presented*, and read the names of the offenders, among whom were the children of many of the "best" people in Northampton, out in church. Later he began to enforce strict rules of church membership. The rules, which had been modified by his beloved predecessor and father-in-law, Solomon Stoddard, to permit church membership without a full declaration of faith, required that anyone applying for church membership, and thus full citizenship in the town and colony, had to make a full and public declaration of faith and a saving experience. By 1750, Edwards' church was in full revolt, and on July 1, 1750, he preached his "Farewell Sermon."

In 1751, Edwards settled in the frontier village of Stockbridge, Massachusetts, where he became minister of the small church there and missionary to the Indians. He also devoted much of his time there to writing, producing, among other works, *The Nature of True Virtue, The Freedom of the Will,* and *Concerning the End for Which God Created the World.* In 1757, he was named president of the new Princeton College. He took office in January 1758 and died of smallpox on March 22 of that year.

THE AUTOBIOGRAPHY

Jonathan Edwards wrote his *Personal Narrative,* the account of his conversion, probably in 1739, long after the actual experience. By this time, Edwards began to rework the material from his diary, in which he had originally recorded an account of his conversion. He had not only led his congregation through the first phases of the great revival, but had also observed carefully and written much about the conversion experience of others. Much of Edwards' intellectual energy in the late 1730s and early 1740s was devoted to the analysis of conversion, and it is no surprise that he turned to his own experience to provide an example of a "true" conversion.

Although Puritan theology admitted that not all conversion experiences were identical, by the eighteenth century, a morphology of conversion, or general pattern for the experience, had developed. Edwards and other ministers held that not every religious emotion or enthusiastic feeling was part of a saving conversion. Although ministers differed on the exact number of steps, nearly all Puritan ministers taught that a true conversion followed a general pattern and order. First was a person's hearing God's word and coming to an understanding of God's law. This was followed by a personal awareness of sinfulness. Next came a period of doubt and despair and a cry for forgiveness. The final step was an assurance of God's mercy and the infusion of saving grace. After the experience came a renewed and changed life. In many instances, applicants for church membership and ministers, as well as later critics of Puritanism, turned this morphology into a mere formula. Edwards, however, in his short *Personal Narrative,* demonstrates that the experience was neither static nor formulaic.

Edwards begins the account of his conversion by announcing

I had a variety of concerns and exercises about my soul from my childhood, but had two more remarkable seasons of awakening before I met with that change by which I was brought to those new dispositions, and that new sense of things, that I have since had. (p. 57)

Two ideas central to Edwards' thought emerge here. First, conversion is a process. Religious concerns and two seasons of awakening precede the change itself. Conversion for Edwards is not one moment, but rather an ongoing event. Second, the result of the conversion is a new disposition and a new sense. Specifically, Edwards uses the word "sense" in psychological terms; literally this means that the converted person senses things in a new way: conversion transforms perception.

When he begins his description of his early life, Edwards remembers that there had been "remarkable awakenings" in his father's congregation and that he and his friends "took delight" in religious duties, building a place of prayer in an isolated spot. He also remembers how he used to go off to pray in private. He comments, however, that he was always easily moved, and that the delight he found in religious practice was not grace.

After a time, these religious affections wore off, and Edwards "returned like a dog to his vomit, and went on in the ways of sin" (p. 57). He writes that God visited him with pleurisy and "shook him over the pit of hell." Shortly after this, Edwards began to have inward struggles and vowed to change his sinful life.

These doubts, struggles, and attempts at religion are consistent with the early stages of the conversion process proscribed by Puritan ideology. The transformation itself Edwards describes in terms of doctrine. He writes that "from my childhood up, my mind had been full of objections against the doctrine of God's sovereignty, in choosing whom he would for eternal life, and rejecting whom he pleased" (p. 58). For the rational Edwards, this fundamental Puritan doctrine seemed horrible. No intellectual approach offered any help. He records, however, reading the words of 1 Timothy 1:17, "Now unto the King eternal, immortal, invisible, the only wise God, be honour and glory for ever and ever. Amen," and feeling "a new sense, quite different from anything I ever experienced before" (p. 59). This sense, which Edwards describes as a "sort of inward, sweet delight in God and divine things," provided a "wonderful alternation" in his mind that made the sovereignty of God now a delightful conviction. No longer was the doctrine an objection; it was now a source of joy.

This "delightful conviction" and "wonderful alteration" is an excellent example of the change in perception brought on by the conversion experience. Before the conversion, Edwards' difficulty with the doctrine of sovereignty was the result of his looking at the impact of sovereignty on man. After the conversion experience, Edwards' emphasis had shifted to God, and as a result, the doctrine seemed not only reasonable, but also just and proper. For Edwards, conversion was affective; it acted on the senses and altered perception, enabling the newly converted to see all of creation in a new light.

Edwards writes that after this experience, he gave an account of his conversion to his father. This is a significant detail. At the time of the composition of the *Personal Narrative*, one of the major questions facing the New England clergy was how to differentiate between true conversion and mere emotional enthusiasm. Edwards' interview with his ministerial father suggests one method of evaluation: Let the church decide.

The impact of the conversion overwhelmed Edwards. He recalls:

The appearance of everything was altered; there seemed to be as it were, a calm, sweet cast, or appearance of divine glory, in almost every thing. God's excellency, his wisdom, his purity and love, seemed to appear in every thing; in the sun, moon, and stars; in the clouds, and blue sky; in the grass, flowers, trees; in the water, and all nature; which used greatly to fix my mind. (p. 61)

The conversion experience, which was first perceived in an altered attitude over church doctrine, now became a mystical experience in which Edwards' very perception of the world had been transformed. Like Gerard Manley Hopkins, Edwards had come to a vision in which he could see that "the world was charged with the grandeur of God."

For Edwards, conversion was not a static experience. The *Personal Narrative* is a record of a continuity of change. Edwards writes that thunder, which formerly frightened him, now seemed to be the voice of God. This change of perception led him to more "vehement longings of the soul for God and Christ." These longings led him to increased prayer and the discovery of more inward delight. For more than a year and a half, Edwards' sense of divine things increased and matured. He felt called to preach in New York, and there he "felt a burning desire to be in every thing a complete Christian; and conformed to the blessed image of Christ; and that I might live, in all things, according to the pure, sweet and blessed rules of the gospel" (p. 62). This desire led him to make a solemn dedication to God, which he wrote down and recorded on January 12, 1723.

Edwards' autobiography clearly demonstrates that conversion is not an instantaneous phenomenon during which a sinner is transformed into a saint. Rather, as he looks back on his own life and conversion, Edwards sees a process of preparation leading up to a dramatic experience that was followed by an ongoing series of interrelated events. He writes, for example, that some time after he had been experiencing these "sweetest joys and delights," his "heart had been much on the advancement of Christ's kingdom in the world" (p. 68). His inner sense of God and God's power, majesty, and beauty led him to commit himself to the work of God in the world; mysticism led to ministry.

The exuberance of the early sections of the narrative are absent from its end. Edwards was well aware that few people could maintain the emotional intensity of the conversion experience over long periods, and he concludes the account of his own conversion from the perspective of an experienced minister writing after the first wave of revival had died down in New England. He notes with some sadness that the sweet sense that had infused him had been replaced by an awareness of his own sinfulness and his need for God's grace and strength. This awareness is as valid as was his earlier overwhelming sense of joy, but Edwards is aware that time and experience transform people. He notes, finally, that

it seems to me, that, in some respects, I was a far better Christian, for two or three years after my conversion, than I am now; and lived in a more constant delight and pleasure; yet, of late years, I have had a more full and constant sense of the absolute sovereignty of God. (p. 71)

With age, wisdom replaced delight.

CRITICISM

Jonathan Edwards may be the best-known American Puritan. His famous Enfield sermon, "Sinners in the Hands of an Angry God," has come to represent Puritanism to generations of American college students. During his lifetime, Edwards was famous as well, and throughout most of the nineteenth century, he was an influential figure in mainstream Protestantism. By the early twentieth century, however, there was little interest in Edwards or Puritanism. That situation changed, with the pioneering work of Perry Miller and the rediscovery of American Puritanism.

Miller's influential scholarship, especially *The New England Mind* and *Jonathan Edwards*, created a renewed interest in the study of the Puritans and placed Jonathan Edwards at the center of early New England studies. In his excellent biography of Edwards, Miller writes:

The truth is, Edwards was infinitely more than a theologian. He was one of America's five or six major artists, who happened to work with ideas instead of with poems or novels. He was much more of a psychologist and a poet than a logician, and though he devoted his genius to topics derived from the body of divinity—the will, virtue, sin—he treated them in the manner of the very finest speculators, in the manner of Augustine, Aquinas, and Pascal, as problems not of dogma but of life. (p. xii)

Although recent critics have disagreed with some of Miller's conclusions, Miller's evaluation of the centrality of Edwards to an understanding of the Puritans remains convincing. His evaluation of the importance of Edwards the artist and philosopher also has withstood critical inquiry.

Jonathan Edwards produced a vast quantity of writing. As William J. Scheick notes in his introduction to the useful *Critical Essays on Jonathan Edwards*, understanding Edwards' life and work "required a keen sensitivity to two and a half centuries of commentary as well as an informed awareness of at least the five disciplines—theology, philosophy, history, American studies, and literary criticism" (p. ix). The study of Jonathan Edwards has become a profession in itself. As M. X. Lesser observes in his *Jonathan Edwards*:

From 1965 to 1975, doctoral candidates in America produced fifty-seven dissertations about Edwards, concerning, among other things; his ideas about glory and grace; typology and teleology, his social and educational theories; continuities beyond Emerson and comparisons with Stoddard; studies of his rhetoric and his symbolic system and his style. (p. 125)

What emerges from all these studies is a complexity that was obvious during Edwards' own life. Jonathan Edwards was a frontier pastor who was an original philosopher; he was a mystic and a rationalist; he was a quiet speaker and a powerful revivalist; he was a world-class theologian and a failed pastor. Despite, or perhaps because of, these complexities, the works of Jonathan Edwards remain essential to the understanding of religious life in America, and the *Personal Narrative*, one of his most accessible works, is an excellent introduction to and account of religious conversion.

BIBLIOGRAPHY

Aldridge, Alfred Owen. "Edwards and Hutcheson." *The Harvard Theological Review*, 44 (1931): 35–53.

———. *Jonathan Edwards*. New York: Washington Square, 1964.

Alstrom, Sidney. *Theology in America*. Indianapolis: Bobbs-Merrill, 1967.

Anderson, Wallace E. Editor's introduction. Jonathan Edwards. *Scientific Writings*. Edited by Wallace E. Anderson. Vol. 6 of *The Works of Jonathan Edwards*. John E. Smith, general editor. New Haven, Conn.: Yale University Press, 1980.

Bercovitch, Sacvan. *The Puritan Origins of the American Self*. New Haven, Conn.: Yale University Press, 1975.

———. "The Ritual of American Autobiography: Edwards, Franklin, Thoreau." *Revue Francaise d'Etudes Americaines*, 14 (May 1982): 139–50.

Brumm, Urusla. *American Thoughts and Religious Typology*. Translated by John Hoaglund. New Brunswick, N.J.: Rutgers University Press, 1970. Excerpted as "Jonathan Edwards and Typology." In *Early American Literature*. Edited by Michael T. Gilmore. *Twentieth Century Views Series*. Series Editor Maynard Mack. Englewood Cliffs, N.J.: Prentice-Hall, 1980.

Bushman, Richard L. "Jonathan Edwards and Puritan Consciousness." *Journal for the Scientific Study of Religion*, 5 (1966): 383–96.

Caldwell, Patricia. *The Puritan Conversion Narrative*. London: Cambridge University Press, 1983.

Carpenter, Frederick I. "The Radicalism of Jonathan Edwards." *New England Quarterly*, 4 (October 1931): 631–33.

Carroll, Peter N. *Puritanism and the Wilderness*. New York: Columbia University Press, 1969.

Carse, James. *Jonathan Edwards and the Visibility of God.* New York: Charles Scribner's, Sons, 1967.

Cherry, Conrad. *Nature and Religious Imagination.* Philadelphia: Fortress, 1980.

Cragg, Gerald R. *Puritanism in the Period of the Great Persecution, 1660–1688.* Cambridge, Mass.: Harvard University Press, 1957.

———. *Reason and Authority in the Eighteenth Century.* Cambridge, Mass.: Harvard University Press, 1964.

Davidson, Edward H. *Jonathan Edwards, The Narrative of a Puritan Mind.* Cambridge, Mass.: Harvard University Press, 1960.

Delattre, Roland. *Beauty and Sensibility in the Thought of Jonathan Edwards.* New Haven, Conn.: Yale University Press, 1968.

DeProspo, R. C. "The 'New Simple Idea' of Edwards's Personal Narrative." *Early American Literature,* 14 (Fall 1979): 193–204.

———. *Theism in the Discourse of Jonathan Edwards.* Newark: University of Delaware Press; London: Associated University Presses, 1985.

Edwards, Jonathan. *Personal Narrative.* In *Jonathan Edwards: Representative Selections, with Introduction, Bibliography, and Notes.* Edited by Clarence Faust and Thomas Johnson. New York: American Book Company, 1935.

———. *The Works of President Edwards, in Eight Volumes.* Edited by Samuel Austin. Worcester: Isiah Thomas, 1808–1809.

———. *The Works of President Edwards: With a Memoir of His Life, in Ten Volumes.* Edited by Sereno E. Dwight. New York: S. Converse, 1829–30.

———. *The Works of Jonathan Edwards.* Edited by Perry Miller and John E. Smith. New Haven, Conn.: Yale University Press, 1957.

Elwood, Douglas J. *The Philosophical Theology of Jonathan Edwards.* New York: Columbia University Press, 1961.

Emerson, Everett, ed. *Major Writers of Early American Literature.* Madison: University of Wisconsin Press, 1972.

Erdt, Terrence. *Jonathan Edwards' Art and the Sense of the Heart.* Amherst: University of Massachusetts Press, 1980.

Fiering, Norman. *Jonathan Edwards's Moral Thought and Its British Context.* Chapel Hill: University of North Carolina Press, 1981.

Gaustad, Edwin Scott. *The Great Awakening in New England.* New York: Harper & Brothers, 1956.

Holbrook, Clyde A. "Jonathan Edwards and His Detractors." *Theology Today,* 10 (October 1953): 384–96.

———. *The Ethics of Jonathan Edwards.* Ann Arbor: University of Michigan Press, 1973.

———. *The Iconoclastic Deity.* Lewisburg, Pa.: Buckwell University Press, 1984.

Howard, Leon. *"The Mind" of Jonathan Edwards: A Reconstructed Text.* Berkeley: University of California Press, 1963.

Kuklick, Bruce. *Churchmen and Philosophers.* New Haven, Conn.: Yale University Press, 1985.

Lee, Sang Hyun. "Mental Activity and the Perception of Beauty in Jonathan Edwards." *Harvard Theological Review,* 69 (1976): 364–96.

Lesser, M. X. *Jonathan Edwards.* Boston: G. K. Hall, 1988.

Levin, David. *Jonathan Edwards: A Profile.* New York: Hill & Wang, 1969.

Lovejoy, Arthur O. *The Great Chain of Being*. Cambridge, Mass.: Harvard University Press, 1942.

Lowance, Mason I. "Typology, Millenial Eschatology, and Jonathan Edwards." In *Literary Uses of Typology from the Middle Ages to the Present*. Edited by Earl Miner. Princeton, N.J.: Princeton University Press, 1977. Reprinted in *Critical Essays on Jonathan Edwards*. Edited by William J. Scheik. Boston: G. K. Hall, 1980.

Lucas, Paul R. *Valley of Discord*. Hanover, N.H.: University Press of New England, 1976.

Miller, Perry. *The New England Mind*. New York: Macmillan, 1939.

———. "Jonathan Edwards on the Sense of the Heart." *Harvard Theological Review*, 41 (1948): 123–45.

———. *Jonathan Edwards*. New York: William Sloan, 1949.

Miner, Earl, ed. *Literary Uses of Typology*. Princeton, N.J.: Princeton University Press, 1977.

Murdock, Kenneth. "The Colonial Experience in the Literature of the United States." In *Early American Literature*. Edited by Michael T. Gilmore. Englewood Cliffs, N.J.: Prentice-Hall, 1980.

Niebuhr, Richard. *The Kingdom of God in America*. New York: Harper & Brothers, 1937.

Opie, John. *Jonathan Edwards and the Enlightenment*. Lexington, Mass.: Heath, 1969.

Owen, H. P. "Morality and Christian Theism." *Religious Studies*, 20, no. 1 (March 1984): 5–17.

Parrington, V. L. *The Colonial Mind*. Vol. 1 of *Main Currents in American Thought*. New York: Harcourt, Brace & World, 1927.

Pierce, David C. "Jonathan Edwards and the 'New Sense' of Glory." *New England Quarterly*, 41, no. 1 (March 1968): 82–95.

Russell, Bertrand. *A History of Western Philosophy*. London: Allen & Unwin, 1948.

Scheick, William J., ed. *Critical Essays on Jonathan Edwards*. Boston: G. K. Hall, 1980.

Shea, Daniel B. "The Art and Instruction of Jonathan Edwards's 'Personal Narrative.' " *American Literature*, 36 (March 1965): 17–32. Reprinted in *Critical Essays on Jonathan Edwards*. Edited by William J. Scheick. Boston: G. K. Hall, 1980.

———. *Spiritual Narrative in Early America*. Princeton, N.J.: Princeton University Press, 1968.

Simonsin, Harold. Introduction. In *Selected Writings of Jonathan Edwards*. Edited by Harold Simonsin. New York: Ungar, 1970.

Stein, Stephen J. "Jonathan Edwards and the Rainbow: Biblical Exegesis and Poetic Imagination." *New England Quarterly*, 47 (3) (Spring 1974): 440–56.

———. Editor's Introduction. In *Jonathan Edwards, Apocalyptic Writings*. Edited by Stephen J. Stein. New Haven, Conn.: Yale University Press, 1977.

———. "The Quest for Spiritual Sense: The Biblical Hermeneutics of Jonathan Edwards." *Harvard Theological Review*, 70 (January–April 1977): 109ff.

Stewart, Randall. *American Literature and Christian Doctrine*. Baton Rouge: Louisiana State University Press, 1958.

Suter, Rufus. "A Note on the Neoplatonism of the Philosophy of Jonathan Edwards." *Harvard Theological Review*, 52, no. 4 (1959): 283–84.

Thomas, Keith. *Man and the Natural World*. New York: Pantheon, 1983.

Tomas, Vincent. "The Modernity of Jonathan Edwards." *New England Quarterly*, 25, no. 1 (March 1952): 60–85.

Tracy, Patricia J. *Jonathan Edwards, Pastor: Religion and Society in Eighteenth Century Northampton*. New York: Hill & Wang, 1980.

Van Doren, Carl. *Benjamin Franklin and Jonathan Edwards*. New York: Charles Scribners' Sons, 1920.

Westfall, Richard S. *Science and Religion in Seventeenth Century England*. New Haven, Conn.: Yale University Press, 1958.

Whittenmore, Robert E. "Jonathan Edwards and the Theology of the Sixth Way." *Church History*, 35 (March 1966): 60–75.

Willey, Basil. *The Eighteenth Century Background*. London: Chatto & Windus, 1946.

Winslow, Ola Elizabeth. *Jonathan Edwards*. New York: Macmillan, 1941.

12 • OLAUDAH EQUIANO (C. 1745–1797)

The Interesting Narrative of the Life of Olaudah Equiano, or Gustavus Vassa, the African

BIOGRAPHY

Olaudah Equiano was born in what is now Nigeria in about 1745. When he was about ten years old, he was captured by slave raiders and taken to the African coast, where he was sold to slave traders. He was shipped to the West Indies and then taken to Virginia. He became the property of a ship captain named Pascal, who gave him the new name Gustavus Vassa, in honor of the king of Sweden. Equiano traveled with Pascal to Canada, England, and the West Indies, becoming an excellent sailor in the process. In time, he was sold to several masters, including a Quaker merchant and a doctor. He had the opportunity to earn money by buying and selling cooking ware, and in 1766, he had saved enough money to buy his own freedom. He continued to work as a seaman, crossing the Atlantic a number of times and also taking part in an Arctic expedition.

After he attained his freedom, Equiano was converted to Methodism. He became an ardent abolitionist and traveled throughout England and Scotland lecturing against slavery. In 1786, he was appointed to assist in the colonization of free slaves returning to Sierra Leone in Africa but was discharged when he spoke out against the dishonesty of the white men who were in charge of the mission. In 1789, he published his autobiography, which became an immediate best-seller and remained a popular text for abolitionists in both England and America. Although there is no agreement on the exact date of his death, April 30, 1797, is most often accepted.

THE AUTOBIOGRAPHY

The Interesting Narrative of the Life of Olaudah Equiano, or Gustavus Vassa, the African was an immensely popular work. One reason for the book's popularity was Equiano's firsthand depiction of the slave system from capture in Africa to eventual freedom in England. A second reason was that the publication of his narrative coincided with increased agitation in England for the abolition of the slave trade. Much of the support for this movement came from members of the dissenting churches, particularly Methodists and Quakers, and Equiano's explicit comments on his conversion and his Christianity made the narrative even more attractive to many readers.

In the first chapter of his autobiography, Equiano begins to develop one of his central themes, the destructive effects of slavery on all who come in contact with it. To do so, he calls on both memory and Anthony Benezet's popular history, *Account of Guinea*, to create a near-Edenic picture of life in Africa. Equiano writes that his father was one of the elders of his community, which was well ordered, peaceful, and prosperous. He records that "our manners are simple, our luxuries are few" (Bontemps, 7) and that "we live in a country where nature is prodigal of her favors, our wants are few and easily supplied" (p. 9).

As Equiano describes the land, rituals, and customs of his country, he remarks:

And here I cannot forbear suggesting what has long struck me forcibly, namely, the strong analogy which even by this sketch, imperfect as it is, appears to prevail in the manners and customs of my countrymen, and those of the Jews, before they reached the land of promise, and particularly the patriarchs while they were yet in that pastoral state which is described in Genesis. (p. 16)

Equiano's reference to the Jews is significant. Like nearly all writers of slave narratives, Equiano compares his slavery with the bondage of the Israelites in Egypt and sees in their deliverance a type of his own. Equiano's use of this analogy provides the basic structure for his entire narrative because in his autobiography, he describes being taken into bondage, coming to freedom in a promised land, and finding the truth of Christianity by conversion. In writing his autobiography, Equiano transforms his life into a type of both the Old and the New Testaments.

In his description of his capture and removal to the coast and eventually the West Indies and Virginia, Equiano charts a fall from paradise. The farther he is moved from his own village, the stranger are the customs and the crueler his treatment. Although a slave in his first remove after capture, he discovers that he is treated kindly, almost as a member of an extended family. By the time he nears the African coast, he discovers that the inhabitants have been corrupted by contact with white men: They ate without washing, the men fought among themselves, and the women were "immodest." Equiano writes that worse followed, for he was soon put aboard a slave ship and brought to the West Indies.

The description of the slave voyage is one of the most dramatic passages in Equiano's narrative. Equiano presents not only the strangeness of being aboard a ship for the first time, but also the violence of the sailors and the terrible conditions of the hold. His noting that a number of slaves committed suicide rather than continue to endure the voyage suggests how horrible the infamous middle passage was. He finally arrived in the islands. Looking back at this part of his life, Equiano breaks from his narrative to address his readers: "O, ye nominal Christians! might not an African ask you— Learned you this from your God, who says unto you, Do unto all men as you would men should do unto you?" (p. 33). The question here is who is the savage and who the Christian?

The sections that follow chronicle Equiano's life and adventures, and as several critics have observed, they read like passages from a picaresque novel. Equiano records his being purchased by Captain Pascal, acquiring his new name, Gustavus Vassa, time served aboard various war ships, and fighting for the British navy against the French in the Atlantic and Mediterranean. In these passages, Equiano establishes his character as a brave soldier who considered his situation fortunate. He was still a slave, but because his master apprenticed him to the navy, Equiano had the opportunity to live like a seamen and develop a variety of skills that he would later put to good use.

Equiano eventually was sold to a Mr. King, a wealthy Philadelphia Quaker engaged in shipping to and from the West Indies. King recognized Equiano's skill and made him first a clerk on his island plantation and later a sailor on one of his ships. In describing his work for King, Equiano is careful to record both the mistreatment of slaves in the islands and the ability of slaves to work for themselves. He writes, for example, that all the skilled labor in the West Indies was slave labor, and that many of the slaves taught themselves to be carpenters, mechanics, and coopers. In this context, he begins to record his own developing skills as a merchant. Beginning with an investment of three pence, Equiano saved more than forty pounds by selling pots, pans, dishes, and cups throughout the islands, and with that money, he was able to buy his freedom.

After attaining his freedom, Equiano returned to England and continued to work as a sailor. He made voyages to Jamaica, Grenada, Turkey, and Martinique. In addition, he was a member of the crew of the *HMS Race Horse*, which attempted to find the Northwest Passage and journey to the North Pole. After returning from that voyage of exploration, he began another, this time internal, one. Equiano records:

[I] began seriously to reflect on the dangers I had escaped, particularly those of my last voyage, which made a lasting impression on my mind, and, by the grace of

God, proved afterwards a mercy to me; it caused me to reflect deeply on my eternal state, and to seek the Lord with full purpose of heart, ere it was too late. I rejoiced greatly, and heartily thanked the Lord for directing me towards London, where I was determined to work out my own salvation, and, in doing so, procure a title to heaven. (p. 139)

Equiano then proceeded to work at salvation with the same earnestness as he worked at freedom. He began visiting various churches, but he found more comfort at home reading the Bible. He asked different people how to get to heaven, and was told a variety of answers. He then began a campaign of righteousness, during which he attempted to keep perfectly all the commandments. He eventually realized that this was not sufficient. Discouraged, he continued to search for the way to salvation. He eventually was told by a Methodist friend, "The law is a schoolmaster to bring us to Christ" (p. 146). This was his first awareness that salvation came not through works, but through faith, and after that realization, he saw himself as a sinner, prayed, and finally felt the spirit of God's grace pour out on him.

Equiano's description of his conversion is important for a number of reasons. First, it is consistent with the standard Protestant morphology of conversion: desire for salvation, reading of scripture, awareness of sinfulness, acknowledgment of God's power, and, finally, emotional release. In addition, Equiano's account records conversion as a process leading up to a moment. More interesting is the change of perception that Equiano records. Before his conversion, Equiano believed that he was far more sinned against than sinning. He had been taken from his home, made a slave, and mistreated. He had, in response, been faithful, hardworking, earnest, prosperous, and brave. When he began to look after his salvation, he was convinced that works were sufficient. Only when he was willing to radically reform his perception of himself, to see even the virtuous ex-slave as a "condemned criminal under the law" and unworthy of salvation, and to place himself at the mercy of Christ does he experience God's grace.

After his conversion, Equiano turned to the work of the Lord. He became an outspoken advocate of abolition and petitioned the bishop of London for ordination as a missionary to Africa. When he discovered that a governmental expedition to return freed slaves to Africa was being planned, he agreed to serve as one of the commissioners, and the final chapters of the autobiography record the failure of that mission and Equiano's continuing work for the abolition of the slave trade. He ends his narrative with an appropriately religious message, hoping that his readers will find in the story of his life a "lesson of morality and religion" (p. 192).

CRITICISM

Equiano's autobiography, like many other slave narratives, has become the object of serious criticism after years of neglect. In his introduction to

Great Slave Narratives, Arna Bontemps writes that while growing up, he was taught that "the only meaningful history of the Negro in the United States (possibly even in the world) began with the Emancipation Proclamation of 1863" (p. vii). This misconception helped to ensure the neglect of an entire genre of black writing, but with the revived interest in black culture during and after the Harlem Renaissance, scholars and readers have turned to the slave narrative in an attempt to rediscover an important part of American history and to reinterpret the relation between blacks and whites in America.

Serious criticism has emerged, and the study of the slave narrative and black autobiography has become a significant field of literary and cultural study. Such works as William Andrews' *To Tell a Free Story: The First Century of Afro-American Autobiography, 1760–1865*, John Blassingame's *Slave Testimony: Two Centuries of Letters, Speeches, Interviews, and Autobiographies*, Francis Smith Foster's *Witnessing Slavery: The Development of Ante-Bellum Slave Narratives*, Edward Margolies' *Ante-Bellum Slave Narratives: Their Place in American Literary History*, John Sekora and Darwin Turner's *The Art of the Slave Narrative: Original Essays in Criticism and Theory*, Sidione Smith's *Where I'm Bound: Patterns of Slavery and Freedom in Black American Autobiography*, Marion Wilson Starling's *The Slave Narrative: Its Place in Literary History*, and Robert Stepto's *From Behind the Veil: A Study of Afro-American Narrative* demonstrate the breadth and depth of the field.

The most complete study of Equiano and his writing is Angelo Costanzo's excellent *Surprising Narrative: Olaudah Equiano and the Beginnings of Black Autobiography*. Costanzo not only provides a thorough introduction and bibliography, but also gives an intelligent reading of the autobiography, noting, for example, that Equiano's autobiography combines elements of the picturesque, narrative of success, and conversion narrative.

As many critics have pointed out, ex-slaves told their stories for a variety of reasons—to condemn slavery, to praise God for their deliverance, to establish their own identities, to chronicle their own amazing transformations. Equiano's autobiography provides a complex and intelligent narrative in which all these motives can be seen. It remains one of the most dramatic tales of bondage and escape and records the continual transformations of an unusual man.

BIBLIOGRAPHY

Andrews, William. *To Tell a Free Story: The First Century of Afro-American Autobiography, 1760–1865*. Urbana: University of Illinois Press, 1986.
Benezet, Anthony. *Some Historical Account of Guinea*. London: J. Phillips, 1788.
Blassingame, John. *Slave Testimony: Two Centuries of Letters, Speeches, Interviews, and Autobiographies*. Baton Rouge: Louisiana State University Press, 1977.

Costanzo, Angelo. *Surprising Narrative: Olaudah Equiano and the Beginnings of Black Autobiography*. New York: Greenwood, 1987.

Duffield, Edward, and Ian Duffield. "Equiano's Turks and Christians: An Eighteenth Century African View of Islam." *Journal of African Studies*, 2 (1975–76): 433–44.

Equiano, Olaudah. *The Interesting Narrative of the Life of Olaudah Equiano, or Gustavus Vassa, the African*. 1813. In *Great Slave Narratives*. Edited by Arna Bontemps. Boston: Beacon, 1969.

———. *Equiano's Travels: His Autobiography*. Edited by Paul Edwards. New York: Praeger, 1967.

———. *The Life of Olaudah Equiano*. Edited by Paul Edwards. London: Dawson, 1969.

Foster, Frances Smith. *Witnessing Slavery: The Development of Ante-Bellum Slave Narratives*. New York: Greenwood, 1979.

Margolies, Edward. *Ante-Bellum Slave Narratives: Their Place in American Literary History*. New York: Harper & Row, 1975.

Sekora, John, and Darwin T. Turner. *The Art of the Slave Narrative: Original Essays in Criticism and Theory*. Macomb: Western Illinois University Press, 1982.

Smith, Sidione. *Where I'm Bound: Patterns of Slavery and Freedom in Black American Autobiography*. New York: Greenwood, 1974.

Starling, Marion Wilson. *The Slave Narrative: Its Place in Literary History*. Boston: G. K. Hall, 1981.

Stepto, Robert B. *From Behind the Veil: A Study of Afro-American Narrative*. Urbana: University of Illinois Press, 1979.

13 • JERRY FALWELL (1933–   )

Strength for the Journey

BIOGRAPHY

Jerry Falwell was born in Lynchburg, Virginia, on August 11, 1933. The Falwells had lived in Virginia since the seventeenth century and were among the original settlers in and around Lynchburg. His father was an entrepreneur who owned small restaurants, stores, an inn, and a bootlegging business. His mother, one of sixteen children, grew up in a pious Baptist family. Falwell's early years were not particularly religious, and during high school, he engaged in typical adolescent pranks. In 1950, he enrolled in Lynchburg College, intending to major in mechanical engineering. On Sunday morning, January 20, 1952, Falwell became a born-again Christian.

After his conversion, Falwell transferred to Baptist Bible College, in Springfield, Missouri, where he graduated in 1956. He returned to Lynchburg to become founding pastor of the Thomas Road Baptist Church. From 1956 through 1972, Falwell led one of the fastest-growing church organizations in the United States. In 1956, Falwell began a television ministry, "The Old-Time Gospel Hour," which grew along with his congregation. In 1959, he established the Elim Home for Alcoholics; in 1964, he opened Lynchburg Christian Academy, a full-time day school. In 1971, Falwell started Lynchburg Baptist College, which has become Liberty University, and in 1972, he began the Thomas Road Bible Institute.

During the past two decades, Falwell has become a national figure. In 1971, Falwell made headlines when the Securities and Exchange Commission filed charges against the Thomas Road Baptist Church for fraud and deceit in the sale of bonds. The charges were later dropped. In 1978, Falwell launched the "Clean Up America" campaign, and in 1979, he founded and became president of the Moral Majority, now the Liberty Foundation. In 1987, after scandals had forced Jim Bakker to resign as head of the PTL television ministry, Falwell attempted to keep the ministry alive, but the growing moral and financial scandals of Bakker's stewardship compelled him to resign. Falwell remains one of the most influential pastors, televangelists, and conservative activists in America today.

THE AUTOBIOGRAPHY

Strength for the Journey takes its title from a traditional Christian metaphor that compares

the Christian life to a journey that began at my second birth. That journey or Christian walk took a lifetime and ended only upon my physical death, when I would stand before the Lord to be rewarded for my faithfulness. The lifelong journey was fraught with danger. I had to make my way through two different and competing worlds simultaneously: the world of God and the world of man. (p. 123)

Other Christian writers have used the same metaphor, most notably John Bunyan in *A Pilgrim's Progress*, and Falwell, like Bunyan, takes his metaphor seriously. The idea of a journey through "two different and competing worlds" provides Falwell with one of the two controlling ideas of his narrative. Throughout *Strength for the Journey*, Falwell moves from descriptions of events in the world of man to interpretations from the world of God, the latter providing meaning for the events in the former. Of equal importance to Falwell is the idea of evangelization, or spreading the gospel. As he tells of his life, Falwell moves from personal experience to a scriptural commentary and, finally, to a call to his readers to accept Christ themselves. The autobiography thus becomes an extended sermon, with Falwell bringing together the Bible, his family history, and his own life to demonstrate God's actions in the affairs of men.

Although Jerry Falwell includes his conversion experience in his autobiography and uses it as the turning point in his narrative, *Strength for the Journey* is not primarily a story of conversion. Rather, it is the memoir of a public religious man. Falwell is aware of his notoriety, and in telling the story of his life, he places himself within both familial and religious contexts. By establishing himself as a member of both a particular family—traditional Virginian—and a particular faith—Baptist—Falwell is able to establish credentials that provide a frame of reference for the moral and political positions he has taken throughout his public ministry.

In the opening chapters of *Strength for the Journey*, Falwell provides his readers with a family history. After briefly referring to his revolutionary and pioneer ancestors, Falwell begins the family history that "forms and informs" him with the end of the Civil War and the murder of his great-grandfather John Falwell, an ex-Confederate soldier. After describing the murder, Falwell comments:

John's murder is just one more personal reminder that the enemy pursues us even in the quiet paradise of Lynchburg nestled safely in the shadow of the Blue Ridge Mountains where the Blackwater creek meets the James River.... Man was not created to murder his fellow man.... Evil is at work in the world, and no family can be protected from it. (p. 9)

Falwell continues to use these Old Testament metaphors of paradise, temptation, and the fall as he chronicles the lives of his grandfather, who turned away from God after the death of his wife, and his father, who killed his own brother with a shotgun on December 28, 1931. As he describes his grandfather's atheism and his father's confrontation with his brother, Falwell not only makes a case for the reality of sin but also establishes a comfortable but empty way of life that he contrasts with his mother's poor, yet faithful Baptist upbringing. The images of death and sin that are part of his family history also establish a perspective that will change dramatically when Falwell undergoes his own conversion experience.

Falwell calls the chapter in which he presents his own conversion "The Prodigal Son"and the one that precedes it, "The Prodigal Father." In the latter, he presents his father's deathbed conversion and death and in the former, his own. Using the New Testament parable as a model, Falwell describes his own and his father's return from the world to God. To establish the drama of his own conversion, Falwell depicts himself as a bright, joking youngster who was a leader of one of Lynchburg's (rather nonviolent) youth gangs. After graduation from high school, he lived at home and attended Lynchburg College. He remembers that although he took six hours of Bible and theology classes, he did not know the Old Testament from the New nor had he any notion of sin or its consequences. He did, however, listen to Charles Fuller's "Old Fashioned Revival Hour," which his mother tuned in on the family radio every Sunday morning. He writes that on Sunday morning, January 20, 1952, he felt strangely moved while listening to the program, and later in the day went to afternoon services in Fuller's Park Avenue Baptist Church, where he walked to the altar and accepted Christ.

Falwell notes that at the time of conversion, he didn't know a thing about the Holy Spirit or the God that had pursued him through Lynchburg that day. Instead, he writes that he felt himself drawn to the church. Falwell is a fundamentalist, not a Pentecostal, and he does not describe his conversion experience as an event filled with voices or visions. He tells of this crucial event in his life quite simply and in a plain style. The implications are far from simple, however, for after his conversion, Falwell sets out on his journey of faith, a journey that would lead him to the pulpit and, eventually, politics.

Falwell's presentation of the first part of his Christian journey is quite traditional. As he describes his experiences at Baptist Bible College, his first attempts at ministering to youth, his struggles over his calling, and his eventual decision to return to Lynchburg to preach, Falwell writes of experiences that could be that of almost any young person entering religious life. Falwell depicts his younger self as energetic, committed, and inexperienced, and the young Falwell emerges as a sympathetic character. Likewise, Falwell's narration of the first years of his ministry is both simple and sympathetic. As Falwell describes the establishment of the Thomas Road Baptist Church in 1956 and the development of radio and television ministries in the late 1950s and early 1960s, he drops his evangelistic tone and becomes a recorder of events. The early years of his ministry were prosperous and peaceful, and in writing about them, Falwell creates a kind of golden age of his ministry, a reference point from which he can measure the distance.

As Falwell sees it, the end of the golden age of innocence in Lynchburg came with the civil rights movement. He writes that he grew up in the segregated South and that he believed in segregation and never thought of the injustices of the system; it was, he observes, a matter of Southern culture in which he was fully immersed. Falwell describes how he pulled into the confrontation. As the national civil rights movement grew in 1963 and 1964, the relation between church and state began to change. In July of 1964, after the march of 250,000 persons to Washington, D.C., to urge Congress to pass civil rights legislation, President Lyndon Johnson signed the Civil Rights Act and asked Baptist leaders and clergy to support civil rights. Falwell responded in a sermon entitled "Ministers and Marches," in which he declared that "preachers are not called to be politicians but soul winners. ... I feel we need to get off the streets and back into the pulpits and into the prayer rooms" (pp. 276–77). Later, in an interview with the *Lynchburg News*, he said that the Civil Rights Act was misnamed: "It is a terrible violation of human and property rights. It should be considered civil wrongs rather than civil rights" (p. 277). Excerpts from the sermon and interview were published, and Falwell found himself in the middle of the national controversy.

Writing about his position on civil rights, Falwell admits that he was wrong, and he describes the pleasure he had when he later integrated his church. He is well aware of the irony in his early position of separation of church and state as he writes from the vantage point of one of the most politically active ministers in the United States. In *Strength for the Journey*, it becomes clear that Falwell learned not only that segregation was wrong, but also that the pulpit could be an effective political tool. The extent of its effectiveness Falwell describes in a chapter titled "The Moral Majority."

In describing his decision to become active in national politics, Falwell depicts himself as a type of Old Testament prophet, chosen to call an erring nation to return to the faith of the fathers. Falwell sees America as under attack by Satan and cites abortion, pornography, moral permissiveness, a breakdown of family values, military unpreparedness, and a softness toward Marxism-Leninism as evidence of America's turning away from God. In 1979, Falwell called a meeting of national conservatives in Lynchburg, and the Moral Majority was born. For the next seven years, political-social action became the focal point of Falwell's life. He writes with pride of the impact of the Moral Majority on national politics, citing with special pleasure the impact of his movement on the elections and policies of Ronald Reagan. In summarizing the impact of the Moral Majority, Falwell notes that conservatives have become the largest voting bloc in the nation and that America had moved to the right both politically and theologically. Falwell writes that after having taken part in returning the nation to the paths of righteousness, he became convinced that it was time to return to his primary duties as a pastor and teacher and was preparing to withdraw from the public view when he became involved in the PTL scandal.

In March 1987, the PTL (Praise the Lord) television network was facing a major crisis as the Reverend Jim Bakker, its founder and chairman, was confronting charges of sexual misconduct and financial irregularities. In the face of pressure to resign and in an effort to save his ministries, which included a Christian theme park in addition to the television network, Bakker, an Assemblies of God minister, asked Falwell to take over as chairman of the board of PTL. Falwell agreed, and in the final chapter of his autobiography, Falwell describes how he attempted to hold together the ministry during a time when such major televangelists as Bakker, Jimmy Swaggart, and Oral Roberts came under close scrutiny as a result of personal, emotional, and financial irregularities. Falwell writes that when he accepted Jim Bakker's request to take over the troubled ministry, he began a long, risky journey, but that life is just such a journey. As he describes the ongoing series of revelations about Jim Bakker and Bakker's attempts to return to PTL, Falwell emerges as a straightforward and honest man trying to make the best out of an impossible situation. For many people, especially those who were not supporters of his conservative politics, Falwell acquitted himself most courageously in his failure at saving PTL rather than in his more successful ventures.

CRITICISM

In *Prime Time Preachers: The Rising Power of Televangelism*, Jeffrey K. Hadden and Charles E. Swann call Jerry Falwell one of the "elder statesmen of fundamentalist religious telecasting" (p. 20). In their profile of Falwell, they draw a distinction between the politician and the preacher: The politician they see as a conservative crusader against the evils of American modernism; the preacher they see as a conventional fundamentalist Baptist, whose television program, "The Old-Time Gospel Hour," "is a bastion of frontier fundamentalism moved uptown" (p. 28). In most of the commentary about Falwell in the media, this distinction holds true. In examinations of Falwell and the Moral Majority, for example, the mainstream press tends to depict Falwell as a member of a right-wing extremist group whose views on such topics as sex education and the Equal Rights Amendment remain far outside the American consensus. In fact, most of the coverage of Falwell is within this context. When the media does look at Falwell the preacher, he does appear to be far closer to the mainstream, especially since Falwell's Baptist fundamentalism is much more comfortable to most people than the Pentecostal enthusiasm of such contemporary figures as Pat Robertson and Oral Roberts.

The conflicting images of Jerry Falwell in the popular press arise, to a great extent, from the conflicting callings of the Reverend Jerry Falwell. On one hand, he is a mainstream Protestant preacher whose fundamental theology and careful use of the electronic media have enabled him to build one of the largest churches in the country. On the other hand, he is one of the most visible and articulate spokesmen for political and social position at odds with the beliefs of many Americans. In a curious way, in his particular configuration of church and state, Jerry Falwell is both in the mainstream and on the margin.

BIBLIOGRAPHY

Ajeminan, R. "Jerry Falwell Spreads the Word." *Time*, 2 September 1985, 58–59 + .

"Americans Disagree with Rev. Jerry Falwell's Views on South Africa." *Jet*, 30 September 1985, 37.

Capouya, J. "Jerry Falwell's Team." *Sport*, September 1986, 72–74 + .

Cheers, D. M. "Rev. Jesse Jackson Travels to Lynchburg to Take Issue with Rev. Jerry Falwell." *Jet*, 23 September 1985, 6–9.

"Circuit Rider to Controversy." *US News & World Report*, 2 September 1985, 11.

Clifford, G. "His Critics Speak Out and Jerry Falwell's Home Base Becomes a Flock Divided." *People Weekly*, 10 January 1983, 27–38.

"The Court Denies a 'Distress' Call." *Newsweek*, 7 March 1988, 8.

Cryderman, L. "Jerry Falwell Is Not Just Another Baptist Minister." *Christianity Today*, 18 March 1988, 36.

Doan, M. "Jerry Falwell Anti-Aids Dollar Drive." *US News & World Report*, 4 May 1987, 12–13.

Doerr, E. "Falwell's Farewell." *The Humanist*, January/February 1988, 40–41.

Emerson, S., and G. Witkin. "For Falwell: New Job, New Questions." *US News & World Report*, 6 April 1987, 60–61.

Falwell, Jerry. *Listen, America!* Garden City, N.Y.: Doubleday, 1980.

———. *Fasting*. Wheaton, Ill.: Tyndale, 1981.

———. *Finding Inner Peace and Strength*. Garden City, N.Y.: Doubleday, 1982.

———. *Twenty-five of the Greatest Sermons Ever Preached*. Grand Rapids, Mich.: Baker Books, 1984.

———. *When It Hurts Too Much to Cry*. Wheaton, Ill.: Tyndale, 1984.

————. *Wisdom for Living*. Wheaton, Ill.: Victor Books, 1984.

————. *Champions for God*. Wheaton, Ill.: Victor Books, 1985.

————. *If I Should Die Before I Wake*. Nashville: Thomas Nelson, 1986.

————. *My Favorite Verse*. Denver: Accent Books, 1987.

————. *Strength for the Journey: An Autobiography*. New York: Simon & Schuster, 1987.

Falwell, Jerry, Ed Dobson, and Edward Hinson, eds. *The Fundamentalist Phenomenon: The Resurgence of Conservative Christianity*. Garden City, N.Y.: Doubleday, 1981.

Falwell, Jerry, and Edward Hinson, eds. *The Liberty Bible Commentary*. Nashville: Thomas Nelson, 1983.

Falwell, Jerry, and Elmer Towns. *Church Aflame*. Nashville: Impact Books, 1971.

————. *Capturing a Town for Christ*. Old Tappan, N.J.: Fleming H. Revell, 1973.

————. *Stepping Out on Faith*. Wheaton, Ill.: Tyndale, 1984.

"Falwell Backs Away from Politics." *Christianity Today*, 17 October 1986, 46.

"Falwell Drops Out of Financial Accountability Organization." *Christianity Today*, 8 April 1983, 50.

"Falwell: Fighting Fundamentalist." *Time*, 6 April 1987, 62.

"Falwell: Lambasted About His Remarks About Tutu." *Jet*, 9 September 1985, 16.

"Falwell Puts Politics Behind Him—for the Most Part." *Christianity Today*, 11 December 1987, 53–54.

"Falwell Says Media Ministers Need More Accountability." *Christianity Today*, 10 July 1987, 42.

"Falwell Wants Southern Baptists to Sever Their Liberal Schools." *Christianity Today*, 18 March 1983, 26–27.

Fields, H. "Court Rebuffs Falwell, Affirms Right to Spoof Public Figure." *Publishers Weekly*, 11 March 1988, 18–19.

Greenfield, M. "Strange Bedfellows." *Newsweek*, 17 October 1983, 100.

Hadden, J. K. "Silence Does Not a Statement Make." *US News & World Report*, 13 April 1987, 8.

Hadden, Jeffrey K., et al. "Why Jerry Falwell Killed the Moral Majority." In *The Godpumpers*, 101–15. Bowling Green, Ohio: Popular Press, 1987.

Hadden, Jeffrey K., and Charles E. Swann. *Prime Time Preachers: The Rising Power of Televangelism*. Reading, Mass.: Addison-Wesley, 1981.

Hansell, Grace. *Prophecy and Politics: Militant Evangelists on the Road to Nuclear War*. Westport, Conn.: Hill, 1986.

"Heaven Can Wait." *Newsweek*, 8 June 1987, 58–62+.

"Jerry Falwell's New Legion." *US News & World Report*, 13 January 1986, 7.

"Jerry Falwell vs. Larry Flint." *Newsweek*, 14 December 1987, 76.

"The Jim Bakker Affair." *Christianity Today*, 17 April 1987, 36–37.

Lacayo R. "Taking the Peril Out of Parody." *Time*, 7 March 1988, 49.

Lee, R. "Falwell's College Strives to Become a Fundamentalist University Serving 50,000." *Christianity Today*, 25 November 1983, 40+.

Martz, L. "Gospelgate II: Target Falwell." *Newsweek*, 1 June 1987, 56–57+.

————. "TV Preachers on the Rocks." *Newsweek*, 11 July 1988, 26–28.

"A Moral Victory?" *Newsweek*, 17 October 1983, 30–31.

"The Moral Majority: Dial 800-REVENGE." *Newsweek*, 6 January 1986, 23.

Ostling, R. N. "Jerry Falwell's Crusade." *Time*, 2 September 1985, 48–52+.

———. "Of God and Greed." *Time*, 8 June 1987, 70–72 +.

———. "Falwell Throws in the Towel." *Time*, 19 October 1987, 74.

———. "A Jerry Built Coalition Regroups." *Time*, 16 November 1987, 68–69.

"Over the Line." *America*, 26 March 1988, 316–17.

"The Renquist Court Smiles on Satire." *US News & World Report*, 7 March 1988, 11–12.

"The Reverend vs. the Hustler." *Newsweek*, 17 December 1984, 101.

Shaffer, James, and Colleen Todd. *Christian Wives: Women Behind the Evangelists Reveal Their Faith in Modern Marriage*. Garden City, N.Y.: Doubleday, 1987, 27–48.

Spring, B. "Falwell Raises a Stir by Opposing Sanctions Against South Africa." *Christianity Today*, 4 October 1985, 52–54 +.

"Ted Kennedy a Hit in Falwell's Lynchburg." *Christianity Today*, 11 November 1983, 55.

Waas, M. "Falwell's New Name." *The New Republic*, 31 March 1986, 16–17.

Wilentz, S. "God and Man at Lynchburg." *The New Republic*, 25 April 1988, 30–34 +.

Witkin, G. "Stones Fly in the TV Temple." *US News & World Report*, 8 June 1987, 10–11.

14 • CHARLES GRANDISON FINNEY (1792–1875)

The Memoirs of Charles Grandison Finney

BIOGRAPHY

Charles Grandison Finney, one of the most important revivalists in American history, was born on August 29, 1792, in Warren, Connecticut. He was the seventh child of the family. His father was a Revolutionary War veteran whose ancestors were among the first settlers in Plymouth Plantation. In 1792, the family moved to Oneida County, New York. There Finney attended common schools and the Hamilton Oneida Academy. From 1808 to 1816, Finney taught school in western New York and New Jersey, taking some time out in 1812 to 1814 to study in preparation of entering Yale College.

In 1816, Finney decided not to attend Yale and returned to Henderson, New York. In 1818, he began studying law under Benjamin Wright, of Adams, New York, and he was admitted to the New York State Bar in 1820 and began to practice law. In 1821, Finney experienced a dramatic conversion. He immediately gave up his law practice and began to study for the ministry with the Reverend George Washington Gale, pastor of the Presbyterian church in Adams. In 1824, he was ordained as an evangelist by the Oneida Presbytery.

Beginning in 1824, Finney began conducting revival meetings in small towns throughout western New York. Finney met with immediate success, and in 1826 and 1827, he moved his operations to the larger towns of Utica and Troy. By this time, Finney's success had attracted attention, and in 1827, he was attacked by Asahel Nettleton for using nontraditional methods during his revivals. For the rest of the decade, Finney continued to conduct revivals throughout the Northeast, including meetings in Wilmington, Philadelphia, and New York. In 1830–1831, Finney held a series of spectacular revivals in Rochester, New York. His success there made him the most famous evangelist of his day.

From 1832 to 1837, Finney worked in New York City, first as pastor of the Chatham Street Chapel and then as pastor of the Broadway Tabernacle. In both positions, Finney aligned himself with the Protestant reform movement that advocated temperance, women's rights, and the abolition of slavery. In 1837, he gave up his position in New York to become pastor of the Oberlin, Ohio, Congregational Church and take up his position as professor of theology at Oberlin College. At Oberlin, Finney trained young ministers, taught revival and reform, and from 1851 to 1866, served as president of Oberlin College.

In 1857, Finney conducted a series of popular revivals in New England, and in 1859–1860, he conducted a revival tour of England and Scotland. Finney died in Oberlin on August 16, 1875.

THE AUTOBIOGRAPHY

Charles Grandison Finney was the most popular, and perhaps the most successful, evangelist of nineteenth-century America. His early success as a frontier revivalist in western New York made him a celebrity, and his work in New York City demonstrated his organizational skills and ability to work with a wide range of people. At Oberlin College, Finney directed the careers of a generation of ministers. He finished his memoirs in 1868, and they were published after his death. In the *Memoirs*, Finney presents the life of a man who believed that the world could be changed through revival and spent his life attempting to change the world. During the height of Finney's career, there were mass migrations to the West; reform agitation for abolition, women's rights, and temperance; and the beginning of the immigrant influx into American cities. Finney was involved with all of this. He remains best known, however, for his evangelism.

Charles Finney begins his autobiography with a specific reference to the cause of his celebrity:

It has pleased God in some measure to connect my name and labors with an extensive movement of the Church of Christ, regarded by some as a new era in its progress. Especially this has been supposed to be true in respect to revivals of religion. (p. 1)

He continues to observe that this "extensive movement" involved some modified views of Christian doctrines and some changes in the means of evangelization. As a result, he received considerable criticism. Finney chose to write his memoirs in defense of his work, and to give such an account of the doctrines which were preached, and of the measures which were used ... as to enable the church hereafter, partially at least, to estimate the power and purity of those great works of God. Purer and more powerful revivals I never saw than those that have been most spoken against. (p. 3)

Finney's revival work had been attacked as early as 1826, when reports of enthusiastic behavior on the part of young converts and public prayers led by women were circulated by opponents. In essence, the controversy between Finney and such opponents as Lyman Beecher and Asahel Nettleton was one of degree. Both sides emerged from the Calvinist tradition and worked within the Presbyterian-Congregational institutional framework. Finney, living on the frontier, was more willing than either Nettleton or Beecher to experiment with methods of evangelization such as introducing the sinners' pew—a special pew reserved for those who wished to be saved—and allowing women to have a more active role in the ministry and church services. He also believed that the key to all revivals was the "annointing of the Holy Spirit" (p. 57). As a result, he was less tied to old-line Presbyterian doctrines of total depravity and limited atonement than his opponents; he also was more successful.

In writing his defense of his evangelism, Finney begins with a narrative of his own upbringing and conversion. He writes that his family moved to the "wilderness" of central New York when he was two. The family found few religious privileges; there were no sabbath schools, and few religious books were available. Finney recalls that his parents were not professors of religion and that few neighbors were religious. The only time he heard the gospel preached was from an occasional traveling minister who happened to pass through the community. This situation continued until Finney moved to Adams, New York, to study law with Benjamin Wright. At Adams, Finney met George Washington Gale, a Presbyterian minister with whom Finney began to study religion and read the Bible.

In 1821, Finney decided that the would make up his mind about salvation and make peace with God. He writes that he shut himself in his room and began praying earnestly and reading the Bible. After two days of this, he began to feel nervous and a strange feeling came over him, as if he were going to die. The next morning, on his way to his law office, he heard an inward voice say: "What are you waiting for? Did you not promise to give your heart to God? And what are you trying to do? Are you endeavoring to work out a righteousness of your own?" (p. 18). Finney recalls that at that moment, the question of salvation seemed clear to him and that he understood "the reality and the fullness of the atonement of Christ" (p. 18). He knew that there was nothing he had to do but accept Christ and salvation was his. He then realized that he had been standing in the middle of a street for an unknown period of time. He immediately accepted Christ and walked to the woods north of town and began to pray.

Finney spent the rest of the day in what he recalls as a "profoundly tranquil state," thinking about the condition of his soul. In the evening, he received a "mighty baptism of the Holy Ghost." Finney records the experience carefully because it was one of the most significant moments in his life and determined the nature of his revivals.

Without expecting it, without ever having the thought in my mind that there was any such thing for me, without any recollection that I had ever heard the thing mentioned by any person in the world, at a moment entirely unexpected by me, the Holy Ghost descended upon me in a manner that seemed to go through me body and soul. I could feel the impression, like a wave of electricity, going through and through me. (p. 23)

Finney's account of his dramatic conversion conforms to the pattern established by Calvinist theologians, and is in fact similar to that of Jonathan Edwards. Finney first becomes aware of the gospel and his need for salvation. This period of preparation and prayer is followed by a recognition of his own sinfulness and the power of Christ. Only then comes an emotional release and an assurance of salvation. Finney, like Edwards before him, describes the conversion as both a process and a dramatic event, and both men, unlike other theologians, emphasize the emotional rather than the intellectual elements of the experience. Both ministers who had exceptional success preaching the revival of religion, Edwards and Finney were aware that conversion must be felt. The intensity of the emotional experience transformed Finney and provided him with a standard with which to measure his own work. Finney immediately gave up the law and began to study for the ministry with George Washington Gale, and because of the nature of his own conversion, he always stressed the primacy of the Holy Ghost in his work and writing.

In the chapters that follow, Finney describes his preparation for the ministry and early missionary work. Early in his studies, Finney disagreed with Gale over the doctrine of atonement. Gale and traditional Calvinists believed in limited atonement, or the salvation of only a small number of people, or the elect. Finney, on the other hand, believed in a more universal atonement. Finney was not alone in this belief, and one of the major developments in American Protestantism during the late eighteenth and early nineteenth centuries was the rejection of the idea of limited atonement by increasing numbers of believers. In describing his disagreement with Gale, Finney uses such significant phrases as "I was but a child in theology" and "unused as I was to theological discussions" to emphasize his differences with his Princeton-trained mentor. He also comments that Gale, for all his education, had failed to receive the annointing of the Holy Ghost. This was, for Finney, a crucial failure because for Finney, the power of the Holy Ghost was much more important than theological correctness.

In describing his early missionary work, Finney addresses those who accused him of heresy and emotional enthusiasm. He writes that he always taught the basic doctrines of the gospel: moral depravity, the necessity of a radical change of heart, the divinity of Christ, justification by faith, and the power of the Holy Ghost. He also notes that one reason for his success was his experience as a lawyer. Finney saw preaching in the same light that he saw the practice of law; both were rhetorical acts with the purpose of convincing audiences. He writes that many of the preachers he heard during his study lost their listeners with dry theological discourses. He always spoke in a plain style and used repetition and careful choice of topics addressed to specific audiences in his revivals. He also mentions that he often was inspired by the Holy Ghost. Whether from divine inspiration or effective rhetoric, Finney was immediately effective. His revivals throughout western New York produced large numbers of converts; his revivals throughout the new settlements brought in Methodists, Baptists, Congregationalists, and Presbyterians. In fact, Finney was one of the first evangelists to actively encourage cross-denominational revivals. A typical meeting often would produce fits and shakes in his listeners, as well as a "wonderful conviction of sin and an alarm for souls."

Throughout his narrative, Finney argues that his real enemy was not traditional or old-school Presbyterianism, but rather deism and universalism. Finney saw both as attacks of rationalism on Christian religion, and fought them throughout his career. Universalism and Unitarianism, offshoots of deism, tended to emphasize the intellect and discount the emotional and mysterious in Christianity. For Finney, who based his entire program of evangelization on his own emotional experience of the Holy Ghost, such a platform was to dismiss religion. Like Jonathan Edwards, Finney believed that the intellect was not the seat of religious emotions. He writes, for example, that schools were spoiling the ministry by producing educated, but spiritually dead, churchmen.

As he describes his revival work, Finney both defends his theology, several times listing the basic doctrines he taught, and outlines the effects of his preaching. In describing his successful revival at Antwerp, New York, for example, Finney recalls that all the members of the congregation fell out of their seats onto the floor of the church and cried out for mercy. Finney remarks that one of the first serious attacks on his revivals came after his successful meetings at Utica and Rome, New York. Reports had reached the East that women spoke at Finney's meetings, and Nettleton wrote to New England ministers of this objectionable conduct. In his autobiography, Finney responds that this was true, that in some social prayer meetings held in the houses of church members, women, when moved by the spirit, would lead groups in prayer. Finney, who based his program on the movings of the spirit, had no objection. The New England ministers, who based their program on Paul's admonitions against women speaking in church, did.

Perhaps Finney's most famous revival occurred in Rochester, New York, in 1830. In his autobiography, Finney provides an overview of it as a response to the criticism that he was only successful with the ignorant men and women who lived in isolated small towns on the frontier. Finney records that his Rochester revival produced the same marked conversions among the prominent men and women of the city as his earlier revivals had produced in the small towns. He notes, for example, that "the lawyers, physicians, merchants, and indeed all the most intelligent class of society, became more and more interested, and more and more easily influenced to give their hearts to God" (p. 307). Finney concludes his account of the Rochester revival by noting that its success was so wide throughout the city among all classes of people that there was no local opposition whatsoever.

In the final chapters of his autobiography, Finney chronicles his work after the dramatic events at Rochester. Finney moved his ministry to New York City, where he led popular revivals at the Chatham Street Chapel and later at the Broadway Tabernacle, which he designed himself as a theater for revival meetings. Again, Finney was successful, as he was later as professor of theology and president of Oberlin College, which was established as a seminary to train ministers for the growing Western population. In these chapters, Finney continues to present evidence in defense of his work, noting that in New York City, at Oberlin, and later in his life during a visit to England, whenever he held revivals, he was successful at producing significant conversions. These revivals were far less dramatic than his earlier ones, and as a result, the final sections of the autobiography are more the record of the good works of Charles Grandison Finney than the dramatic defense of the first sections.

CRITICISM

Charles Grandison Finney was one of the most significant evangelists in American history, and a large body of scholarship is available about the man and his work. He was a figure of controversy throughout his career, and as a result, critics and supporters wrote about Finney and his revival as early as the 1830s. Two significant early works are Calvin Colton's *History and Character of American Revivals* and William Sprague's *Lectures on Revivals of Religion*. This early interest has continued, and such works as Alice Felt Tyler's *Freedom's Ferment: Phases of American Social History to 1860* (New York: Harper & Brothers, 1944) and Timothy L. Smith's *Revivalism and Social Reform: American Protestantism on the Eve of the Civil War* (Baltimore: Johns Hopkins University Press, 1980) place the revival movement within the context of American social history.

The best edition of Finney's autobiography is *The Memoirs of Rev. Charles G. Finney: The Complete Restored Text*. Editors Garth M. Rosell and Richard A.G. Dupuis have reconstructed the text from various manuscript and early sources. In addition, they have included an insightful introduction and elaborate notes and bibliography.

Another important edition is Finney's *Lectures on Revival of Religion*, edited by William G. McLoughlin. Finney's lectures can be read as a commentary on his autobiography, as they also define and defend his doctrines and method. In addition, in his introduction, McLoughlin provides an excellent overview of the Second Great Awakening and Finney's place in it.

Charles Grandison Finney remains a significant figure in American history for a number of reasons. First, his impact on American culture during the first half of the nineteenth century was immense. The Finney-led revival movement in New York State helped to energize the Protestant community at a time when some ministers were insisting on historical rigidity and others abandoning Presbyterianism and Congregationalism for Unitarianism. Second, Finney was able to link the religious emotionalism of early pentecostalism with the reform movement, establishing a powerful moral force that helped to influence the temperance, abolitionist, and women's movements. Finally, Finney became a figure of national reputation around whom the members of the evangelical community not tied to a specific denomination could rally. His *Memoirs* also remain important. In his narrative of his own life and works, Finney not only chronicles the history of the revivals of the 1820s and 1830s, but also provides one of the most dramatic accounts of a personal conversion available to the modern reader.

BIBLIOGRAPHY

Beardsley, Frank G. *A History of American Revivals*. New York: American Tract Society, 1912.

———. *A Mighty Winner of Souls: Charles Grandison Finney*. New York: American Tract Society, 1927.

Belt, R. A. *Charles Finney, a Great Revivalist*. Des Moines: Boone, 1944.

Carwardine, Richard. *Transatlantic Revivalism: Popular Evangelicalism in Britain and America, 1790–1865*. New York: Greenwood, 1978.

Cheesebro, Roy Allen. "The Preaching of Charles G. Finney." Dissertation, Yale, 1948.

Cole, Charles C. *The Social Ideas of the Northern Evangelists, 1826–1860*. New York: Columbia University Press, 1954.

Colton, Calvin. *History and Character of American Revivals*. London, 1832.

Cross, Whitney R. *The Burned-Over District: The Social and Intellectual History of Enthusiastic Religion in Western New York, 1800–1850*. Ithaca, N.Y.: Cornell University Press, 1950.

Day, Richard Ellsworth. *Man of Like Passions. A Dramatic Biography of Charles Grandison Finney*. Grand Rapids, Mich.: Zondervan, 1942.

Drummond, Lewis A. *Charles Grandison Finney and the Birth of Modern Evangelism*. London: Hodder & Stoughton, 1983.

Edman, V. Raymond. *Finney Lives On*. Minneapolis: Bethany, 1971.

Finney, Charles Grandison. *Sermons on Various Subjects*. New York: Taylor, 1834.

————. *Lectures on Revivals of Religion.* 1835. Reprint. Edited by William G. McLoughlin. Cambridge, Mass.: Harvard University Press, Belknap Press, 1960.

————. *Sermons on Important Subjects.* New York: Taylor, 1836.

————. *Lectures to Professing Christians.* London: Molner, 1837.

————. *Skeletons on a Course of Theological Lectures.* Oberlin, Ohio: Steele, 1840.

————. *Views of Sanctification.* Oberlin, Ohio: Steele, 1840.

————. *Letters on Revivals.* New York: Wright, 1845.

————. *Lectures on Systematic Theology.* Oberlin, Ohio: Fitch, 1846–1847.

————. *The Reviewer Reviewed: Or Finney's Theology and the Princeton Review.* Oberlin, Ohio: Fitch, 1847.

————. *Guide to the Savior: or Conditions Attaining to and Abiding in Entire Holiness of Heart and Life.* Oberlin, Ohio: Fitch, 1848.

————. *The Character, Claims, and Practical Workings of Freemasonry.* Cincinnati: Western Tract & Book Society, 1869.

————. *The Memoirs of Rev. Charles G. Finney.* 1876. Reprint. Edited by Garth M. Rosell and Richard A.G. Dupuis. Grand Rapids, Mich.: Academie, 1989.

————. *Sermons on Gospel Themes.* Oberlin, Ohio: Goodrich, 1876.

Fletcher, Robert S. *A History of Oberlin College from Its Foundation through the Civil War.* 2 vols. Oberlin, Ohio: Oberlin University Press, 1943.

Harding, William H. *Finney's Life and Lectures.* London: Oliphant, 1943.

Hendricks, Tyler O. "Charles Finney and the Utica Revival of 1826: The Social Effect of a New Religious Paradigm." Dissertation, Vanderbilt University, 1983.

Johnson, James E. "The Life of Charles Grandison Finney." Dissertation, Syracuse University, 1959.

Marty, Martin E. *Righteous Empire: The Protestant Experience in America.* New York: Dial, 1970.

McClelland, William L. "Church and Ministry in the Life and Thought of Charles Grandison Finney." Dissertation, Princeton Theological Seminary, 1967.

McLoughlin, William G. *Modern Revivalism: Charles Grandison Finney to Billy Graham.* New York: Ronald, 1959.

————. *Revivals, Awakenings, and Reform.* Chicago: University of Chicago Press, 1978.

Miller, Basil W. *Charles Grandison Finney: He Prayed Down Revivals.* Grand Rapids, Mich.: Zondervan, 1942.

Opie, John. "Conversion and Revivalism: An Internal History from Jonathan Edwards through Charles Grandison Finney." Dissertation, University of Chicago, 1964.

Sprague, William B. *Lectures on Revivals of Religion.* Albany, 1832.

Sweet, William Warren. *Religion on the American Frontier, 1783–1850. The Presbyterians.* Chicago: University of Chicago Press, 1936.

————. *Religion on the American Frontier, 1783–1850: The Congregationalists.* Chicago: University of Chicago Press, 1939.

Tuveson, Ernest Lee. *Redeemer Nation: The Idea of America's Millennial Role.* Chicago: University of Chicago Press, 1968.

Walzer, William C. "Charles Grandison Finney and the Presbyterian Revivals of

Northern and Western New York." Dissertation, University of Chicago, 1944.

Weddle, David L. *The Law as Gospel. Revival and Reform in the Theology of Charles G. Finney.* Metuchen, N.J.: Scarecrow, 1985.

Weisberger, Bernard A. *They Gathered at the River: The Story of the Great Revivalists and Their Impact Upon Religion in America.* Boston: Little, Brown, 1958.

Wright, George Frederick. *Charles Grandison Finney.* Boston: Houghton Mifflin, 1891.

15 • ALEXANDER IRVINE (1863–1941)

From the Bottom Up

BIOGRAPHY

Alexander F. Irvine was born in Antrim, Ireland, on January 19, 1863. Irvine's family was poor; Irvine worked as a groom in Ireland and then followed his older brother to Scotland, where he worked twelve-hour days in a coal pit for $1.50 a week. In 1883, he joined the British army and was sent to Egypt, receiving The Queen's Medal and the Khedive's Bronze Star for his service. In 1888, he emigrated to the United States.

Irvine was ordained as a Congregational minister in 1894, and he served as a pastor in Omaha, Nebraska; Avoca, Iowa; Cleveland, Ohio; and New Haven, Connecticut. While in New Haven, Irvine studied theology at Yale University and continued his ministry for the poor and working classes as religious work director at the YMCA. His advocacy of the poor led him to establish the People's Church of New Haven and to become a member of the Socialist party of Connecticut.

After leaving New Haven, Irvine was commissioned by *Appleton's Magazine* to write a series of articles on labor conditions in the South; he traveled to Bessemer, Alabama, where he worked in the iron mines of the Tennessee Coal and Iron Company while gathering information for his articles.

In 1907, while living and writing in New York City, Irvine met the Reverend Percy Stickney Grant, rector of the Episcopal Church of the Ascension and supporter of the labor movement. Grant invited Irvine, who was making a comfortable living writing and working for the Socialist party in New York, to become a lay reader in the church. From 1907 until 1910,

Irvine used his position to bring together church members and working-class socialists. His autobiography, *From the Bottom Up*, was quite popular. During World War I, Irvine served as a "morale raiser" with the British troops in France. His description of those events appeared in his book *A Fighting Parson*. Irvine died on March 15, 1941.

THE AUTOBIOGRAPHY

From the Bottom Up: The Life Story of Alexander Irvine is an interesting religious autobiography. Not only does it provide information about the religious experiences of a man who was part of the development of the social gospel in the United States, but it also provides a context for an understanding of the social gospel movement. For Irvine, socialism and Christianity were not only not incompatible, but also two sides of the same coin. Irvine writes that he first discovered a church, then a theology, and finally a belief in mankind. He organizes his autobiography in a similar manner. Although the idea of conversion is essential to Irvine, he views convention as an ongoing process, each conversion leading to new insights and developments. The dramatic before-and-after structure of many conversion narratives is not to be found in *From the Bottom Up*; rather, Irvine uses the metaphor of a pilgrimage to structure his autobiography. He also borrows from the Franklinesque narrative of success, a form highly popular during the first decades of the twentieth century. Irvine not only writes of his developing social and religious consciousness, but he also describes the story of a poor immigrant lad from Ireland who rose to a position of some consequence in his adopted land.

Irvine begins his autobiography with a description of his life in Antrim, Ireland, the starting point of his pilgrimage. Like many other ethnic and immigrant writers, Irvine emphasizes both the poverty and the ignorance of the old country. His recollections include a description of an intense religious experience, one that changed his perception of himself and his world. Irvine describes working as a scarecrow in a potato field. After the day's work, he writes:

As I sat on the fence and watched the sun set over the trees, an emotion swept over me, and the tears began to flow. My body seemed to change as by the pouring into it of some strange life-giving fluid. I wanted to shout, to scream aloud; but instead, I went rapidly over the hill into the woods, dropped on my knees, and began to pray. (p. 11)

This experience, similar in setting and intensity to Jonathan Edwards' famous conversion experience, was more than an emotional overflow. Irvine writes that his perception of who he was changed. For the first time, he writes, he realized that he was dirty, that he was hungry, that he had no shoes, and that he could not read. He describes setting out to transform himself. Working as a groom in a local stable allowed him to earn enough money for himself but not enough to help support his family. Looking for better-paying work, he left Ireland for Scotland, where he found worse conditions and pay working in a coal mine. He soon left the mine, and facing starvation, he joined the British army.

Stationed as a marine aboard the *Alexandra*, the flagship of the Mediterranean squadron, Irvine had access to both a school and a library. He also suffered discrimination. English sailors made fun of his heavy Irish accent, his inability to read, and his refusal, on religious grounds, to take his share of grog. In defense, Irvine seriously studied boxing and reading, acquiring skill in both. After defeating one of his tormentors, Irvine began devoting his free time to evangelization, telling the story of his conversion.

After finishing his military service, Irvine emigrated to the United States in 1888. His depiction of his arrival in New York is similar to those left by other immigrant writers. Irvine found poverty, unemployment, discrimination, and, eventually, a calling. About a year after his arrival, Irvine began working for the YMCA. He recalls:

[I] spent my afternoons in the lodging houses, pocket Bible in hand, going from man to man as they sat there, workless, homeless, dejected and in despair. I very soon found that there was one gospel they were looking for and willing to accept— it was the gospel of work; so in order to meet the emergency, I became an employment agency. I became more than that. They needed clothing and food—and I became a junk store and soup kitchen. (p. 92)

In 1894, Irvine was ordained a Congregational minister, and he planned his work to combine individual and social salvation. He writes that he found no fellowship of the saints in New York except as "the poor saints have it by themselves" (p. 157). Irvine writes that he discovered the "new theology," which abandoned such tenants of Calvinism as universal depravity and limited atonement in favor of universal salvation and the efficacy of works. Irvine writes of a new awakening, of being born again and saying to himself, "Soul, if this multitude is doomed to hell, be brave; gird up your loins and go with them" (p. 157). Following that commitment, Irvine continued to serve the immigrant community of New York for a time before becoming a missionary in the West, where, he recalls, he saw a vision of political independence that changed his life.

As a missionary minister in Nebraska and Iowa, Irvine studied the social conditions of the communities as he lived and worked with the poor. He was attracted to the independence of the workers he discovered, and when he was in charge of The Friendly Inn, a charitable Christian institution in Cleveland, he first joined a labor union. By this time in his life, Irvine was committed to social action, political change, and religious life; by 1898, when he was appointed religious works director of the New Haven YMCA and pastor of the Second Congregational Church, Irvine was prepared to engage in radical Christian social action.

In New Haven, Irvine discovered that his commitment to both the established church and social reform caused a good deal of confusion. Some of his parishioners believed that his support of the labor movement made him unfit to lead his congregation, and a number of union members questioned whether a man whose salary was paid by the wealthy members of his congregation could be trusted. Nevertheless, Irvine continued to try to bridge the gap between his two interests. After joining one labor union, becoming the chaplain of a second, and supporting several strikes in New Haven, Irvine was forced to leave the Second Congregational Church and establish the People's Church of New Haven, a "self-governing community for the worship of God and the service of man" (p. 223).

By 1907, Irvine believed that his usefulness in New Haven was at an end; there was division in the People's Church over Irvine's movement from labor supporter to socialist, and Irvine also wanted to devote more of his time to writing. He was offered a YMCA position in New York City that allowed him to help support workers in Manhattan, and he soon combined that work with the position of lay reader at the Episcopal Church of the Ascension, where he found institutional support for his work with the unemployed.

Throughout his autobiography, Irvine acknowledges that most people saw his dedication to labor and religion as a contradiction. He writes, for example, that in New Haven, members of his People's Church often were considered anarchists, not Christians. In the final chapter of his autobiography, "My Socialism, My Religion, My Home," Irvine attempts to resolve the contradiction. He writes: "My vision spiritual came to me out of the unknown. The facts and experiences of life led me to Socialism. In each case it was a rebirth" (p. 285). Irvine calls both "The Way of Jesus" and socialism states of mind and points of view. Both, he asserts, are expanding perspectives that force the individual out of himself and finally, in a dialectical pattern that he sees as a continuing series of rebirths, come together without difference. He summarizes these ideas near the end of his narrative when he writes that the study of the life of Christ led him to a rediscovery of himself that taught him that "the secret of Jesus is to find God in the soul of humanity. The cause of Jesus is the righting of the world's wrongs; the religion of Jesus the binding together in the souls of the solidarity of the race" (p. 294).

CRITICISM

There is little criticism about Alexander Irvine. After he published his autobiography, which was relatively popular, he devoted himself to writing.

And when he is noted, in the 1932 edition of *Who's Who in America,* for example, it is as the author of such works as *A Yankee with the Soldiers of the King* and *A Fighting Parson,* rather than as one of the leading figures in the development of the social gospel. Nevertheless, Irvine's autobiography is a significant work. First, Irvine's adaptation of the narrative of success from a story of the rise to wealth made popular by the work of such writers as Benjamin Franklin and Andrew Carnegie to a story of continuing religious and social maturity demonstrates the adaptability of the form of the personal narrative. Second, Irvine's concept of conversion as an ongoing process rather than as a onetime event shows a considerable psychological and theological sophistication. Finally, Irvine's ability to wed Christian belief and social action is an illustration of the development of the social gospel, one of the main developments of twentieth-century Christianity.

BIBLIOGRAPHY

"Alexander Irvine Biography." *Who's Who in America: A Biographical Dictionary of Notable Living Men and Women in the United States,* vol. 17 (1932–1933). Edited by Albert Nelson Marquis. Chicago: Marquis, 1932.

Irvine, Alexander. *The Master and the Chisel.* New Haven, Conn.: The People's Church, 1904.

———. *Jack London at Yale.* Westwood, Mass.: Ariel, 1906.

———. *From the Bottom Up: The Life Story of Alexander Irvine.* New York: Doubleday, 1910.

———. *The Magyar: A Story of the Social Revolution.* Girard, Kans.: Socialist, 1911.

———. *Revolution in Los Angeles.* Los Angeles, 1912.

———. *My Lady of the Chimney Corner.* New York: Century, 1913.

———. *God and Tommy Atkins.* 4th ed. London: Hutchinson, 1918.

———. *The Carpenter and Some Educated Gentlemen.* London: Evans, 1921.

———. *The Souls of Poor Folk.* London: Collins, 1921.

———. *The Carpenter and His Kingdom.* New York: Charles Scribner's Sons, 1922.

———. *A Yankee with the Soldiers of the King.* New York: Dutton, 1923.

———. *The Life of Christ.* London: Collins, 1924.

———. *A Fighting Parson. The Autobiography of Alexander Irvine.* Boston: Little, Brown, 1930.

———. *My Cathedral: A Vision of Friendship.* Belfast: Quota, 1945.

———. *Anna's Wishing Chair, and Three other Chimney Corner Stories: The Tinker of Tubercurry, Ordeal by Prayer, and a Causerie in Shadowland.* Belfast: Quota, 1947.

Jenison, M. C. "Church and Social Unrest: Church of the Ascension." *Outlook,* 16 May 1908, 112–14.

Miller, Wayne Charles, et al. *A Comprehensive Bibliography for the Study of American Minorities.* New York: New York University Press, 1976.

"Obituary." *Current Biography: Who's News and Why, 1941.* Edited by Maxine Block. New York: Wilson, 1941, 432.

"Obituary." *Publishers Weekly,* 7 June 1941, 2304.

16 • REBECCA COX JACKSON (1795–1871)

Gifts of Power: The Writings of Rebecca Jackson, Black Visionary, Shaker Eldress

BIOGRAPHY

Rebecca Cox was born a free black woman near Philadelphia in 1795. She lived with her older brother, Joseph Cox, who was a member of the Bethel African Methodist Episcopal (A.M.E.) Church in Philadelphia, before and during her marriage to Samuel Jackson. In 1830, Rebecca Cox Jackson underwent an intense religious conversion during a thunderstorm. She began to have visions, hear voices, and take an active part in the Holiness movement of the A.M.E. Church. She also became convinced that sex was a result of the fall of Adam and made a vow of celibacy.

After persuading her husband of the seriousness of her conversion and vow, Jackson continued to receive visions as well as such spiritual gifts as the gift of healing, the gift of prophecy, and the gift of literacy. During the 1830s and early 1840s, she traveled throughout Pennsylvania, New York, Connecticut, and Massachusetts as an itinerant Holiness Methodist minister. This led to a confrontation with her brother, who was suspicious of the Holiness movement and supported the more orthodox elements within the A.M.E. Church.

1n 1842, Jackson visited the Shaker community in Watervliet, New York. She was immediately attracted to the Shaker form of worship, the commitment to celibacy, and the belief in the female presence in God. After resolving some doubts about the need for public confession and reconciling Shaker beliefs with the directions of her own inner voice, Jackson joined the community.

In 1851, feeling called to evangelize, Jackson left Watervliet to establish a Shaker community in Philadelphia. At first not recognized by the community at Watervliet, the group established by Jackson and her companion, Rebecca Perot, became interested in spiritualism and incorporated knockings, moanings, and visions into their form of Shaker worship. The black Shaker sisterhood in Philadelphia eventually was reconciled with the home community at Watervliet. Jackson died in 1871.

THE AUTOBIOGRAPHY

Rebecca Cox Jackson left a large body of autobiographical writing that was not published until 1981. At her death in 1871, Jackson had written an incomplete autobiographical account and other personal writing. These were collected and edited into a draft narrative by Alonzo G. Hollister. In addition, two manuscripts in Jackson's own handwriting survive: one in the Berkshire Athenaeum in Pittsfield, Massachusetts, and the other in the Western Reserve Shaker Collection in Cleveland. Working from these sources, Jean McMahon Humez assembled Jackson's personal writings under the title *Gifts of Power: The Writings of Rebecca Jackson, Black Visionary, Shaker Eldress.* Humez' edition is outstanding. It contains an excellent introduction to Jackson's life and overview of Shaker belief and practice as well as useful secondary documents and bibliography.

Humez divides the autobiography into six major sections, each chronicling a period of development in Jackson's spiritual life. The first is called "Awakening and Early 'Gifts,' " and records Jackson's intense conversion.

Jackson begins her narrative by describing awakening to a dawn thunderstorm and, while feeling afraid, hearing a voice say, "This day thy soul is required of thee" (p. 71). Believing that she was going to die, she fell to her knees and began to pray for forgiveness of her sins. She recalls:

The fearful foreboding of my sudden destruction caused me to cry out in the bitterness of my soul, "Lord, I never will rise from my knees till thou for Christ's sake has mercy on my poor sinking soul or sends me to Hell." For I felt as though my soul had come into the chamber of death. (p. 72).

She immediately felt despair depart, and the love of God filled her with peace, joy, and consolation. She told her brother of her experience and then felt a strong desire to tell the world of the love and power of God.

Although not included in the text, there obviously was a period of preparation before such an intense emotional experience. As Humez notes in her introduction, Jackson was a member of the Bethel A.M.E. community and a member of her religious brother's household. For Jackson, the preparation was far less important than the conversion and results, for in the first section of her narrative, she records not only the dramatic conversion, but also the equally dramatic fruits of the conversion.

Soon after the conversion, Jackson felt compelled to pray for her neighbors, who were both "wicked" and sick. As a result of her prayers, they recovered from their illnesses and their evil ways. She began to lead prayer meetings during which "the house was filled and the floor covered with the slain in the Lord" (p. 75). Finally, in accordance with Methodist practice, she received sanctification, or a public experience of the Lord's power similar to her private conversion.

Jackson recalls that her husband did not believe in her conversion and was opposed to celibacy, but after she laid her hands on a hot stove and removed them without injury, he was compelled to believe that her behavior was more than merely natural. In the remainder of the first section of her narrative, Jackson records her early visions, gifts, and works. Her ecstatic visions, often full of such domestic images as baking cakes and making quilts, provided her with guidance as she interpreted them as messages from God. She writes that her gift for healing was soon followed by a more dramatic one, the gift of literacy. Before her conversion, she could not read, but about a year after her conversion, she picked up the Bible and discovered that she could read. Convinced that she was called by the Lord to evangelize, Jackson put off her normal clothing and adopted the simple dress worn by Quakers and Shakers and began to travel with a Holiness praying band.

In the second part of the narrative, which Humez calls "Breaking Away from Family and Churches," Jackson records her experiences from 1833 to 1836, during which time she first discovered the Shakers and began to grow dissatisfied with her husband, brother, and orthodox Christianity.

Jackson begins this section with a continuation of her record of visions and gifts. Among the most memorable visions recorded are those of her own death, a beatific vision of God and Christ, and a prophetic vision of "God's true people on earth," whom she later identified as the Shakers. Among the most memorable practices of her gifts is the healing of a blind old woman. The major theme of this section of the narrative is her introduction to and growing fondness for the Shakers, about whom she had been given a book by a friend.

The Shakers, one of the millennial groups to establish themselves in the late eighteenth and early nineteenth centuries, were founded by Ann Lee, whom her followers believed was the physical representation of the second coming of Christ. Shaker doctrine held that since Lee's death, the millennium had already begun, sex was sinful, celibacy was necessary for spiritual perfection, and there were female as well as male aspects of God, God the father and Christ being paralleled by Holy Mother Wisdom and Ann Lee. In practice, Shakers opposed slavery, called for complete equality between men and women, incorporated visions and rhythmic movement—shakings—into their services, and held property in common. It was natural that

Jackson, who already was convinced of the necessity of celibacy and stressed direct inspiration over scriptural authority, would be attracted to the Shakers. In her autobiography, she records her first meeting with a Shaker community, her attraction but uneasiness about subjecting her own visions and voices to the direction of others, and her growing dissatisfaction with her brother, husband, and the authorities of the A.M.E. Church. She records, in particular, that she was accused of preaching false doctrine and of coming between "a great many men and their wives" (p. 149). This was not an unusual response by married men to a woman preaching celibacy and women's equality before the Lord. Because of her pentecostal emphasis and belief in celibacy, Jackson was criticized, and many of the male trustees and ministers refused to let her speak in churches. Jackson's persecution can be seen as part of the larger movement to reorganize the A.M.E. Church, which, during the 1830s, 1840s, and 1850s, moved away from its primitive and pentecostal roots and adopted a more formal structure and doctrine. Faced with this primarily male opposition, Jackson received a dramatic vision at a meeting she was conducting at a private home.

I saw that night, for the first time, a Mother in the Deity. This indeed was a new scene, a new doctrine to me. But I knowed when I got it, and I was obedient to the heavenly vision—as I see all that I hold forth, that is, with my spirit eye. And was I not glad when I found that I had a Mother! And that night She gave me a tongue to tell it! The spirit of weeping was upon me, and it fell on all the assembly. And though they never heard it before, I was made able by Her Holy Spirit of Wisdom to make it so plain that a child could understand it. (p. 154)

Shortly after preaching this doctrine, Jackson left the A.M.E. Church.

The next section of the narrative is called "Finding 'God's True People on Earth' " and records Jackson's growing interest in the Shakers. Following her visions and voices, Jackson continued to travel as an itinerant preacher, no longer formally associated with the A.M.E. Church. She became convinced that she should visit a Shaker community and soon became convinced of the correctness of their way of life. She writes that she had difficulty with one aspect of Shaker doctrine, public confession. She records that she was asked to make an open confession to Eldress Paulina before she could testify to the group of Shaker women she was meeting with. This troubled her because it appeared to interfere with the direction of her own inner voice, and she left the community troubled. She writes, however, that her voices and visions continued, all pointing to the Shakers. In her narrative, she provides examples of visions that are all part of Shaker doctrine: visions of the Mother, visions of the Bride and Groom, and visions of the doctrine of celibacy. Her inner voice eventually overpowered her hesitancy over the authority of another, and in 1844, she moved to the Shaker community at Watervliet, New York.

In the fourth section of the autobiography, "Shaker Doctrine and First Residence at Watervliet," Jackson continues to record her dreams, most of which are now concerned with aspects of Shaker doctrine. The most significant occurred on March 1, 1850. Jackson writes that while reciting a Shaker prayer, she had a vision of her Heavenly Parents and Mother Lee. She recalls that she was immediately comforted and filled with a desire to spread the good news to the world. This was a deviation from mainstream Shaker practice, which encouraged personal holiness and prayer for the self, not for the world. Jackson remained at Watervliet for seven years and then left for Philadelphia with a fellow black woman Shaker, Rebecca Perot, to establish a Shaker community there.

The fifth section of the narrative, "Interim in Philadelphia: Experiments in Seance Spiritualism," records the two Rebeccas' work in Philadelphia from 1851 to 1857. Again Jackson includes examples of her visions, including one in which God tells her to return to the world and bring all her brothers and sisters. During this period of Shaker history, the communities placed a great value on spiritualism, believing that members could communicate directly with those who had died and could in fact convert the dead to the faith. As a result, Shakers permitted the use of mediums and seances. Jackson records her experiments with spiritualism in this section and includes the successful conversion of her now-dead former husband. Throughout this period, there were strained relations between the Shaker home community at Watervliet and Jackson's Philadelphia group. Jackson eventually was persuaded to return to Watervliet. She includes, near the conclusion of this chapter, an intense dream of Holy Mother Wisdom that ends with the following declaration:

I am thankful, I am little, I am humble, I am meek and lowly in heart and in mind and in spirit. And I will be good, I will be faithful, I will forsake all for Christ's sake and the Gospel, and I will be one of Mother's little, humble children. (p. 264)

Soon after this dream of submission to the will of the Mother, Jackson left Philadelphia to return to "Zion," or the home community at Watervliet.

In the final section of the autobiography, "Second Residence at Watervliet: Establishment of the Philadelphia Shaker Community," Jackson records her submission to the community and Eldress Paulina, her superior. After this public submission of faith and obedience, Jackson received a vision that commanded her again to leave Watervliet and "labor with the people." This time she received Eldress Paulina's blessing, and when she and Rebecca Perot returned to Philadelphia, they returned with the support of the Shaker community. In the final few pages of the narrative, Jackson continues to record her visions, here primarily explications of Shaker doctrine.

CRITICISM

Although there is relatively little criticism about Rebecca Cox Jackson, two significant sources are available. First, Richard E. William's *Called and Chosen: The Story of Mother Rebecca Jackson and the Philadelphia Shakers* provides a useful history of Jackson and her life. Jean McMahon Humez' edition of Jackson writings, *Gifts of Power: The Writings of Rebecca Jackson, Black Visionary, Shaker Eldress*, is an outstanding work of scholarship. Humez includes a lengthy introduction that places Jackson within the perfectionist, abolitionist, and feminist movements of the nineteenth century, and she also outlines basic Shaker doctrine. In addition, she provides a useful bibliography and selections from Shaker writing.

Gifts of Power is a fascinating document. As Humez points out, Rebecca Cox Jackson's writings

are centrally concerned with how religious vision and ecstatic experience functioned for her and other women of her time as a source of personal power, enabling them to make radical change in the outward circumstances of their lives. (p. 1)

Convinced that God was speaking directly to her, Jackson, after her dramatic conversion, became active in the A.M.E. Church as an itinerant preacher, took a leadership position in the Holiness movement, and finally became a Shaker. Each step involved confronting authority, measuring that external authority against her own inner voice, and then moving on. Her writings can be seen as a record of the quest for autonomy, something seldom attained by blacks and women in the nineteenth century. In addition, when read against the background of such more orthodox narratives as Daniel Payne's *Reflections of Seventy Years* and Lyman Beecher's *The Autobiography of Lyman Beecher*, *Gifts of Power* reveals both the strong attraction of enthusiastic religion in the nineteenth century and the impact that those religions had on the lives of women.

BIBLIOGRAPHY

Andrews, Edward D. *The People Called Shakers: A Search for the Perfect Society.* 1953. Reprint. New York: Dover, 1963.
―――. *Work and Worship: The Economic Order of the Shakers.* Greenwich, Conn.: New York Graphics Society, 1974.
Campbell, D'Ann. "Woman's Life in Utopia: The Shaker Experiment in Sexual Equality Reappraised 1810–1860." *New England Quarterly*, 51.1 (March 1978): 23–38.
Culley, Margo, ed. *A Day at a Time: The Diary Literature of American Women from 1764 to the Present.* New York: Feminist, 1985.
Filley, Dorothy M. *Recapturing Wisdom's Valley: The Watervliet Shaker Heritage 1775–1975.* New York: Albany Institute of History and Art, 1975.

Jackson, Rebecca Cox. *Gifts of Power: The Writings of Rebecca Jackson, Black Visionary, Shaker Eldress*. Edited by Jean McMahon Humez. Amherst: University of Massachusetts Press, 1981.

Pike, Kermit J. *A Guide to Shaker Manuscripts in the Library of the Western Reserve Historical Society*. Cleveland: Western Reserve Historical Society, 1974.

White, Anna, and Leila S. Taylor. *Shakerism: Its Meaning and Message*. Columbus, 1904.

Williams, Richard E. "Mother Rebecca Jackson: One of the Black Shakers in Philadelphia." *Shaker Messenger*, 1.3 (Spring 1979).

———. *Called and Chosen: The Story of Mother Rebecca Jackson and the Philadelphia Quakers*. Edited by Cheryl Dorschner. Metuchen, N.J.: Scarecrow, 1981.

17 • PETER JENKINS (1951–)

A Walk Across America

BIOGRAPHY

Peter Jenkins was born in Greenwich, Connecticut, in 1951 and grew up in a suburban, upper-middle-class environment. In 1969, Jenkins enrolled at Alfred University. While at Alfred, Jenkins majored in art and married. On graduation in 1973, his marriage broke up, and Jenkins decided to begin what he thought would be an eight-month walk across America.

On October 15, 1973, Jenkins started his walk at Alfred, heading for New Orleans. Along the way, he had a conversion experience, and in New Orleans, while staying at the New Orleans Baptist Theological Seminary and working on an article about his adventures while walking for *National Geographic*, he met and married Barbara Jo Pennell. On July 5, 1976, Jenkins and his wife began a walk from New Orleans to the Pacific coast. In 1979, the account of the first part of his transcontinental walk, *A Walk Across America*, was published. In 1981, part two, *The Walk West*, was published. Since the publication and popular reception of these two books, Peter Jenkins has continued to write. Among his later books are *The Road Unseen* (1985), *The Tennessee Sampler* (1985), *Across China* (1986), and *Close Friends* (1989).

THE AUTOBIOGRAPHY

A Walk Across America is an unusual conversion narrative. In fact, most readers would not at first identify it as a religious autobiography. When

Jenkins' book appeared in 1979, readers responded favorably to the story of a young man's leaving society to walk across the country in search of its soul. Although some people Jenkins met on his walk considered him nothing more than a hippie, his renunciation reminded others of Henry David Thoreau, whose narrative of nineteenth-century withdrawal, *Walden*, has become a classic American narrative. Like Thoreau, Jenkins created a personal narrative of spiritual growth and environmental concern, and the popularity of both works suggests an affinity between the two subjects.

Jenkins begins his autobiography with a brief description of his life at Alfred University from 1969 to 1973. His references to Woodstock, Vietnam, drugs, the antiwar movement, and Richard Nixon provide a background for Jenkins' depiction of his disintegrating marriage and unhappiness with himself and his culture. The juxtaposition of public and personal malaise dominates the beginning of the book, creating a world without order or meaning from which Jenkins would withdraw. After describing leaving his wife, Jenkins writes:

I realized one sure thing. I knew I was going to have to get my head together and I would have to do it by myself. It was important for me to get away from her, our friends, Alfred, my parents, Greenwich, and from everyone and everything I knew. (p. 21)

To get away from everything and to get his head together, Jenkins decided to walk across America with his dog, Cooper. The motivation for this act of withdrawal from society and search for value is similar to Thoreau's, which he described in his famous statement in *Walden*: "I went to the woods because I wished to live deliberately, to front only the essential facts of life, and see if I could not learn what it had to teach, and not, when I came to die, discover that I had not lived" (p. 61). Both Jenkins' assertion and Thoreau's declaration can be seen as the first step in the process of conversion, an awareness of an emptiness or dislocation, called a sense of sin in traditional theology, and a decision to begin to search for meaning.

Once Jenkins announces his intention to begin his pilgrimage, he describes his plans and preparations. These sections of the narrative become a hiker's guide as Jenkins writes about his training, organization, and equipment. He also describes his test walk, from Alfred University to Washington, D.C. Finally, after meeting with the editors of *National Geographic* and receiving a commission to write about his experiences and a camera to record them, Jenkins sets out on the main part of his walk.

At the offices of *National Geographic* Jenkins had been told, "The more time you spend with the people out there, the better you will get to know them and America" (p. 52). As Jenkins chronicles his walk through Virginia, West Virginia, Tennessee, North Carolina, Georgia, Alabama, Mississippi, and Louisiana, he focuses on the people he meets. As a result, his narrative becomes more than the hiking adventures of one man; instead, especially where Jenkins describes at length some of the memorable people he met, *A Walk Across America* takes on some of the intensity of James Agee's classic examination of rural Southern life, *Let Us Now Praise Famous Men*.

In the first third of *A Walk Across America*, Jenkins barely mentions religion. As Jenkins describes his adventures along the Appalachian Trail in Virginia, he provides his readers with a series of portraits of rural America. In describing such places as Sperryville and Bluefield and such people as Homer Davenport, "the greatest mountain man alive," Jenkins establishes his credibility as an honest observer of American life, and the life he observes in rural Virginia is rich in landscape and people. By the time Jenkins reaches North Carolina, his emotional exhaustion has been replaced by a spirit of adventure.

In the central chapters of his autobiography, Jenkins begins to describe the changes that took place in him and led to his conversion. These chapters are the most dramatic in the narrative and are set in the mountains of western North Carolina.

Jenkins' drama began as he arrived in Robbinsville, North Carolina, looking for a job. He was recovering from the flu and needed money to continue his walk. Soon after his arrival, a rumor spread throughout the town that he was a drug pusher aiming to corrupt the town children. Jenkins remained in town for a week looking for a job until he was confronted by two men on a lonely dirt road. One of the men approached him, demanding identification:

"Listen, you troublemaking hippie," he shouted as he grabbed the cards from my hand. "I don't give a damn who in the hell you say you are. I'm with the State Bureau of Investigation and my phone's been ringin' off the wall and every one of them about you and that grubby dog." He sneered as he stuck his face in mine. "What are you trying to prove? You ain't gonna get a job in this county, I'll guarantee you that!" (pp. 110–11)

Jenkins left Robbinsville quickly, hiking southwest until he reached Murphy, North Carolina, where he found work, friends, family, and God.

Jenkins' depiction of Robbinsville, complete with bigotry, racism, and threats of violence, marks the low point of the walk. Jenkins' depiction of Murphy, on the other hand, is the emotional center of the narrative, marking the point at which Jenkins' life is turned around. In Augustinian terms, Robbinsville is the City of Man, corrupt and sinful, whereas Murphy approaches the City of God, at least in some of it aspects.

Tired and hungry, Jenkins arrived in Murphy and was immediately made welcome by the Olivers, a black family. He was fed, given a room in the family house, and soon became an adopted member of the family. He found a job in a local sawmill and soon was able to help provide money for the family. He wore family members' clothes and went to the Mount Zion Baptist Church with the Olivers, where he began to undergo the process of conversion.

With the Olivers in Murphy, Jenkins discovered, for the first time in his life, a family and community in which religion played a central and vital role. Jenkins realized that this was one of the things he was looking for. One Sunday morning, after returning from a service, Jenkins thought:

This whole church trip didn't make sense. Before Mount Zion, with its tiny black congregation, I had always known the only way my restless generation could be moved or get high was at a rock concert. Also, I had always known church was a dead place where you were expected to sit still through a thirty- or forty-minute monotone sermon about social ethics. Every Sunday our parents woke us up early and made us wear stiff clothes, and with every hair in place we were loaded into the car and taken to church. . . .

These poor folks, who barely scratched enough together to pay their pastor, had something I was looking for. Of all the cool things, this service surpassed every far out and turned on experience I always held close to my snobby heart. (pp. 137–38)

Jenkins recognized that he had discovered something special. His stay in Murphy was the longest on his pilgrimage, and he even invited his parents to come visit his new "family." He eventually realized that he "could not put off walking any longer," and on a hot August morning, he started down the road away from Murphy.

Jenkins' interest in spirituality continued. The next stop on his walk was The Farm, a commune located in eastern Tennessee. Founded by Stephen Gaskin and 250 followers from San Francisco, The Farm was one of the more famous communes of the early 1970s. More than 750 persons lived there by the time Jenkins arrived, and in that summer, more than 13,000 persons visited The Farm. While on The Farm, Jenkins worked in the fields, listened to talks of Eastern spirituality and meditation, ate vegetarian food, and shared his belongings with his fellow Farmers. The primary purpose of The Farm, Jenkins discovered, was to simplify life so that the members of the commune would have time left over to look for God, who was, according to Gaskin and his followers, something vague and undefinable of which all people were a part. Jenkins immediately was attracted by the integrity and honesty of the members of the commune, and he admired their decision to leave the materialism of urban America behind. He never felt comfortable, however, with the non-Western direction of the spiritual search on The Farm. And when his dog, Cooper, was killed by a truck there, Jenkins knew it was time to move on again.

In the final sections of A Walk Across America, Jenkins describes his walk south across Alabama to the Gulf of Mexico and New Orleans. He also begins to pull together the various themes of the narrative. As he continues to describe the places he visited and the people he met, including an interview with Alabama governor George Wallace, who had heard about the Yankee boy and wanted him to have a safe visit in his state, Jenkins realizes that the major events of his pilgrimage are forming a pattern. He has learned independence from a mountain hermit, love and the importance of faith from a poor black family, and the sense of the spiritual from hippies in a commune. He discovers that he is at peace with himself, the world weariness and confusion of the beginning of the autobiography are gone. Walking south through Alabama to the sea, Jenkins senses that something is happening to him. That something comes to a head in Mobile on Friday, March 21, 1975.

To earn money to continue his walk, Jenkins had found a job as a tree surgeon. Walking that Friday evening, Jenkins "felt a call" to attend a Christian crusade led by James Robison. Jenkins writes that he attended his first revival as an outsider and an observer, intending to record it as one of the many experiences he had had on the road, but when Robison asked his audience, "Have you ever repented of your sin and turned your life over to Jesus Christ? Are you saved?" Jenkins recalls:

I was going to die. The deepest corners of my being were lit with thousand-watt light bulbs. It were as if God himself were looking into my soul, through all my excuses, my dark secrets. All of me was exposed in God's searchlight.

When the question ended its roaring echo, I decided for the first time I needed God. This must be the God I had been searching for, and the One they worshiped back in Murphy at Mount Zion. . . .

Now I knew what people meant when they sang "Amazing Grace." (pp. 260–61)

Jenkins' depiction of his conversion uses a number of traditional elements: the feeling of being called, emotional involvement, senses of sight and sound sharpened, and a feeling of deep peace. Like a number of other writers of conversion narratives, most notably Thomas Merton and Thomas Shepard, Jenkins sees the moment of his actual conversion as part of a longer process, a process going back to Murphy, North Carolina, and beyond. In fact, the entire walk is a long, complex process of the rebirth of Peter Jenkins.

The final short sections of A Walk Across America describe Jenkins' life in New Orleans after his conversion. After walking along the Gulf Coast from Mobile to New Orleans, Jenkins found a room at the New Orleans Baptist Theological Seminary. There he began to work on the story of his walk for National Geographic. There he also met Barbara Pennell, a student who became his wife. The autobiography ends with a marriage and a plan to begin the walk again, this time with Barbara, westward to the Pacific.

CRITICISM

There is almost no criticism available on the work of Peter Jenkins. Several short notices appeared when A Walk Across America first appeared. Patricia

Newman's *People* feature, "Peter Jenkins Sets Out to Walk Across America and Ended Up Finding a New Wife," represents the main response. Readers, however, responded enthusiastically, making Jenkins' narrative a best-seller. The United States Information Agency excerpted sections of Jenkins' work, and it was adapted by the Reader's Digest Condensed Books.

Published in 1979, *A Walk Across America* attracted readers for several reasons. First, Jenkins' narrative celebrates the American landscape. His depictions of rural America, both the land and the people who live in it, are intimate and affectionate. Jenkins set out to "look for America," an America that seemed to have lost its sense of direction, or soul, in the early part of the decade, and in looking at the wilderness along the Appalachian Trail and the people of small Southern towns, he appeared to find it. Throughout his autobiography, Jenkins expresses an environmental sensitivity awareness that links the places with the people he writes about.

Second, readers found in Jenkins' description of his own conversion a contemporary example of a traditional conversion experience. Jenkins begins his narrative isolated and uncertain but moves through a series of experiences to the point where he comes to both an awareness of and a need for God. Jenkins avoids theological discussions and sectarian arguments as he writes; he simply writes about how he found God in the land and its people.

BIBLIOGRAPHY

"A Conversation with Peter Jenkins." *US News & World Report*, 9 May 1983, 130.

Jenkins, Peter. *A Walk Across America*. New York: Morrow, 1979.

———. *The Road Unseen*. Nashville: Nelson, 1985.

———. *The Tennessee Sampler*. Nashville: Nelson, 1985.

———. *Across China*. New York: Morrow, 1986.

———. *Close Friends*. New York: Morrow, 1989.

Jenkins, Peter, and Barbara Jenkins. *The Walk West: A Walk Across America*. New York: Morrow, 1981.

Mitgang, Herbert. "Behind the Best Sellers: Peter Jenkins." *New York Times Biographical Service*, April 1979, 486–87.

Newman, Patricia. "Adventure: Peter Jenkins Sets Out to Walk Across America and Ended Up Finding Himself a New Wife." *People*, 19 March 1979, 67+.

18 • MALCOLM X (1925–1965)

The Autobiography of Malcolm X

BIOGRAPHY

Malcolm X was born on May 29, 1925, in Omaha, Nebraska. His father, the Reverend Earl Little, was a Baptist minister and an organizer for Marcus Garvey's Universal Negro Improvement Association. Little moved his family to Lansing, Michigan, shortly after Malcolm was born. In 1931, Malcolm's father died, and after struggling to keep the family together, Malcolm's mother was committed to the Michigan State Mental Hospital in Kalamazoo. The Little children were sent to live in foster homes, and in 1941, Malcolm moved to Boston at the invitation of his aunt.

In Boston, Malcolm discovered both the black bourgeoisie and the black street life. He immediately was attracted to the latter, and in Boston, and later in New York, Malcolm alternated ordinary jobs with a career as a street hustler. In 1946, he was arrested for robbery, and after his conviction, he was sentenced to serve ten years.

While serving his sentence, Malcolm became aware of the teachings of Elijah Muhammad, and through the influence of his brother, he became a member of the Nation of Islam. In addition, he used his time in prison to educate himself, reading widely in philosophy and history. On his release, he became a spokesman for the Nation of Islam, and he quickly rose to the position of an influential and powerful leader within the Black Muslim community.

Malcolm began his organizational work in Harlem in 1954, and by the early 1960s, he had become one of the best-known black spokesmen in the

United States. He eventually disassociated himself from Muhammad's Nation of Islam and was in the process of establishing a new organization, the Organization of Afro-American Unity, when he was assassinated at the Audubon Ballroom in Harlem on February 21, 1965.

THE AUTOBIOGRAPHY

The Autobiography of Malcolm X is a complex narrative and a major American autobiography. The first complexity of the narrative concerns authorship. Malcolm worked with Alex Haley on the manuscript, and as in any collaboration, there is a question of how much of the narrative is Malcolm's and how much is Haley's. Haley himself acknowledges that Malcolm provided all the information and initialed every page of the manuscript, and he insists that the work is Malcolm's own autobiography, not a biography written by Alex Haley.

A second complexity is the use at the center of the autobiography, the question of what is an American. Like the Quaker and Puritan autobiographers who provided the foundations for the genre in America, Malcolm X created a narrative in which the first half shows him to be a member of a persecuted minority, whereas the second half emphasizes the autobiographer's role as a member of and spokesman for a religious and political community that literally offers him a new life. Again, like Puritan autobiographers, Malcolm X saw his conversion as the crucial event in his life and saw history as a theological adventure. The conversion experience led him to a belief in the brotherhood of man, and although there are great differences between the ideologue of progress and the black nationalist prophet, Malcolm's narrative, like Benjamin Franklin's *Autobiography*, is a version of a success story that draws a parallel between the development of a sense of self and the liberation of a colonized people. Although the setting and material seem far removed from Puritan conversion narratives and colonial success stories, its structure is classically American. Malcolm's narrative opens with an account of his family and early life, which leads to a moment of crisis and illumination. A dramatic conversion follows, and that conversion leads to study, preparation, and then the assumption of the role of the prophet and spokesman for the entire community of believers.

The Autobiography of Malcolm X is, however, more than a simple conversion narrative. The autobiography shows both a conversion and an analysis of that conversion. It is both a black narrative and a tale of a universal experience. The book was begun in 1963 when Malcolm was still a member of the Nation of Islam, the original dedication was to Elijah Muhammad, and all the proceeds from the sale of the autobiography were intended to go to the Black Muslims. At this early stage in the project, Malcolm saw himself as a propagandist rather than as an autobiographer, and his narrative was to be completely orthodox. As coauthor Alex Haley later said of the

notebook that Malcolm kept, "it contained nothing but Black Muslim philosophy, praise of Mr. Muhammad, and the evils of the 'white devil.' He
would bristle when I tried to urge him that the proposed book was *his* life"
(p. 388). Haley's arguments with Malcolm about the didactic nature of the
autobiography, along with Malcolm's own unhappiness with the movement
and his eventual excommunication from the Nation of Islam, compelled
him to reexamine his life, and the product of that reexamination is *The
Autobiography of Malcolm X*, a book that uses the conventional forms of
the conversion narrative but goes beyond the usual limitations of that mode.

The conventions of the conversion narrative demand a contrast built
around the conversion experience, and in describing his transformation from
street hustler and shoeshine boy to minister and spokesman for a large
segment of the black community in the United States, Malcolm X juxtaposes
black and white in American society. He begins in the first chapter of his
narrative, "Nightmare," where he presents both Ku Klux Klan riders and
members of Marcus Garvey's United Negro Improvement Association. The
effects of racism in America dominate the early sections of the narrative.
Malcolm provides his readers with examples of violence, poverty, and the
destruction of his family in the first twenty pages of the book. Four of his
uncles were killed, and he suspects that his father as well. After his father's
death, the Little family was forced to subsist on homegrown food and
welfare until Malcolm's mother finally broke under the strain and was
committed to an institution. Malcolm and his brothers and sisters were then
sent to different homes. This life of poverty and limitations changed when
Malcolm visited the city for the first time.

Malcolm describes his first impressions of urban life effectively.

I couldn't have feigned indifference if I had tried to. People talked casually about
Chicago, Detroit, New York. I didn't know the world contained as many Negroes
as I saw thronging downtown Roxbury at night, especially on Saturdays. Neon
lights, nightclubs, poolhalls, bars, the cars they drove! Restaurants made the streets
smell—rich, greasy, down-home black cooking! Jukeboxes blared Erskine Hawkins,
Duke Ellington, Cootie Williams, dozens of others. (p. 35)

The nightlife provided Malcolm with one alternative, and his Aunt Ella
provided him a second, life as a member of the black bourgeoisie, who,
according to Malcolm, prided themselves on being more cultured and cul-
tivated than their neighbors in the ghetto. "Under the pitiful misapprehen-
sion that it would make them 'better," these Hill Negroes were breaking
their backs trying to imitate white people" (p. 40).

Malcolm's descriptions indicate that the fast life of the street was more
attractive to him. He documents how he learned about the "cats" and
adopted their way of life. He soon found work as a shoeshine boy in a
dance hall and made extra money selling drugs, alcohol, and girls. The
homeboy had come to town in a big way.

As he describes the life of a black hustler in Harlem during the 1940s, Malcolm creates a new persona in his autobiography. No longer is he Malcolm Little, homeboy from Michigan; instead, he is Detroit Red, street-wise and tough. In the hustler sections of *The Autobiography of Malcolm X*, Malcolm demonstrates his ability to survive in a hostile environment, a central part of black autobiographical writing. These chapters also show Malcolm's initiation into a subculture set apart from the white mainstream in America. In addition, they serve to set up the major transition in the narrative, Malcolm's religious conversion.

After his arrest and conviction for robbery, Malcolm was sentenced to ten years in prison, where he was converted to the Nation of Islam. Malcolm describes the experience quickly and effectively. In 1948, after he had been transferred to Concord Prison, he received a letter from his brother Philbert urging him to join the Nation of Islam. In another letter from his family, this one from his brother Reginald, he was advised not to eat pork or smoke cigarettes.

Malcolm was interested. Conversion is a process of casting off and taking on, and Malcolm uses this convention of breaking habits, a device used by other writers of conversion narratives, in the description of his own conversion:

Quitting cigarettes wasn't going to be difficult. I had been conditioned by days in solitary without cigarettes. Whatever this chance was, I wasn't going to fluff it. After I had read that letter, I finished the pack I then had open. I haven't smoked another cigarette to this day, since 1948.

It was about three or four days later when pork was served for the noon meal. I wasn't even thinking about pork when I took my seat at the long table. Sit-grab-gobble-stand-file out; that was the Emily Post in prison eating. When the meat platter was passed to me, I didn't even know what the meat was; you usually couldn't tell anyway—but it was suddenly as though don't eat any more pork flashed on a screen before me....

Later I would learn, when I had read and studied Islam a good deal, that, unconsciously, my first pre-Islamic submission had been manifested. I had experienced, for the first time, the Muslim teaching, "If you will take one step toward Allah—Allah will take two steps toward you." (p. 156)

Malcolm then describes the years he spent in prison, but he emphasizes his growth in faith rather then the difficulties of confinement. All the standard conventions of the conversion experience are present in the narrative: the descent into the depths of sin, confusion, despair, and prison; the direct illumination of the sinner, much like Jonathan Edwards' sweet infusion of saving grace; and an outer transformation to match the inner conversion. The use of external changes to mirror internal conversion continues in the narrative as Malcolm describes in detail his purchase of new clothes, new glasses, and a new watch as he leaves prison. He also has taken on a new name to match his new awareness of himself. Malcolm Little is no more; Malcolm X has been born.

What follows also is part of the traditional conversion narrative. Malcolm presents himself as the convert who becomes a spokesman for the community, defending the faithful from attack and supporting them and the faith. Again, like many earlier conversion narratives, *The Autobiography of Malcolm X* depicts the oppressed community's conflicts with the larger, unconverted part of society. After the conversion, it is time for the acts.

Malcolm's depiction of his work as a minister of the Nation of Islam chronicles a dramatic rise from the depths of prison to the heights of power and fame. Malcolm is not interested in recounting his achievements for their own sake; instead, the narrative of his work for the Nation of Islam emphasizes the position of blacks in a hostile white culture and the impact that faith can have on the lives of those who accept it.

In the second half of his autobiography, Malcolm X changes the tone of his writing, adapting his language to his message. In the first half of his story, he used the language of the street and the rhythms of jazz as he recounted events of his early life. Later, as he describes building his faith and converting people to the Nation of Islam, he uses the language of a preacher and teacher. He is aware of his double audience: While recalling the way he spoke in storefronts to black audiences in Harlem, he now addresses the black and white audience reading his autobiography. His life story becomes, then, another opportunity to convince and convert.

Malcolm's success was remarkable. Beginning as an assistant minister in Detroit in 1953, he became, by 1959, the editor of *Muhammad Speaks* and one of the best-known spokesmen for the black community in the United States. He was at the height of his power in November of 1963 when, after the assassination of President Kennedy, he gave a speech linking the assassination to white violence against blacks called "God's Judgment on White America" with the theme "as you sow, so shall you reap" (p. 301).

Malcolm X had been speaking about the violent nature of American society for more than decade, but the reaction to his comments was so strong that Elijah Muhammad silenced him for ninety days and ordered him to submit to the total authority of the Nation of Islam. Later, Malcolm discovered that he was being driven from the Nation of Islam because some of its leaders perceived him as a threat. He eventually was excommunicated.

The final sections of *The Autobiography of Malcolm X* treat Malcolm's life after his split with the Nation of Islam. In this part of the narrative, Malcolm reexamines the conversion he has undergone. Again Malcolm is in a state of confusion and crisis: "I felt as though something in nature had failed, like the sun or stars" (p. 304). His expulsion has denied him the support of the community he had served for more than a decade, and while he never abandoned his conversion to Islam, he began to see it in a new light, especially after his pilgrimage to Mecca. Like his earlier conversion in prison, a second, or an affirmation of the first, takes place in Mecca. And again the result is a renewed sense of self and a rededication to the struggle for racial equality.

Malcolm's pilgrimage to Mecca dominates the final sections of his autobiography. He spends more than fifty pages describing the experience and the lessons he learned. Malcolm details how he discovered the errors in the teaching of Elijah Muhammad, especially his teachings on the nature of the "white devil." On the way to Mecca, Malcolm had discovered the international brotherhood of Islam, what he later calls "the color blindness in the Muslim world" (p. 338).

Malcolm returned from his pilgrimage convinced that a more orthodox Islam would provide the framework for a solution to the racial problems in the United States. In the final months of his life, Malcolm X began to build a new movement, the Organization of Afro-American Unity, which he hoped would eventually represent all the blacks in the United States. He was assassinated on February 21, 1965, before he could put his plans into action.

CRITICISM

The Autobiography of Malcolm X is a conversion narrative transformed by changing events. The simple, single-minded vision of conversion to the Nation of Islam is replaced by a more complex self-examination. Conversion, as Malcolm ultimately came to see it, was an ongoing, creative process, not a single static experience, and his narrative demonstrates this complexity. The final sections show the autobiographer in a continued state of transformation, a state of becoming, moving away from a separatist view of American society to a more complex one that refused to hold, for example, that all whites were "devils."

Literary critics have recognized the importance of this autobiography. G. Thomas Causer, in *American Autobiography: The Prophetic Mode*, places the autobiography within the mainstream of American letters by comparing it with the major American autobiographies written by Puritans and Quakers. C.W.E. Bigsby, in *The Second Black Renaissance*, calls it a crucial document in black literature and a classic example of a survival story. Stephen Butterfield, in *Black Autobiography in America*, calls the work a masterfully crafted political and rhetorical document.

The Autobiography of Malcolm X is an important work of American literature for a number of reasons. First, it is a dramatic narrative of one man's struggle to come to terms with himself and his society. Because the man was black and articulate, the coming to terms with a white society is even more dramatic. Second, Malcolm X's narrative does document survival and speaks for all outcasts in society. Finally, *The Autobiography of Malcolm X* addresses the question of identity, of what it means to be an American and a black American. Malcolm X provides a variety of answers, suggesting that the real answer may well be a process rather than a product.

BIBLIOGRAPHY

Abbott, H. Porter. "Organic Form in the Autobiography of a Convert: The Example of Malcolm X." *CLAJ*, 23 (1979): 125–46.

Adoff, Arnold. *Malcolm X*. New York: T. Y. Crowell, 1970.

Bigsby, C.W.E. *The Second Black Renaissance: Essays in Black Literature*. New York: Greenwood Press, 1980.

Bradley, David. "My Hero, Malcolm X." *Esquire*, 100 (December 1983): 488+.

Breitman, George, ed. *Malcolm X, the Man and His Ideas*. New York: Pathfinder, 1965.

———. *The Last Year of Malcolm X*. New York: Schocken, 1968.

Breitman, George, Herman Porter, and Bexter Smith, eds. *The Assassination of Malcolm X*. New York: Pathfinder, 1976.

Butterfield, Stephen. *Black Autobiography in America*. Amherst: University of Massachusetts Press, 1974.

Causer, G. Thomas. *American Autobiography: The Prophetic Mode*. Amherst: University of Massachusetts Press, 1979.

Clarke, John Henrik, ed. *Malcolm X*. New York: Macmillan, 1969.

Curtis, R. *The Life of Malcolm X*. Philadelphia: MacRae Smith, 1971.

Damerest, David P., Jr. "*The Autobiography of Malcolm X*: Beyond Didacticism." *CLAJ*, 16 (1972): 179–87.

Davis, Lenwood, and Marsha Moore. *Malcolm X: A Selected Bibliography*. New York: Greenwood Press, 1984.

Eakin, Paul John. "Malcolm X and the Limits of Autobiography." *Criticism*, 18 (1976): 230–42.

Goldman, Peter Lewis. *The Death and Life of Malcolm X*. New York: Harper & Row, 1973.

Holte, James. "The Representative Voice: Autobiography and the Ethnic Experience." *MELUS*, 9, 2 (1983): 25–46.

———. *The Ethnic I: A Sourcebook for Ethnic-American Autobiography*. New York: Greenwood Press, 1988.

Malcolm X. *Malcolm X Speaks*. Edited by George Breitman. New York: Grove Press, 1965.

———. *The Speeches of Malcolm X at Harvard*. Edited by Archie Epps. New York: Apollo Editions, 1969.

———. *Malcolm X on Afro-American History*. New York: Pathfinder, 1970.

———. *The End of White World Supremacy*. Edited by Benjamin Goodman. New York: Monthly Review Press, 1971.

Malcolm X, with Alex Haley. *The Autobiography of Malcolm X*. New York: Grove Press, 1965.

Maloney, Stephen R. "Tongues of Flame: A Study of Five Modern Spiritual Autobiographies." *DAT*, 32 (1971): 3314(A)–Rochester.

Ohmann, Carol. "*The Autobiography of Malcolm X*: A Revolutionary Use of the Franklin Tradition." *American Quarterly*, 22 (1979): 131–49.

Stone, Albert E. *Autobiographical Occasions and Original Acts. Versions of American Identity from Henry Adams to Nate Shaw.* Philadelphia: University of Pennsylvania Press, 1982.
Wolfenstein, Eugene Victor. *The Victims of Democracy: Malcolm X and the Black Revolution.* Berkeley: University of California Press, 1981.

19 • AIMEE SEMPLE MCPHERSON (1890–1944)

In the Service of the King

BIOGRAPHY

Aimee Semple McPherson was born in the small town of Ingersoll, Ontario, Canada, on October 9, 1890. She had a typical rural childhood, growing up on the family farm and attending local schools and churches. Although not particularly religious as a young girl, she was a believer but began to have doubts about Christianity in high school. In 1907, however, she had a conversion experience at a Pentecostal meeting, and the next year she married Robert Semple, the evangelist who had converted her, and joined him as an itinerant revivalist. In 1910, the Semples felt themselves called to be missionaries in China. Robert Semple died three months after their arrival, and Aimee, who was eight months pregnant, returned to the United States and began a transcontinental revival tour. In 1912, she married Harold Stewart McPherson, a Providence, Rhode Island, hotel clerk.

In 1915, after her marriage to McPherson ended, she returned to Ingersoll. There she felt called by the Lord to return to evangelism and began a series of Pentecostal revivals, practicing healing by laying on of hands. She toured throughout the United States, ending her tour in Los Angeles, where she decided to establish her headquarters. In 1921, she began construction of the Angelus Temple in Los Angeles; in 1922 she was the first woman to use radio to deliver a sermon; in 1924, she established her own radio station, KFSG, and began a successful radio ministry; and in 1926, she founded the Lighthouse of International Evangelism Bible College. By that time, she had become the most popular evangelist in the United States.

In May 1926, McPherson disappeared while swimming at a Los Angeles beach. She was thought to have drowned, but she reappeared in Mexico in June, claiming to have been kidnapped. McPherson's disappearance was the media event of the year; although a number of people claimed that she had run off with Kenneth Ormiston, who was employed at KFSG, McPherson maintained that she had been kidnapped. McPherson eventually was charged with corruption of public morals, obstruction of justice, and conspiracy to manufacture evidence. Despite several investigations by California officials, no one was ever convicted of anything in the case.

Although her reputation was damaged by the incident, McPherson continued to have a strong following. In 1927, she founded the International Church of the Foursquare Gospel as an independent Pentecostal denomination, and she continued to preach from the Angelus Temple and on the radio until her death in 1944.

THE AUTOBIOGRAPHY

In the Service of the King is one of three autobiographical works by Aimee Semple McPherson. Written just after the famous disappearance, it borrows much material from the earlier *This is That* (1923) and adds several chapters on McPherson's disappearance. After her death, a collection of autobiographical pieces was published as *The Story of My Life. In the Service of the King* is the most dramatic of the three autobiographies. In retelling the story of her life less than a year after her disappearance, McPherson develops the story of her religious life against the context of mystery and scandal.

The disappearance and reappearance of the most popular evangelist in the United States created a large audience for her autobiography, and McPherson takes advantage of that interest by opening her narrative with a dramatic chapter called "The Escape." Here and in her concluding chapters McPherson confronts the allegations that her kidnapping was actually a romantic adventure with an employee of the Angelus Temple. McPherson outlines in general terms her imprisonment, escape, trial, and triumphant return to the Angelus Temple. Although the frame narrative of *In the Service of the King* is a defense, the body of the work takes the form of a traditional conversion narrative.

McPherson's depiction of her rural Canadian childhood is openly romantic. She recalls "rolling meadows," "fertile acres," and "orchards in full bloom." She writes that her parents told her that "they had prayed the Lord would send a baby girl who would some day preach the Gospel" (p. 61). The church, school, and family farm are the settings of McPherson's recalled Edenic childhood until, during high school, she discovered the theory of evolution in one of her textbooks and began to doubt her faith. McPherson remembers that in the depths of her struggle with the "viper" of evolution, she asked God for help and saw, the next day, a sign for "Full Gospel Revival Services." After attending the services, she asked God's mercy. She writes:

Instantly the light streamed over my soul. I had a peculiar sensation of something warm, cleansing and healing flowing over me from head to foot, and the great peace, the "Peace that passeth understanding," flooded my heart. (p. 79)

Immediately after this experience, McPherson consecrated her life to Christ. Praying the next day, she asked what she should do with her life, and in answer she heard "Be a winner of souls" (p. 81).

McPherson's depiction of her conversion, with its acknowledgment of a sense of depravity followed by surrender to the will of God and a physical manifestation of forgiveness, is traditional. Her commitment to religion after the experience also is traditional. She married evangelist Robert Semple and prepared to leave for China with him to help "preach to the pagans."

The Semples' missionary trip was a disaster. They arrived in Hong Kong with no money, few plans, and no local organization. Robert Semple began to study Chinese and hand out gospel tracts. Soon he developed malaria and died, leaving McPherson alone, penniless, and pregnant.

A standard part of traditional conversion narratives is a description of the testing of the converted, and McPherson uses the Chinese chapters of her autobiography for that purpose. After describing her return to Canada, she begins to describe the major theme of her narrative, her development as a soul-winner.

McPherson had been an active partner in her husband's ministry, and on her return, she began to plan a series of revivals. McPherson recognized that it would be unusual for a woman to be an evangelist, but she refused to let that interfere with her plans. She writes:

At the time when I first began my own meetings, women had not taken the place in the affairs of everyday life which they occupy now. The woman in the world of business, the woman before the public eye, was the exception; men still largely abrogated those activities outside the home. Thus it was that a woman preacher was something of a novelty, a dress in the pulpit something new. However, if the Lord chose a woman to attract to Himself those who otherwise might not have come, who shall question the wisdom of the Lord? (p. 151)

McPherson's revival tour was a success. The "novelty" of a woman preacher attracted thousands to her Pentecostal gospel tent. Her services emphasized music, preaching, and healing by the laying on of hands. In her autobiography, McPherson chronicles her tour throughout the United States, which ended in Los Angeles. There she began publishing a monthly magazine, the *Bridal Call*, and constructing the Angelus Temple.

The establishment of the Church of the Foursquare Gospel and the construction of the Angelus Temple as its headquarters were the high points of her career, and in her narrative, McPherson devotes several chapters to her ministry. In "Multitudes and Miracles," she describes the thousands of people who came to her services for healing, noting that she dwells on the healing services "only to show the tremendous effect which they have in the spreading of religion" (p. 230). In "Soul Winning," she describes the need for organization in church services and the importance of evangelization. In "Beautiful Angelus Temple," she describes the planning, construction, and operation of the Angelus Temple itself and its own radio station, KFSG. These chapters not only chronicle the good work of the converted, a standard feature of the conversion narrative, but also provide balance for the criticism, some of which she includes in the final chapters of her narrative, McPherson received after her disappearance.

Near the end of her autobiography, McPherson returns to her disappearance and trial for corruption of public morals, obstruction of justice, and conspiracy to manufacture evidence. In describing her trial, she maintains her innocence, including pages of court testimony to support her assertions of kidnapping and escape. She argues that the state's charges, brought by a grand jury that refused to believe that she was kidnapped at all, were part of the devil's plot against her and her church. She concludes her narrative with a short chapter titled "Rock of Ages," in which she argues "the Church of God is built upon the Rock of Ages and the gates of Hell shall not prevail against it!" and "as for me 'I must be about my Father's business' " (pp. 314–16). With this identification with Christ, Aimee Semple McPherson ends her autobiography.

CRITICISM

Opinion concerning Aimee Semple McPherson is as mixed today as it was in the 1920s. Her inclusion in such works as William R. Hunt's *Dictionary of Rogues*, Ishbel Ross' *Charmers and Cranks: Twelve Famous American Women Who Defied Conventions,* and Irving Wallace's *The Intimate Sex Lives of Famous People* indicates that she is remembered more for her mysterious disappearance than for her ministry. Two works about her, *The Vanishing Evangelist*, by Lately Thomas, and a 1980s made-for-television movie, focus entirely on the alleged kidnapping and famous trial. On the other hand, G. R. Lothrop's "West of Eden: Pioneer Media Evangelist Aimee Semple McPherson in Los Angeles" suggests valid historical reasons for an interest in McPherson.

Aimee Semple McPherson is an important figure in American evangelism for a number of reasons. First, she established a nationwide evangelical media network that served as a model for later radio and television evangelists. Her combination of evangelism and mass media, her use of public relations and national tours with syndicated services remains the basic pattern of popular evangelism to this day. Second, McPherson was one of the first women to become a nationally famous evangelist. Her success and the publicity surrounding her disappearance provide an insight into the public's attitude about the role of women in religion during the early part of the century. Finally, McPherson's establishment of an independent, fundamental, Pentecostal, evangelical church in response to what she saw as the evils of modernism provided an example that other media ministers would follow.

BIBLIOGRAPHY

"Aimee Semple McPherson." *The National Cyclopedia of American Biography*. Vol. 35. New York: White, 1949, 229–30.

Austin, Alvyn. *Aimee Semple McPherson*. Don Mills, Ontario: Fitzhenry & Whiteside, 1980.

Bach, Marcus. *They Have Found a Faith*. Indianapolis: Bobbs-Merrill, 1946, 57–87.

Bahr, Robert. *Least of All the Saints: The Story of Aimee Semple McPherson*. Englewood Cliffs, N.J.: Prentice–Hall, 1979.

Barr Mavity, Nancy. *Sister Aimee*. New York: Doubleday, Doran, 1931.

Douglas, George H. *Women of the 20s*. Dallas: Saybrook, 1986, 32–58.

Hunt, William R. *Dictionary of Rogues*. New York: Philosophical Library, 1970, 82.

Hynding, Alan A. *California History Makers*. Dubuque, Ia.: Kendall/Hunt, 1976, 125–28.

Keatley, V. B. "Siren of the Sawdust Trail." Coronet, August 1957, 52–58.

Lothrop, G. R. "West of Eden: Pioneer Media Evangelist Aimee Semple McPherson in Los Angeles." *Journal of the West*, April 1988, 50–59.

McPherson, Aimee Semple. *This Is That*. Los Angeles: Bridal Call, 1923.

———. *In the Service of the King*. New York: Boni & Liveright, 1927.

———. *The Story of My Life*. Hollywood: International Correspondents, 1951.

McWilliams, C. "Aimee Semple McPherson: Sunlight in My Soul." In *The Aspirin Age, 1919–1941*. Edited by Isabel Leighton. New York: Simon & Schuster, 1949, 50–80.

Melton, J. Gordon. *Biographical Dictionary of American Cult and Sect Leaders*. New York: Garland, 1986, 168–70.

Mencken, Henry Louis, ed. *A Mencken Christomathy*. New York: Alfred A. Knopf, 1949, 289–92.

Morris, Lloyd R. *Postscript to Yesterday; America: The Last Fifty Years*. New York: Random House, 1947, 434–39.

Plagenz, G. R. "Story of Aimee Semple McPherson: Everybody's Sister." *Biography News*, September 1974, 1503–4.

Ross, Ishbel. *Charmers and Cranks: Twelve Famous American Women Who Defied Conventions*. New York: Harper & Row, 1965, 252–82.

Skow, J. "Sister Aimee." *Time*, 12 October 1970, 88 + .

Thomas, Lately (Robert V.P. Steele). *The Vanishing Evangelist: The Aimee Semple McPherson Kidnapping Affair*. New York: Viking, 1959.

————. *Storming Heaven: The Lives and Turmoils of Minnie Kennedy and Aimee Semple McPherson*. New York: Morrow, 1970.

Wallace, Irving, et al. *The Intimate Sex Lives of Famous People*. New York: Delacorte, 1981, 408–9.

"Where Was Aimee?" *Time*, 25 May 1959, 94.

20 • THOMAS MERTON (1915–1968)

The Seven Storey Mountain

BIOGRAPHY

Thomas Merton was born on January 31, 1915, in Prades, a village in the French Pyrenees. His father, Owen Merton, was a painter born in New Zealand; his mother, Ruth Jenkins, also was an artist, and the daughter of a successful Long Island publisher. In face of the growing World War I, the Mertons moved to Flushing, Long Island, where Owen Merton became a gardener. In 1918, Thomas Merton's brother, John Paul, was born. Shortly after, Ruth Merton discovered that she had cancer; she died in 1921.

After his wife's death, Owen Merton devoted himself to painting and travel, taking Thomas first to Bermuda and then to France. His work began to sell, and in 1925, he left the United States again for Europe. Thomas lived in Saint Antonin, in the south of France, until his father took him to England and enrolled him in the Ripley Court School. In 1929, Merton was admitted to the Oakham School. In 1931, his father died. In 1933, Merton was accepted as a student at Cambridge University. Before he matriculated, Merton took a trip to Italy, and while in Rome, he experienced an emotional conversion after viewing Byzantine mosaics. Although he soon discounted the experience, he would later recognize it as a crucial turning point in his life.

Merton left Cambridge after one year, returning to New York City. In 1934, Merton entered Columbia University, where he majored in English. He graduated in 1938 and received his M.A. in English literature in 1939. While at Columbia, Merton immersed himself in the study of both literature and religion. His interest in religion led him to Catholicism, and in November 1938, he was baptized a Catholic. Merton began planning to take religious orders, first as a Franciscan and later as a Trappist. While waiting, he taught English at St. Bonaventure's College. Finally, in December 1941, Merton entered the Trappist monastery, Our Lady of Gethsemani, in Kentucky.

From 1941 until his death in 1968, Thomas Merton was a Trappist monk. While living and working in the monastery under strict silence, Merton wrote more than fifty books and hundreds of essays and poems. His most famous work was his autobiography, *The Seven Storey Mountain*, published in 1948. In his autobiography, Merton, following the pattern of Augustine's *Confessions*, chronicled the dramatic conversion of a worldly intellectual. For his work, Merton became the best-known Catholic writer in America. In 1949, Merton, known as Father Louis in the monastery, was ordained. In 1955, he was named Master of the Choir Novices of the monastery. In 1960, he was given permission by his superiors to spend time in seclusion as a hermit in a cinder-block house on the monastery grounds.

In the late 1950s and 1960s, Merton's interests and writing began to change. In his early work, especially *The Seven Storey Mountain* and such inspirational books as *Cistercian Contemplatives* and *Seeds of Contemplation*, Merton wrote as a contemplative ascetic renouncing the evils of a fallen world. In his maturer writing, Merton turned his attention to the world and its problems, writing about racism, poverty, starvation, and the threat of nuclear war. In addition, he moved away from the conservative Catholicism that rejected non-Catholic thought as error and began to embrace some of the ideas of such writers as Karl Barth and Albert Camus as well as to explore the relation between Eastern and Western systems of mysticism and monasticism. In 1968, while on an Asian trip to attend ecumenical talks with Tibetan Buddhists and Asian monks, Merton presented a speech titled "Marxist Theory and Monastic Theoria." Shortly after his speech, he returned to his room and touched an exposed electric wire. He was killed instantly.

THE AUTOBIOGRAPHY

Writing in *Archetypes of Conversion: The Autobiographies of Augustine, Bunyan, and Merton*, Anne Hunsaker Hawkins points out the complexity of Merton's autobiography when she observes that *The Seven Storey Mountain* is similar to the works of Augustine and Bunyan in its use of the quest motif and yet different in its grounding in sacrament and ritual (p. 15). Merton's narrative has become one of the most studied works of the genre, and the critical attention is deserved. In *The Seven Storey Mountain*, Thomas Merton records a traditional search for God in a nontraditional era.

In several important ways, *The Seven Storey Mountain* is a traditional conversion narrative. Merton uses the three-part structure found in many traditional religious narratives: preconversion history or life of sin, the conversion itself, and finally postconversion life and works. In addition, Merton deliberately uses the metaphor of pilgrimage, another favorite device of authors of traditional religious narratives, to organize his material. What is nontraditional about the autobiography, on the other hand, is the degree of hostility toward the world and the exaltation of the contemplative life expressed in the text. Such attitudes might be expected in a pre-Reformation narrative, but Merton's advocacy of a kind of medieval monasticism in the mid-twentieth century can be disquieting. Also nontraditional is Merton's specific adaptation of the three-part conversion structure. As Hawkins, among other critics, has demonstrated, Merton's narrative is more complex than it first appears. Imbedded within the narrative is a series of illuminations, or moments of conversion, that force Merton to continually grow intellectually and spiritually. Merton's conversion is actually a continuous process, something that his later life and work confirmed.

Thomas Merton begins his autobiography with a depiction of the state of the world on the day of his birth.

On the last day of January 1915, under the sign of the Water Bearer, in a year of a great war, and down in the shadows of some French mountains on the borders of Spain I came into the world. Free by nature, in the image of God, I was nevertheless the prisoner of my own violence and my own selfishness, in the image of the world into which I was born. The world was the picture of Hell. (p. 3)

For Merton, whose autobiography records the renunciation of the world, the world was unredeemed. Later in his life, Merton would abandon that belief, but in writing his autobiography, he uses his introductory chapter, appropriately called "Prisoner's Base," to establish the place from which his religious journey begins.

The narrative voice of Thomas Merton, Trappist monk, dominates *The Seven Storey Mountain*. All the events recorded are filtered through the perspective of a man who believed that contemplative withdrawal from the world was the summit of human perfection. As a result, images of disorder and chaos dominate Merton's recollections of his early life, and when an experience is recalled in a positive manner, Merton emphasizes the religious, specifically Catholic, nature of the experience. For example, when he describes living with his father in the French town of Saint Antonin after the death of his mother, Merton spends three paragraphs describing how the landscape of the village centers on the town church. To ensure that his readers do not miss the metaphoric nature of the passage, he then observes:

The whole landscape, unified by the church, and its heavenward spire, seem to say: this is the meaning of all created things: we have been made for no other purpose than that men may use us in raising themselves to God, and in proclaiming the glory of God. (p. 37)

For Merton the autobiographer, the town church becomes the universal church and the landscape of Saint Antonin the world as it should be.

The first part of *The Seven Storey Mountain*, in addition to describing the world Merton would renounce, records the education of Thomas Merton, or the intellectual, emotional, and spiritual events that would lead him to his conversion. As have many other writers of spiritual narratives, Merton discovered that motif of the journey, or pilgrimage, provided him with a way of ordering events, and in the early sections of *The Seven Storey Mountain*, Thomas Merton depicts himself as continually in motion. The setting of the early chapters of the narrative shifts continually from France to New York to England and then around again. Schools become for Merton crucial places. Merton spent a good deal of his young life in boarding schools, and his depictions of Oakham, Cambridge, and Columbia reveal Merton's spiritual progress at important stages on his journey to the Abbey of Our Lady of Gethsemani.

In 1929, Merton began his studies at Oakham, an English public school. These were difficult years for young Merton, and his father was slowly dying of cancer. Merton writes that at Oakham, he lost his faith and discovered literature. At public school, the Anglican faith in which he was baptized was closely tied to the British class structure, which Merton found alien. Although he came to reject the Church of England, he did turn his interest to English literature, reading voraciously the work of James Joyce, D. H. Lawrence, T. S. Eliot, William Blake, and Gerard Manley Hopkins.

In 1933, after passing the entrance examination to Cambridge University, Merton decided to visit Rome. While there, he began visiting churches in search of Byzantine art. He recalls that he started to pray in the churches and read the Bible at night. He recalls that one night in his hotel room, he sensed the presence of his father, who had been dead for more than a year. He then recalls:

I was overwhelmed with a sudden and profound insight into the misery and corruption of my own soul, and I was pierced deeply with a light that made me realize something of the condition I was in, and I was filled with horror at what I saw, and my whole being rose up at revolt of what was in me, and my soul desired escape and liberation and freedom from all this with an intensity and urgency unlike anything I had ever known before. And now I think for the first time in my life I really began to pray. (p. 111)

Although by the time Merton entered Cambridge the intensity of his experience had been forgotten, this dramatic recognition of his sense of sin and need for redemption would play an important part in his life. He would return to it several years later and see it as part of his progressive movement toward monasticism.

For Merton, Cambridge was a disaster. He calls Cambridge "dark and sinister," and writes that, aside from the discovery of Dante, the virtue of his stay at Cambridge was that he fell so far from grace that he could later appreciate God's love. After one year, Merton left Cambridge and England for New York and Columbia University, which he found to be "full of light and fresh air."

The portions of *The Seven Storey Mountain* dealing with Merton's Columbia experiences are the most positive premonastic sections of the autobiography. It was at Columbia that Merton became both a writer and a Catholic, and it was there that he discovered a happiness he had missed. The thing he liked best about the university, he would later recall, was that it "was glad to turn me loose in its library, its classrooms, its distinguished faculty, and let me make what I liked out of it all" ("Learning to Live," pp. 197–98).

In addition to providing Merton with intellectual stimulation and freedom, his Columbia education set him on his path to Gethsemani. He decided that contemplation was more important than money and fame, and planned to become a college English teacher living his life on a quiet campus reading and teaching. In 1938, he received his B.A. degree and began graduate studies in English, planning to write his thesis on "Nature and Art in William Blake." During his first year of graduate study, Merton enrolled in a seminar on the scholastic philosophy of Thomas Aquinas and Duns Scotus. Moved by the experience and finding in Catholicism a coherent perspective, Merton became a Catholic in November 1938.

Merton writes that he viewed his baptism as a beginning, the first step up a "seven circled mountain of a Purgatory" (p. 221). This reference and Merton's title refer to Dante's *Purgatorio*. The reference also underscores Merton's belief that religious experience is an ongoing process rather than a single event. After his baptism, Merton took a series of additional steps up the mountain, and in his autobiography, he devotes the sections after his becoming a Catholic to a description of his evolving decision to enter the priesthood and a monastery.

Merton initially had planned to become a Franciscan, but after a visit to Cuba, Merton became unsure of his decision, and on his return to New York, he was told by his Franciscan advisor that his permission to enter that order had been canceled. Merton decided to accept a teaching position at St. Bonaventure's College in New York. While teaching there, he made a retreat to the Trappist monastery of Our Lady of Gethsemani Abbey in Kentucky during Easter of 1941. During the summer after the retreat, he worked at Friendship House, a Catholic mission established in Harlem. Merton writes that he was attracted to both the contemplative life and the life of social action, but during the fall of 1941, his desire to enter the monastery proved stronger. In December 1941, he left St. Bonaventure's for Gethsemani.

In the final sections of his narrative, Merton describes his life in the Trappist monastery. Merton calls the monastery "a school in which we learn from God how to be happy" (p. 372). In one of the most significant scenes in the autobiography, Merton records a Trappist brother locking a gate behind him as he steps into the monastery garden. The locked gate literally closes Merton off from the world, and in these parts of the auto-biography, Merton's attention is focused on the observances and prayers of the Trappists rather than on the fallen world at war outside the monastery gates. Although in his later writing Merton would move beyond the simple dichotomy of his autobiography, here he emphasizes the depravity of the world and the necessity of withdrawing from it. As he describes his intro-duction to the monastic life, Merton argues that the contemplative life is superior to the active. To emphasize the contrast, Merton records that while celebrating Easter week at Gethsemani, he received news that his younger brother, John Paul, had died while flying a bombing mission over Germany. Death and loss are part of the world outside the monastery walls, whereas prayer and praise exist within. With these references to death and resur-rection, Merton ends his story.

CRITICISM

Thomas Merton was an influential, prolific, and popular writer. His in-terests were varied, and he wrote on a wide range of topics: spirituality, war, civil rights, nuclear weapons, prayer, art, politics, poetry, psychology. During his lifetime, Merton was best known for his autobiography, but after his death in 1968, his later work began to draw serious attention. Merton's more than fifty books and hundreds of articles and letters have attracted numerous writers and scholars, and Thomas Merton has become one of the most studied contemporary American autobiographers.

Several works are crucial for the study of Thomas Merton and his writing. The most useful is perhaps Michael Mott's excellent biography, *The Seven Mountains of Thomas Merton*, which contains excellent notes and bibli-ography. Other important studies include James Thomas Baker's *Thomas Merton, Social Critic: A Study*, Monica Furlong's *Merton: A Biography*, Anne Hunsaker Hawkin's *Archetypes of Conversion: The Autobiographies of Augustine, Bunyan, and Merton*, Ross Labrie's *The Art of Thomas Mer-ton*, Anthony Padovano's *The Human Journey: Thomas Merton, Symbol of a Century*, and George Woodcock's *Thomas Merton, Monk and Poet: A Critical Study*. Useful bibliographic sources also are available. In addition to the quarterly *Merton Seasonal*, published by Bellarmine College, which lists new Merton titles each issue, Marquita Breit's *Thomas Merton: A Bibliography* and Frank Dell'Isola's *Thomas Merton: A Bibliography* provide Merton students with valuable information. Finally, the Thomas Merton Collection at Bellarmine College in Louisville is a unique depository of source material.

The Merton scholarship is as varied as the man himself and his interests. Merton is studied as a contemplative, a poet, and a social critic. Studies of the man and his work range from simple hagiography to sophisticated literary analysis. What emerges from the scholarship is a consensus that the image of Merton the world-renouncing monk that he created in *The Seven Storey Mountain* is not completely accurate. At the time he was writing his autobiography, Merton was already dissatisfied with that persona, and as he lived, thought, and prayed at Gethsemani, he continued to grow and change. Merton's conversion did not stop at the monastery gate; it continued throughout his life.

BIBLIOGRAPHY

Adams, Daniel J. *Thomas Merton's Shared Contemplation: A Protestant Perspective.* Kalamazoo, Mich.: Cistercian, 1979.

Baker, James Thomas. *Thomas Merton, Social Critic: A Study.* Lexington: University Press of Kentucky, 1971.

Bamberger, J. E. "In Search of Thomas Merton." *America,* 2 October 1982, 165–69.

Burns, R. E. "Salute to a Seven-Storey Memory." *U.S. Catholic,* September 1984, 2.

Christopher, M. "Will the Real Thomas Merton Please Stand Up?" *U.S. Catholic,* January 1981, 48–49.

Conn, W. E. "Merton's 'True Self': Moral Autonomy and Religious Conversion." *The Journal of Religion,* 65 (1985), 513–29.

Cooper, D. D. "Recent Merton Criticism." *Renascence,* 34 (1982), 113–28.

Costello, G. M. "The Monk Heard Round the World." *U.S. Catholic,* May 1985, 48–51.

Cupitt, D. "Turbulent Trappist." *Times Literary Supplement,* 13 February 1981, 156. [no. 4063].

Daggy, R. E. "Whatever May Be of Interest." *America,* 22 October 1988, 288–91+.

Davis, R. M. "Grace Beyond the Reach of Sullen Art: Waugh Edits Merton." *Journal of Modern Literature,* 13 (1986), 163–66.

Dell'Isola, Frank. *Thomas Merton: A Bibliography.* 1st rev. and exp. ed. Kent, Ohio: Kent State University Press, 1975.

Donohue, J. W. "Merton: A Film Biography of Thomas Merton." [TV program review] *America,* 2 June 1984, 422.

———. "A Kind Prophet." *America,* 2 June 1984, 422.

"Essays on Thomas Merton." [cover story; special section] *America,* 22 October 1988, 268–91+.

Ferry, W. H., R. Lax, and J. E. Bamberger. "The Merton We Knew." *Commonweal,* 111 (1984), 553–57.

Forest, James H. *Thomas Merton: A Pictorial Biography*. Mahwah, N.J.: Paulist Press, 1980.

Furlong, Monica. *Merton: A Biography*. 1st ed. New York: Harper & Row, 1980.

Giroux, R. "Editing The Seven Storey Mountain." *America*, 22 October 1988, 273–76.

Grayston, D. "Thomas Merton: The Global Future and Parish Priorities."*The Christian Century*, 29 August (supplement)1984: 802–4.

Groves, G. "Gregarious Hermit." *American Scholar*, 49 (1979), 89–93.

Hart, Patrick, ed. *The Legacy of Thomas Merton*. Kalamazoo, Mich.: Cistercian, 1986.

Hawkins, Anne Hunsaker. *Archetypes of Conversion: The Autobiographies of Augustine, Bunyan, and Merton*. Lewisburg, Pa.: Bucknell University Press, 1985.

Healey, Charles J. *Modern Spiritual Writers: Their Legacies of Prayer*. Staten Island, N.Y.: Alba House, 1989, 47–70.

Kelly, Frederick Joseph. *Man Before God*. 1st ed. Garden City, N.Y.: Doubleday, 1974.

Kramer, Victor A. "Thomas Merton." In *Dictionary of Literary Biography Yearbook: 1981*. Detroit, Mich.: Gale Research, 1982, 217–27.

Labrie, Ross. *The Art of Thomas Merton*. Fort Worth: Texas Christian University Press, 1979.

———. "Thomas Merton: Contemplative and Artist." *Studies in Formative Spirituality*, 4 (1983), 61–82.

———. "Thomas Merton." In *Dictionary of Literary Biography* v. 48. Detroit, Mich.: Gale Research, 1986, 290–98.

Lentfoehr, Thérèse. *Words and Silence: On the Poetry of Thomas Merton*. New York: New Directions, 1979.

Lipski, Alexander. *Thomas Merton and Asia: His Quest for Utopia*. Cistercian Study Series, no. 74. Kalamazoo, Mich.: Cistercian, 1983.

Malits, Elena. *The Solitary Explorer: Thomas Merton's Transforming Journey*. 1st ed. San Francisco: Harper & Row, 1980.

Merton, Thomas. *Thirty Poems*. New York: New Directions, 1944.

———. *A Man in the Divided Sea*. New York: New Directions, 1946.

———. *Figures for an Apocalypse*. New York: New Directions, 1948.

———. *Cistercian Contemplatives*. New York: Marbridge Printing Co., Inc., 1948.

———. *The Seven Storey Mountain*. 1948 1st ed. New York: New American Library, 1963.

———. *What Is Contemplation?* Holy Cross, Ind.: St. Mary's College Press, 1948.

———. *Exile Ends in Glory*. Milwaukee: Bruce, 1948.

———. *Seeds of Contemplation*. 1949 1st ed. New York: Dell, 1960.

———. *The Waters of Siloe*. New York: Harcourt, Brace and Company, 1949.

———. *The Tears of the Blind Lions*. New York: New Directions, 1949.

———. *What Are These Wounds?* Milwaukee: Bruce, 1950.

———. *The Ascent to Truth*. New York: Harcourt, Brace, 1951.

———. *A Balanced Life of Prayer*. Trappist, Ky.: Abbey of Gethsemani, 1951.

———. *The Sign of Jonas*. New York: Harcourt, Brace, 1953.

———. *Bread in the Wilderness*. New York: New Directions, 1953.

——— *The Last of the Fathers*. New York: Harcourt, Brace, 1954.

————. *No Man Is an Island.* New York: Harcourt, Brace, 1955.

————. *The Living Bread.* New York: Farrar, Straus and Cudahy, 1956.

————. *Silence in Heaven.* New York: Studio Publications and Thomas Y. Crowell, 1956.

————. *The Strange Islands.* New York: New Directions, 1957.

————. *The Tower of Babel.* New York: New Directions, 1957.

————. *The Silent Life.* New York: Farrar, Straus, 1957.

————. *Thoughts in Solitude.* New York: Farrar, Straus and Cudahy, 1958.

————. *Monastic Peace.* Saint Paul, Minn.: North Central Publishing Company, 1958.

————. *The Secular Journal of Thomas Merton.* New York: Farrar, Straus, 1959.

————. *Selected Poems of Thomas Merton.* New York: New Directions, 1959.

————. *The Wisdom of the Desert.* New York: New Directions, 1960.

————. *Disputed Questions.* New York: Farrar, Straus, 1960.

————. *The Behavior of Titans.* New York: New Directions, 1961.

————. *New Seeds of Contemplation.* New York: New Directions, 1961.

————. *The New Man.* New York: Farrar, Straus, 1961.

————. *A Thomas Merton Reader.* Ed. Thomas P. McDonnell. New York: Harcourt, Brace, 1962.

————. *Original Child Bomb.* New York: New Directions, 1962.

————. *Breakthrough to Peace.* New York: New Directions, 1962.

————. *Life and Holiness.* New York: Herder and Herder, 1963.

————. *Emblems of a Season of Fury.* New York: New Directions, 1963.

————. *Seeds of Destruction.* New York: Farrar, Straus and Cudahy, 1964.

————. *The Way of Chuang Tzu.* New York: New Directions, 1965.

————. *Gandhi on Non-Violence.* New York: New Directions, 1965.

————. *Seasons of Celebration.* New York: Farrar, Straus and Giroux, 1965.

————. *Raids on the Unspeakable.* New York: New Directions, 1966.

————. *Conjectures of a Guilty Bystander.* Garden City, N.Y.: Doubleday and Company, Inc., 1966.

————. *Redeeming the Time.* London: Burns and Oates Limited, 1966.

————. *Mystics and Zen Masters.* New York: Straus and Giroux, 1967.

————. *Cables to the Ace.* New York: New Directions, 1968.

————. *Faith and Violence.* South Bend, Ind.: University of Notre Dame Press, 1968.

————. *Zen and the Birds of Appetite.* New York: New Directions, 1968.

————. *The Plague.* Religious Dimensions in Literature. The Seabury Reading Program. RDL7. Lee A. Belford, general editor. New York: The Seabury Press, 1968.

————. *Contemplative Prayer.* New York: Herder and Herder, 1969.

————. *The Geography of Lograire.* New York: New Directions, 1969.

————. *My Argument with the Gestapo.* Garden City, N.Y.: Doubleday, 1969.

Mohs, M. "Silent Prophet." *Time,* 3 November 1980, 110+.

Mott, Michael. *The Seven Mountains of Thomas Merton.* Boston: Houghton Mifflin, 1984.

Nouwen, Henri J. M. *Thomas Merton, Contemplative Critic.* Reprint. New York: Harper & Row, 1981.

Ostling, R. N. "Merton's Mountainous Legacy." *Time,* 31 December 1984, 65.

O'Sullivan, Timothy. "Thomas, Merton." In *Makers of Modern Culture*, Facts on File, 1981, 352–53.

Padovano, Anthony T. *The Human Journey: Thomas Merton, Symbol of a Century.* 1st ed. Garden City, N.Y.: Doubleday, 1982.

Pennington, M. B. "Thomas Merton: An Experience of Spiritual Paternity in Our Time." *Studies in Formative Spirituality*, 5 (1984), 229–44.

Plank, K. A. "Mediating on Merton's Eichmann." *The Christian Century*, 9 October 1985, 894–95.

Powaski, Ronald E. *Thomas Merton on Nuclear Weapons.* Chicago: Loyola University Press, 1988.

Rubin, Michael. *Men Without Masks.* Reading, Mass.: Addison-Wesley, 1980, 242–52.

Shannon, W. H. "The Future of Thomas Merton." *Commonweal*, 115 (1988), 649–52.

———. "Thomas Merton's Three Gifts: A Review Essay." *America*, 21 October 1989, 267–73+.

Shannon, W. H., and B. Shore. "Many Mertons, Many Meads." *Commonweal*, 111 (1984), 560–63.

Sussman, Cornelia Silver, and Irving Sussman. *Thomas Merton.* Rev. ed. Garden City, N.Y.: Doubleday, 1980.

Teahan, J. F. "Solitude: A Central Motif in Thomas Merton's Life and Writings." *American Academy of Religion Journal*, 50 (1982), 521–38.

Wilkes, Paul, ed. *Merton, by Those Who Knew Him Best.* 1st ed. San Francisco: Harper & Row, 1984.

Woodcock, George. *Thomas Merton, Monk and Poet: A Critical Study.* New York: Farrar, Straus, Giroux, 1978.

Woodward, K. L. "The Seven-Storey Merton." *Newsweek*, 10 December 1984, 87.

21 • WILLIAM MILLER (1782–1849)

Apology and Defense

BIOGRAPHY

William Miller was born in Pittsfield, Vermont, in 1782. The eldest of sixteen children, Miller loved reading, and although he did not attend college, he acquired a good education by reading avidly. From 1803 to 1810, Miller lived a normal and successful life, marrying, farming, becoming a mason, and serving first as a constable and then as sheriff of Poultney, Vermont. In 1810, Miller, after reading the works of Hume, Paine, and Voltaire, denounced his Baptist faith, calling it a superstition. He joined the United States Army, declaring that patriotism was "one bright spot in the human character." During the War of 1812, Miller rose to the rank of captain. After the war, he retired from the army and returned to his farm.

In 1816, Miller returned to a belief in Christianity. He immersed himself in Bible study, spending most of his time on the books of Daniel and Revelation. From 1816 to 1818, Miller worked on a plan to determine the date of the end of the world. In 1818, he selected the year 1843 as that date, and from 1818 to 1832, he worked on proving the correctness of his date.

In 1831, after spending thirteen years working on his proofs, Miller became convinced that he should let the public know of his conclusions. In what he came to see as a divine coincidence, as soon as he decided he must speak, he was invited to speak on the end of the world in the neighboring town of Dresden. From 1831 to 1839, he traveled throughout New England and New York lecturing. He convinced and converted thousands.

In 1840, the Reverend Joshua V. Himes, pastor of the Second Christian Church in Boston, became Miller's publicity agent and general manager. Himes established two periodicals, *The Sign of the Times* in Boston and *The Midnight Cry* in New York City, and persuaded Miller to preach to large urban audiences. Miller became a sensation, giving 627 lectures in 1841.

Miller set the data for the end of the world as April 3, 1843. Before that date, Miller's followers enthusiastically prepared for the end, selling businesses and houses, giving away property, and preparing ascension robes. Thousands of Millerites, as Miller's followers came to be known, gathered on the evening of April 3 to wait for the day of doom. The world did not end. Miller returned to his study, and after recalculating his figures, Miller said that the actual date of the end of the world would be March 21, 1844. Once again, Millerites gathered in white ascension robes, waiting for the end. Again, the world did not end. Most of his followers abandoned Miller, returning to their original Baptist, Methodist, and Congregational denominations. Miller again recalculated his figures and determined that October 22, 1844, was the actual date. Again he was disappointed. Until his death in 1849, Miller continued to believe that the Second Coming was at hand. Several sects of Second Adventists formed following Miller's preaching, shaping the foundation of the Seventh-Day Adventist Church.

THE AUTOBIOGRAPHY

William Miller's *Apology and Defense* is a fascinating document. Published by J. V. Himes in 1845, shortly after Miller's predicted day of doom failed to appear, the *Apology and Defense* reflects both Miller's disappointment at his failure to discern the time of the Second Coming of Christ and his continued faith in his method of biblical study, the correctness of his general principle, and belief the end of time was at hand. Miller was aware that he was considered by many to be a false prophet, and at the beginning of his narrative, he addresses his readers frankly:

All men are responsible to the community for the sentiments they may promulgate, the public has a right to expect from me, a candid statement in reference to my disappointment in not realizing the Advent of Christ in A.D. 1843—4, which I had confidently believed. I have, therefore, considered it not presumptuous in me to lay before the Christian public a retrospective view of the whole question, the motives that actuated me, and the reasons by which I was guided. (p. 2)

After this statement of intentions, Miller begins to describe his life, conversion, and the studies that led him to his pronouncement.

Miller writes that he "was early educated to reverence the Scriptures as revelation of God to man" (p. 2) but was perplexed with what he saw as contradictions and inconsistencies in the Bible. Miller was unable to "harmonize" views on the Bible, and when he was twenty-two, he moved to Vermont, where he became acquainted with a number of "professed Deists," who introduced him to the works of Voltaire, Hume, and Paine. After his readings, Miller became convinced that the Bible was superstition.

Miller then briefly describes his service in the army during the War of 1812. He writes that his confidence in many of his Deistical principles was shaken and that after his release from the army, at the rank of captain, he moved to Low Hampton, New York, and retired from public life. Miller records that he was still bothered by religious doubts, finding assurance neither in Deisim nor in Christianity. He dates his conversion to May 1816, when he detected himself taking the name of God in vain. Miller writes that he instantly was convicted of the sinfulness of this, and was led to despair, which lasted for several months. After musing on his condition, Miller became convinced of the goodness of God, the friendship of Jesus, and the necessity of belief in the Bible.

After this classic description of a conversion experience, Miller writes that he was determined to understand the scriptures. He undertook a two-year period of study during which he put aside his previous beliefs and read the Bible in a "regular and methodical manner," reading verse by verse until he discovered something obscure. At that point, he would move to collateral passages, reading again until all was harmonized. When he had finished his study, Miller became convinced that the Bible plainly taught that there would be a literal Second Coming of the Lord at which time the righteous would be taken up to heaven, and that this personal premillennial advent could come at any time, since, according to Miller's calculations, all the necessary prophesies had been fulfilled. In fact, after further study and calculation, focusing on prophetical periods of time, Miller became convinced that the Second Coming of the Lord would occur in 1843.

For five years, Miller examined objections to his discovery, and finding none, he became convinced that it was his duty to "go tell the world of their danger" (p. 15). Miller writes that this was a difficult period for him. He spoke to all who came in contact with him about his discovery, but he did all he could to "avoid the conviction that anything else was required" of him (p. 16). Miller writes that finally, in 1833, fifteen years after his first inspiration, he heard a voice say, "Go and tell it to the world" (p. 17), and as a result, he made a solemn covenant with God to speak publicly in any place if he should receive an invitation. He records that in less than a half hour, he received an invitation to preach in a neighboring church. On the first Sunday in August 1833, Miller delivered his first lecture on the Second Advent, and soon the churches of Congregationalists, Baptists, and Methodists throughout New York, Vermont, and parts of Canada were open to him.

In the central part of his narrative, Miller describes his public ministry, which began with a series of lectures in small rural churches and grew after he published his views in pamphlet form until he was giving more than one hundred lectures a year and had at least eight Baptist elders using his calculations. Miller records that the transformation of his ministry occurred in 1840 with his association with Brother J. V. Himes, pastor of the Second Christian Church in Boston, who established two periodicals—*The Sign of the Times* and *The Midnight Cry*—to spread Miller's views. In addition, Himes convinced Miller to preach to urban audiences as well as rural ones. As a result, Miller's message became known throughout the country.

In the final sections of his autobiography, Miller comes to grips with the fact that the last day did not come in April 1843. In describing prophetic time, he writes: "I had never been positive as to any particular day for the Lord's appearing, believing that no man could know the day and the hour. In all my published lectures, it will be seen on the title page 'about the year 1843' " (p. 24). He admits to predicting that the Lord would come sometime between March 21, 1843, and March 21, 1844, and admits to disappointment over the passing of his "published time." Still, he asserts that his faith was unchanged in any essential feature of his belief.

Miller also confronts his critics in this part of his *Apology and Defense*. He recalls that during 1843, he and his followers were attacked in the press and also from many pulpits. He remembers that as time passed, "our motives were assailed, our principles were misrepresented, and our characters traduced.... Our disappointment was great; and many walked no more with us" (p. 24). Looking back, he also describes a major error of many of his followers, who began calling their home denominations Babylon and preaching that it was the duty of Adventists to come out of them. Although he defends his doctrine and method, Miller attacks the spirit of sectarianism and bigotry that arose from his teachings.

Miller ends his narrative with a summary of his beliefs, restating the fact that he was living in the end of times, and an exhortation to Christians to read the scriptures, do good, be humble, and be vigilant. The end, he was still preaching, was near.

CRITICISM

William Miller is best known as a historical curiosity. At the height of the religious enthusiasm in late 1842 and early 1843, Miller and the Millerites were the object of derision. After the world did not come to an end and Miller continued to preach his gospel of the Second Advent, he and his followers were seen as deluded fanatics. Even many modern descriptions of Miller and his movement approach the subject with humor, presenting Miller as a country bumpkin who led uneducated rural fundamentalists astray. Miller's movement is part of a serious American phenomenon as well, and such writers as Charles Francis Potter (*Great Religious Leaders*

[New York: Simon & Schuster, 1958]) and Larry Gragg ("The Days of Delusion," *American History Illustrated*, July 1978) point out that Miller's activities were part of a recurring series of revivals in America that began in the seventeenth century and continue to this day.

Miller's emphasis on the Second Advent continues to have influence in the culture as well. The Seventh-Day Adventist Church is a direct descendant of the Millerite movement, and Joseph Smith's Church of Jesus Christ of the Latter-Day Saints is related as well. In addition, interest in end-time theology has grown dramatically in the late 1970s and 1980s. A number of fundamental Protestant denominations have adopted Miller's method and theology, although changing the expected date of the Second Advent. In addition, awareness of such concepts as premillennialism and prophetic time have moved into the secular culture with the publication of such works as Hal Lindsey and C. C. Carlson's *The Late Great Planet Earth*, which is a contemporary popular version of Miller's basic argument. In fact, the idea of the rapture, or Christ's taking up the true believers before the day of doom, is essentially Miller's, and the contemporary interest in the rapture can be seen as part of the continuing series of revivals in America.

BIBLIOGRAPHY

Bliss, Sylvester. *Memoirs of William Miller*. New York: AMS Press, 1972.

Gale, Robert. *Urgent Voice: The Story of William Miller*. Review and Herald Pub. Assn., Independence, Mo.: 1975.

Holbrook, Stewart, H. "The Bridegroom Cameth Not." *American Mercury*, May 1949, 600–606.

Larrabee, Harold A. "The Trumpeter of Doomsday." *American Heritage*, April 1964, 35–37 +.

Lindsey, Hal, and C. C. Carlson. *The Late Great Planet Earth*. Grand Rapids, Mich.: Zondervan, 1976.

Malachy, Y. "Seventh Day Adventists and Zionism." In *Herzl Year Book*, Vol. 6. New York: Herzl Press, 1965, 267–79.

Miller, William. *Evidences from Scripture and History of the Second Coming of Christ, About the Year A.D. 1843, and of His Personal Reign of 1000 Years*. Syracuse, N.Y.: Smith, 1835.

———. *Evidence from Scripture and History of the Second Coming of Christ, About the Year 1843; Exhibited in a Course of Lectures*. Troy, N.Y.: Kemble, Hooper, 1836.

———. *A Familiar Exposition of the Twenty-Fourth Chapter of Matthew, and Fifth and Sixth Chapters of Hosea*. Edited by Joshua V. Himes. Boston: Himes, 1841.

———. *Dissertations on the True Inheritance of the Saints, and the Twelve Hundred and Sixty Days of Daniel and John, with an Address to the Conference of Believers in the Advent Near*. Boston: Himes, 1842.

———. *Evidence from Scripture and History of the Second Coming of Christ, About* the Year 1843; Exhibited in a Course of Lectures. Vol. 2. Edited by Joshua V. Himes. Boston: Himes, 1842.

————. The Kingdom of God. Boston: Himes, 1842.

————. A Lecture on the Typical Sabbaths and the Great Jubilee. Boston: Himes, 1842.

————. Letter to Joshua V. Himes, on the Cleansing of the Sanctuary. Boston: Himes, 1842.

————. Remarks on Revelations Thirteenth, Seventeenth and Eighteenth. Boston: Himes, 1844.

————. Apology and Defense. Boston: Himes, 1845.

————. Correspondence and Notes, 1814–1849. Chicago: University of Chicago Library, 1967. [Microfilm]

Nichol, F. D. "Growth of the Millerite Legend." Church History, 21 (1952): 296–313.

Potter, Charles Francis. Great Religious Leaders. New York: Simon & Schuster, 1958, 415–21.

22 • CARRY NATION (1846–1911)

The Use and Need of the Life of Carry A. Nation

BIOGRAPHY

Carry Amelia Moore Nation was born on November 25, 1846, on a farm in Garrard County, Kentucky. Her father, a relatively prosperous cattle trader until the outbreak of the Civil War, moved his family about Kentucky, Missouri, Texas, and Arkansas. Nation's mother, Mary Moore, related to revivalist Alexander Campbell, had a history of mental and emotional illness, and proved little security for her daughter, who was a semi-invalid during much of her childhood and received little formal education. In November 1867, Nation married Charles Gloyd, a Civil War veteran, physician, teacher, and alcoholic. Her husband abandoned her shortly after she became pregnant, and he died soon after. In 1877, she married David Nation, an attorney, newspaper editor, and minister to a Christian (Disciples of Christ) Church. The family moved from Missouri and attempted to establish a cotton plantation in Texas.

In 1889, after the failure of the cotton venture, the Nations moved to Medicine Lodge, Kansas, where David Nation became pastor of the local Christian Church and Carry Nation began reform work. In 1892, she co-founded a local branch of the Woman's Christian Temperance Union and began to work for prohibition and women's suffrage. In 1899, she moved from opposition to direct action against the sale of liquor and began to have success shutting down "joints." The next summer she escalated her attack and used physical force, including her famous hatchet, in her attempts to close down saloons. In December 1900, Nation destroyed the Hotel Carey bar in Wichita, Kansas, and as a result spent two weeks in jail for the destruction of property. This event also gained her national attention.

In 1901, Nation temporarily gave up "joint-bashing" to go on a lecture circuit to spread her gospel of militant prohibitionism and pay off her jail fines. In 1903, she appeared in the play *Hatchetation* and sold small pewter hatchets inscribed "Carry Nation, Joint Smasher" at her lectures. In the same year, her husband was granted a divorce on the grounds that his wife's constant travels constituted a form of desertion.

In 1904, she published her autobiography, *The Use and Need of the Life of Carry A. Nation,* and moved to the Oklahoma Territory. In 1908, she traveled to England, where she lectured on the evils of liquor, tobacco, and women's fashions. Two years later, she was beaten by a woman owner of a Montana saloon and gave up her hatchet and joint-smashing. She died in Kansas on June 9, 1911.

THE AUTOBIOGRAPHY

The Use and Need of the Life of Carry A. Nation is not a carefully constructed narrative of the life of Carry Nation. It is a hastily written anthology of Nation's memories, ideas, speeches, and poetry put into chronological order. She wrote her autobiography during her lecture tours and sold copies of it to finance her prohibition activities. Although not an elegant book, Nation's autobiography is important because it does express the passions and ideas of one of America's most famous moral crusaders.

Nation begins her autobiography with two chapters—"My Old Kentucky Home and What I Remember of My Life Up to the Tenth Year" and "My Experience with the Negroes as Slaves—Their Superstitions—A Beautiful Fairy Tale"—that establish a golden age, an almost mythical paradise, from which Nation is expelled and for which she searches for the rest of her life. Nation's memories of her childhood are selective; she remembers a ten-room house with white columns, gold-leaf wallpaper, red-plush furniture, and contented slaves who cheerfully sang while they worked in her father's fields and cared for the children of the master. This idealized picture of the prewar South is fantasy but it is a fantasy in which Nation believes; it is her depiction of the way things should be.

Nation had her first conversion experience when she was ten, and she continued to be "marvelously affected" throughout her life. In *The New Birth: A Naturalistic View of Religious Conversion,* Joe Edward Barnhart and Mary Ann Barnhart argue that not only is conversion a relatively common experience, but also that people who undergo strong conversions are likely to experience them in series. Nation includes numerous references to dramatic religious experiences in her autobiography, and they provide both motivation and content for her prohibition actions.

Nation's initial conversion is quite traditional. She describes how she was taken to a protracted church meeting in Jackson County, Missouri, when she was ten, and at the close of the sermon, she began to cry. The next day her father's cousin's wife arranged for her baptism, which left her with "the peace that is past understanding." She then comments that Protestant churches make a grave mistake by not providing new converts with care and instruction, for although she remained a nominal Christian, her enthusiasm quickly died.

In describing her second conversion experience, Nation is more dramatic. Nation calls the fifth chapter of her narrative "The Baptism of the Holy Spirit," and she begins it by writing simply, "In this chapter I will tell of God's leading." This is perhaps the most significant sentence in her autobiography, as it both marks the turning point in her life from wife and mother to activist and gives that transformation divine sanction.

Nation records that while attending a Methodist conference in Richmond, Texas, in 1884, she heard a minister read the sixty-second chapter of Isaiah. She remembers that she felt rapt in ecstasy and felt her heart expand to an enormous size. She decided that "from henceforth all my time, means and efforts should be given to God" (p. 47). Nation recalls that she had not been taught about Pentecost or the gifts of the Holy Spirit at that time, but looking back at her experience she realizes that is what she had experienced. She had been a Sunday school teacher in both of Richmond's churches, one Methodist and one Episcopal, but after her conversion, she refused to accept or teach Methodist or Episcopal theology. Like Pentecostals before and since, Nation felt the direct inspiration of the Holy Spirit and followed where that voice led.

In 1889, David Nation moved his family from Texas to Medicine Lodge, Kansas, to become pastor of a Christian Church. Carry Nation began her reform work there and continued to have religious experiences. She reports that once she was in a heavenly rapture for three days, with the Lord as her constant companion. Later she records what she calls her divine call:

On the 6th of June, before retiring, as I often did, I threw myself face downward at the foot of my bed and told the Lord to use me any way to suppress the dreadful curse of liquor.... I told Him I wished I had a thousand lives, that I would give Him all of them, and wanted Him to make it known to me in some way. The next morning, before I awoke, I heard these words very distinctly: "Go to Kiowa and" (as in a vision and here my hands were lifted and cast down suddenly) "I'll stand by you." (p. 69)

She left for Kiowa, twenty-five miles from her home, and used rocks, bricks, and billiard balls to demolish the saloons she found there.

Before June 6, 1900, Carry Nation had, like other militant members of the Woman's Christian Temperance Union, confronted tavern owners and patrons with prayer, picket lines, and placards. Nation found that nonviolence was not always successful, and with the Lord's word that he would support her and reasoning that because selling liquor was illegal in Kansas, the destruction of private property used for such purposes would not be a crime, Nation took her assault on dives and joints from Kiowa to Wichita, where she destroyed the Hotel Carey bar, was arrested, and served two weeks in jail. In January 1901, she spoke before the state temperance convention in Topeka and was awarded a gold medal inscribed "To the Bravest Woman in Kansas." She also became convinced that she could use her fame to argue for prohibition (as well as pay off her fines), and ceased smashing to give public lectures about her actions and prohibition.

Nation was well aware that her actions were considered outrageous by many people, and both on the lecture circuit and in her autobiography, she addresses that issue. In a chapter titled "Spiritual Authority for My Christian Work," Nation cites chapter and verse concerning famous "smashers" in the Old and New Testaments. On page 125, for instance, she lists thirty-six specific references to "smashings" and then proceeds to demonstrate how those biblical actions can be applied to herself. Deliberately and carefully she depicts herself as a modern type of Old Testament prophet, smashing idols to bring the children of Israel back from the corruption of liquor to innocence and peace.

Although Nation continued to smash joints after 1901, she dedicated most of her time to the suppression of vice through lectures and public appearances. In addition to advocating prohibition, Nation spoke vehemently against the use of tobacco and for women's suffrage. In the final chapters of her autobiography, Nation provides her readers with examples of her enthusiasm for reform. She recounts her arrest in the Senate chamber as she cried out "Treason, anarchy, conspiracy" from the visitors' gallery and demanded that the Senate discuss prohibition. She calls Theodore Roosevelt a "dive-keeper" for his refusal to see her or support her cause, and she attacks both Harvard and Yale for the use of tobacco and liquor by students and faculty.

Nation ends her autobiography with a call to elect a prohibition president. She asserts that both the Democratic and Republican parties, as well as the Anti-Saloon League, are in league with saloon owners, and announces that she has formed a national Prohibition Federation to prohibit the use of alcohol and tobacco. In addition, she writes, members of the federation "want to prohibit the tyranny and unlawfulness in preventing women from a voice in the government, compulsory education, no games on the Lord's Day, no profanity on the highways" (p. 171). After this exhortation, Nation includes a copy of the by-laws of the federation, a "scientific article" on liquor drinking in health and disease and a "scientific testimony" on beer, and twelve poems, including the classic temperance poem, "The Lips That Touch Liquor Must Never Touch Mine."

CRITICISM

Carry Nation's reputation was never beyond reproach, and time has done little to change that. *American Reformers: An H. W. Wilson Biographical Dictionary*, edited by Alden Whitman, notes:

To many respectable citizens of her day, Carry Nation was a dangerous eccentric or a pious fraud. Her resort to physical force, which may be seen as an application of the frontier vigilante tradition to new goals, offended and thrilled a nation that still had pretensions about chivalry. (p. 604)

And Paul Messbarger, in *Notable American Women*, observes:

Carry Nation's carnival tactics publicized the prohibition cause more widely than any previous personality or organization had done. . . . Yet by the 1920s her grim, iron-jawed figure had become, for many Americans, a symbol of prohibition not as reform, but as a bigotry to be overthrown. (p. 611)

Despite the general evaluation that Nation was a radical extremist of the reform movement and the suspicion that some of her religious enthusiasm stemmed from mental instability, she remains an important figure in American culture. First, Carry Nation had become a symbol for an entire social and political movement, and as such deserves study. More important, she articulated a sense of outrage at the exclusion of women from almost all spheres of nineteenth-century American society that many women felt. Finally, her movement from nonviolent opposition in the face of perceived social wrongs to direct physical confrontation provided a model for a number of groups engaged in social action who believed in the righteousness of their causes and felt compelled to act.

BIBLIOGRAPHY

Asbury, Herbert. *Carry Nation*. New York: Alfred A. Knopf, 1929.

Barnhart, Joe Edward, and Mary Ann Barnhart. *The New Birth: A Naturalistic View of Religious Conversion*. Macon, Ga.: Mercer University Press, 1981.

Beals, Carleton. *Cyclone Carry: The Story of Carry Nation*. Radnor, Pa.: Chilton, 1962.

Boyer, D. "Carry Nation and Her Campaigns Against Almost Everything." *Critic*, May 1975, 26–37.

Braniff, E. A. "How I Ran Out on Carry Nation." *Commonweal*, 19 March 1948, 558–60.

Holbrook, Stewart Hall. *Dreamers of the American Dream*. New York: Doubleday, 1957, 94–105.

———. "Bonnet, Book, and Hatchet." *American Heritage*, December 1957, 53–55 +.

Hynd, A. "Hatchet Lady from Medicine Lodge." *Reader's Digest*, April 1948, 123–26.

Johnson, Geraals. *Lunatic Fringe*. Philadelphia: J. B. Lippincott, 1957, 207–21.

"Lady and the Hatchet." *Time*, December 1956, 20+

Messbarger, Paul R. "Carry Nation." *Notable American Women 1607–1950*. Vol. II. Edited by Edward T. James. Cambridge, Mass.: Harvard University Press, Belknap Press, 1973, 609–11.

Nation, Carry. *The Use and Need of the Life of Carry A. Nation*. Revised ed. Topeka, Kans.: F. M. Stevens, 1905.

———. "Carry Nation, Saloon-Wrecker Extraordinary: Personal Memoirs." In *From the Horses Mouth*. Edited by George Mandel. Hartford, Conn.: 1956, 148–65.

Ross, Ishbel. *Charmers and Cranks: Twelve Famous American Women Who Defied Conventions*. New York: Harper & Row, 1965, 173–95.

St. Johns, Adela (Rogers). *Some Are Born Great*. New York: Doubleday, 1974, 29–41.

Taylor, Robert Lewis. *Vessel of Wrath: The Life and Times of Carry Nation*. New York: New American Library, 1966.

Wallace, Irving, et al. *The Intimate Sex Lives of Famous People*. New York: Delacorte, 1961, 545–47.

White, William Allen. "Carry Nation and Kansas." In *Saturday Evening Post Treasury*. New York: Simon & Schuster, 1954, 55–59.

Whitman, Alden, ed. *American Reformers: An H. W. Wilson Biographical Dictionary*. New York: Wilson 1985, 603–5.

23 • Daniel Alexander Payne (1811–1893)

Reflections of Seventy Years

BIOGRAPHY

Daniel Alexander Payne was born of free black parents in Charleston, South Carolina, on February 24, 1811. His parents were active members of the Methodist Episcopal Church, and they provided Payne with a solid education and formal religious training early in his life. By the time Payne was nine, both his parents had died, and he was raised by his grandaunt, who also believed in the importance of education and sent him to the Minor's Moralist Society School. In 1823, Payne began to study under a private tutor, Thomas Bonneau, a well-educated black native of Charleston. Payne soon became acquainted with the educational theories of the Reverend John Brown, Scottish author of the *Self-Interpreting Bible*, who advocated self-education. Payne began a program to teach himself astronomy, botany, chemistry, geography, and natural history.

Payne had always been religious, but in 1829, when he was eighteen, he underwent a conversion. While attending the Cumberland Street Church in Charleston, he felt the presence of God and heard a voice saying that he had been chosen to be an "educator of his people." He soon opened a school for blacks in Charleston.

In 1835, education for blacks was outlawed in South Carolina by the General Assembly because the members believed that education encouraged notions of equality and insurrection. As a result, Payne left South Carolina.

Following the advice of John Bachman, a white Lutheran friend in Charleston, Payne enrolled in the Lutheran Seminary at Gettysburg, Pennsylvania, after being assured that he would not have to accept Lutheran doctrine or the then-popular idea of colonization, or returning all freed slaves to Africa. In 1837, he left the seminary without a degree because of an eye strain, but on hearing a voice again, he joined the Lutheran Church and was ordained in 1839.

In 1841, Payne was convinced by Bishop Morris Brown to join the African Methodist Episcopal (A.M.E.) Church. In 1843, he wrote five "Epistles on the Education of the Ministry," in which he argued for an educated ministry. The response was an immediate attack by many of the clergy, some of whom were uneducated ex-slaves. In 1847, Payne married Julia Farris, who died while giving birth to their daughter. The next year his daughter died, and Payne was named historian of the A.M.E. Church.

In 1852, Payne was named bishop of the A.M.E. Church and began a series of pastoral visits throughout the United States and Canada. In 1863, he was instrumental in the purchase of Wilberforce College in Columbus, Ohio, for the church. During the ensuing years, he continued to argue for the education of the black ministry and visit A.M.E. churches. In 1881, he presided, as the first black, over the Methodist Ecumenical Conference in London, and in 1893, he was a delegate to the World Parliament of Religions, held in Chicago. He died in the same year.

THE AUTOBIOGRAPHY

Daniel Alexander Payne's life coincided with the period of the most dramatic changes in the political, social, and religious status of blacks in America. In 1811, when Payne was born, slavery was a well-established institution in half the nation, free blacks were in danger of being kidnapped and sold into slavery, and in many places, it was illegal for blacks to be educated or own property. By 1893, the year Payne died, slavery had been abolished, the Civil War fought, and civil rights granted to blacks; a number of black Americans also had earned national and international reputations.

Almost all conversion narratives conform, to some degree, to a three-part pattern: preconversion life, the conversion experience, and life and acts of the awakened convert. Individual autobiographers emphasize different aspects of their lives. In his *Life and Times*, Frederick Douglass stresses his life before conversion as he emphasizes the horrors of growing up in slavery, and Jonathan Edwards' famous *Personal Narrative* is an examination and recollection of the conversion process itself. Payne, while including depictions of his early life and conversion in *Recollections of Seventy Years*, emphasizes his life after his conversion as he records his personal and spiritual growth and the growth of the A.M.E. Church.

Payne begins his narrative by describing his ancestry, a traditional nineteenth-century autobiographical convention. He writes that his father's parents fought against the British during the Revolution, and that his father, who was a free black, was kidnapped as a child and sold into slavery in Charleston, where he lived as a slave until he earned enough money to purchase his freedom. The attention to family also is a significant element in black autobiography. Frederick Douglass notes, for example, that he barely knew his mother and that his father was rumored to be a white man. Because the institution of slavery constantly threatened the black family, many black autobiographers often devoted significant attention to family in their writing.

Payne believed that education and religion were the two avenues available to blacks to improve their condition in America, and in the early sections of his autobiography, he describes his enthusiasm for both. His parents and grandaunt insisted on his education, and Payne recalls that at an early age he was teaching himself both languages and sciences. He also was a member of the Methodist Episcopal Church. In presenting his conversion, Payne describes how these two interests came together in his life. When Payne was eighteen, he took part in a series of revival meetings at the Cumberland Street Church. He remembers that God "poured out his awakening and converting power upon his wanting children, and many souls were converted and sanctified by it" (p. 17). Payne was one of them. He continues to describe his conversion:

Several weeks after this event, between twelve and one o'clock one day, I was in my humble chamber, pouring out my prayers into the listening ears of the savior, when I felt as if the hands of a man were pressing into my shoulders and a voice speaking within my soul saying: "I HAVE SET THEE APART TO EDUCATE THYSELF IN ORDER THAT THOU MAYEST BE AN EDUCATOR TO THY PEOPLE." The impression was IRRESISTIBLE and DIVINE; it gave a new direction to my thoughts and efforts. (p. 17)

This conversion, a literal change in direction and perception, determined the rest of Payne's life, and in the rest of his autobiography, Payne records his work as "an educator to his people."

In the chapters that follow this description of conversion, Payne outlines his educational activities in Charleston. He records a conversation he had with a slave owner who told him that the only difference between a slave and a master was "superior knowledge." This insight helped him to continue his efforts as a private teacher to blacks in Charleston until, as a result of the South Carolina General Assembly's decision to close all black schools in the state, he was forced to leave.

After leaving Charleston, Payne traveled to New York, where he met Charles Ray, a black Congregational minister involved in city missions and the abolition movement. Ray and other influential New York blacks convinced Payne that a career in the church was the most effective way for him to assist in advancing the black cause. Payne enrolled in the Lutheran Seminary at Gettysburg, Pennsylvania, and began serious study for the ministry. While he was studying, he continued teaching, offering classes to free black women and children from the neighboring communities. Both his study and teaching were interrupted by a strained optic nerve in his left eye, which left him in pain and unable to read. Payne recalls that this was one of the worst moments of his life. Unable to read, he wondered what he would do with his life. He recalls that in this depression, he suddenly "felt a pressure from on high that constrained me to say with the Apostle Paul: "Woe is me if I preach not the Gospel" (p. 62). Shortly after, Payne discovered that darkened glasses relieved his eye strain, and he agreed to be ordained a Lutheran minister.

In 1840, Payne opened a school for blacks in Philadelphia, and while there, he came into contact with the leading members of the city's black community, most of whom were members of the Bethel A.M.E. Church. Payne realized that the A.M.E. Church was the most influential black denomination in the country; he soon joined it, and in 1843, he was called to be an itinerant minister of the church.

The A.M.E. Church was established by blacks in Philadelphia in 1816 after black members had been expelled from white congregations. The A.M.E. Church adopted the doctrines of the Methodist Episcopal Church and grew rapidly during the first half of the nineteenth century. The church drew many of its clergymen from the ranks of ex-slaves, and many of the ministers were uneducated or poorly educated. In 1843, Payne, in a series of five epistles, called for the establishment of an educated ministry. In his autobiography, Payne recalls that even though he wrote the epistles for the benefit of the church, he immediately was criticized. His writing was called "infidelity in its rankest form"; he was called a "devil" and charged with "branding the ministry with infamy" (p. 76). Payne records with satisfaction his vindication. He writes that soon after the debate over his proposals, he was named chairman of the church's Committee on Education, which was established to plan for the education of future ministers.

In 1852, Payne was elected the sixth bishop of the A.M.E. Church. For the next decade, he traveled throughout the country visiting A.M.E. churches and working for the education and social improvement of black Americans. Much of the material in the central chapters of his autobiography describes Payne's travels as a missionary bishop.

By the outbreak of the Civil War, Payne had established himself as one of the most influential black men in the United States. He continued his missionary work throughout the North during the war, and he met with Frederick Douglass and President Lincoln. Like Douglass, Payne argued with the president for the abolition of slavery. During 1862, the North had achieved some success on the battlefield and had met with some defeats. Slavery had not yet been abolished. Bishop Payne, looking at the state of the country in that year, wrote in his autobiography:

But the most extraordinary thing of all, and that which forms the greatest anomaly, is the circumstances that the South was earnestly invoking God against the North, the North invoking God against the South, and the blacks invoking God against both! (p. 145)

Payne recalls that this attitude changed dramatically after the Emancipation Proclamation was signed by Lincoln.

In 1865, Payne was named president of Wilberforce College in Columbus, Ohio. At last he was able to engage in the education and training of black leaders. In addition, he had the opportunity to travel to Europe to raise funds and support for the church and the college. For the rest of his life, as president of Wilberforce College and bishop of the A.M.E. Church, Payne devoted himself to the education and inspiration of black Americans.

Payne's dedication to the education and improvement of black church members brought him into a second controversy with many of the rank-and-file church members. In 1878, Payne began to introduce responsive scripture reading into Sunday services, believing that

the colored race, who had been oppressed for centuries through ignorance and superstition, might become intelligent, Christian and powerful through the enlightenment and sanctifying influences of the word of God. (p. 253)

Payne's conception of a proper service was properly Victorian; it should be rational and ordered. Throughout the A.M.E. Church, however, other forms of worship were popular. In his narrative, Payne describes visiting a "bush meeting" on one of his missionary tours.

After the sermon they formed a ring, and with coats off sung, clapped their hands, and stamped their feet in a most ridiculous and heathenish way.... They stopped their dancing and clapping of hands, but remained singing and rocking their bodies to and fro.... I then went, and taking their leader by the arm requested him to desist and sit down and sing in a rational manner. I told him also that it was a heathenish way to worship and disgraceful to themselves, the race, and the Christian name. (pp. 253–54)

This tension between reason and emotion, scripture and inspiration, has been part of Protestantism since Calvin and Luther. In this passage, Payne, "the educator to his people" and apostle of education, comes down firmly on the side of reason and order. Again there was a controversy within the church, and again Payne prevailed.

In the final pages of his autobiography, Payne completes the description of his own efforts on behalf of the church and the black community in the United States and turns to a history of the A.M.E. Church during the last half of the nineteenth century. He records with pride the increased education of church leaders and calls for young blacks to become educated for their own good and to serve as leaders of the church.

CRITICISM

Most of the criticism available about Bishop Daniel Payne is biographical. Short reference pieces appear in such works as Adams' *Great Negroes, Past and Present*; Simmons' *Men of Mark: Eminent, Progressive, and Rising*; and Young's *Major Black Religious Leaders*. A major work that treats Payne in the context of religion and education is Paul R. Griffin's *Black Theology as the Foundation of Three Methodist Colleges: The Educational Views and Labors of Daniel Payne, Joseph Price, and Isaac Lane*.

Recollections of Seventy Years is an important autobiography. In telling the story of his life, Daniel Payne chronicles not only the work of one man, but also the development of the black church during the nineteenth century. In addition, he describes the important roles that education and religion had in the black community before and after emancipation. Finally, in describing his own career from private teacher in Charleston to president of Wilberforce College, Payne demonstrates the potential political and social impact of both education and religion.

BIBLIOGRAPHY

Adams, Russell L. *Great Negroes, Past and Present*. Chicago: Afro-American, 1963.

Griffin, Paul R. *Black Theology as the Foundation of Three Methodist Colleges: The Educational Views and Labors of Daniel Payne, Joseph Price, and Isaac Lane*. Lanham, Md.: University Press of America, 1984.

Killian, C. "Daniel A. Payne and the A.M.E. General Conference of 1888: A Display of Contrasts." *Negro History Bulletin*, 32 (1969): 11–14.

———. "Wilberforce University: The Reality of Bishop Payne's Dream." *Negro History Bulletin*, 34 (1971): 83–87.

Payne, Daniel Alexander. *Recollections of Seventy Years*. 1888. Reprint. New York: Arno, 1968.

Redding, Jay Saunders. *Lonesome Road*. New York: Doubleday, 1958.

Simmons, William J. *Men of Mark: Eminent, Progressive, and Rising*. New York: Arno, 1968.

Strange, D. C. "Note on Daniel Payne." *Negro History Bulletin*, 28 (1964): 9–10.

Thorpe, Earl E. *Black Historians*. New York: Morrow, 1971.

Toppin, Edgar A. *Biographical History of Blacks in America Since 1528*. New York: McKay, 1971.

Young, Henry J. *Major Black Religious Leaders: 1755–1940*. Nashville: Abingdon, 1977.

24 • PAT ROBERTSON (1930–)

Shout It from the Housetops

BIOGRAPHY

Marion Gordon Robertson was born in Lexington, Virginia, on March 22, 1930. Both of Robertson's grandparents were Baptist preachers, and his father, Absalom Willis Robertson, represented Virginia in the United States Congress, first in the House of Representatives and later in the Senate, for thirty-four years. The *Current Biography Yearbook* describes Senator Robertson as a "Democrat of the old-school South, ready with a Biblical quotation for almost all occasions . . . one of the fiercest and most eloquent conservatives in the Southern caucus." Robertson's mother, Gladys Churchill Willis, was an enthusiastic religious woman, who, after a born-again experience, urged her son to give his life to Jesus Christ.

Robertson, nicknamed Pat by his older brother, received an education befitting the son of a United States Senator. He attended the McCallis School in Chattanooga, Tennessee, earned his undergraduate degree from Washington and Lee University, and studied law at the University of London and at Yale. In addition, Robertson served in the Marine Corps from 1950 to 1952, earning the rank of lieutenant. Robertson married Adelia Elmer in 1954, graduated from Yale in 1955, and settled in Staten Island, New York, after failing to pass the New York bar examination.

Robertson's mother prayed for her son and arranged a meeting for him with Cornelius Vanderbreggen, a Baptist missionary. After the meeting, Robertson underwent a profound religious experience in which he received the gifts of the Holy Spirit, including the powers of healing through faith, speaking in tongues, and discernment of God's will. Robertson then attended New York Theological Seminary, graduating in 1959. He was ordained a Southern Baptist clergyman two years later and moved to Portsmouth, Virginia, to purchase a small television station for the purpose of establishing a Christian television ministry.

In 1960, Robertson established the Christian Broadcasting Network (CBN), and in 1961, the first television stations went on the air. In 1963, he appealed for 700 viewers to pledge ten dollars a month, and in the process, established "The 700 Club," one of the most successful productions in religious television. In 1977, Robertson established CBN University, an accredited institution with five graduate schools in such areas as religion, journalism, and law.

Robertson began actively to engage in politics in 1981, when he cofounded the Freedom Council, a tax-exempt foundation with regional chapters, whose primary purpose was to recruit evangelical Christians for conservative political action. As an outgrowth of this activity and support for President Ronald Reagan, Robertson became involved in Republican party politics, declaring on October 1, 1987, his formal candidacy for president. He ran a relatively strong campaign in party caucuses but faired poorly in Republican primaries. After withdrawing from the presidential race, Robertson returned to his positions at CBN and "The 700 Club," from which he withdrew when he was running for office. Pat Robertson remains one of the more visible members of the evangelical right and an influential televangelist.

THE AUTOBIOGRAPHY

Shout It from the Housetops was published in 1972, before Pat Robertson became a national figure or began to take part in politics. As a result, Robertson's autobiography does not chronicle the rise of the religious right as a political force in the United States or the development of personality cults surrounding a number of prominent televangelists. What Robertson does present is a contemporary version of a traditional conversion narrative in which a person changes the direction of his life as a result of a dramatic religious experience. Robertson's autobiography is of special interest because Robertson is one of the best-known Pentecostals in the United States, and his personal narrative provides readers with both a history of the development of Christian television and an example of a Pentecostal narrative. Although the general structure of *Shout It from the Housetops* will be familiar to many readers, Robertson's use of such Pentecostal tropes as demon possession, miracle healing, and speaking in tongues may be unfamiliar.

In describing his life, Pat Robertson uses the three-part narrative structure found in many conversion narratives: life of sin before conversion, the conversion itself, life of grace after the conversion. This basic organizational pattern provides a framework for many religious autobiographers and permits them to emphasize different elements of their lives by manipulating the pattern. Because one of Robertson's intentions is to demonstrate the impact of the Holy Spirit on his life, he stresses his life after his saving experience. As a result, *Shout It from the Housetops* is as much a chronicle of Robertson's works as it is a narrative of conversion.

In his introductory chapter, "Something's Missing," Robertson provides a brief picture of his life before conversion. Living in a chauffeur's cottage on an estate overlooking New York harbor seemed to Robertson "the perfect place for us to live if we were to build our image as sophisticated New York swingers who were rapidly climbing the success ladder" (p. 13). Despite his apparent success, Robertson recalls that his life was empty, and in response to that emptiness, he turned to religion, telling his mother, who had been urging him to turn to God for years, that he was going to enter the ministry. Rather than encouraging her son, Robertson's mother told him that he did not know what he was doing: "How can you go into the ministry until you *know* Jesus Christ?" (p. 18).

Robertson describes how he came to know Jesus Christ in his second chapter, "From Swinger to Saint." Cornelius Vanderbreggen, an evangelical minister and head of the Reaper's Fellowship in Holland and the Miracle Manor in Philadelphia, invited Robertson to dinner, and during the dinner, Robertson experienced his religious awakening. Robertson describes how he had been talking with Vanderbraggen about God in general terms until Vanderbraggen pushed him for a personal response. Robertson then recalls:

Suddenly I was oblivious to the surroundings. "Yes, there is something else. I believe Jesus Christ died for the sins of the whole world." I hesitated. I knew what he wanted, but I had never been able to say it before. Now, to my amazement, I heard myself continue, "...and for my sins, too."

As soon as I had said that, I looked up at my host. A slight smile was playing over his tanned face. A Bible verse I had learned flooded my consciousness. "If thou shalt confess with *thy* mouth the Lord Jesus...thou shalt be saved." (p. 23)

Robertson then draws an important distinction. He observes that before this outward confession of faith, all his experiences were religious rather than spiritual, and only by accepting Jesus as his personal savior was he able to move beyond religion into spirituality. This is a crucial theological point for Pentecostal and evangelical Christians, and Robertson emphasizes it by making it the key element of his conversion and the driving force of the rest of his narrative. For Pentecostal and evangelical Christians (the terms often are used synonymously, although there are important distinctions), adherence to a creed or membership in a church is not true Christianity. Rather, a personal relationship with Jesus Christ followed by an indwelling of gifts of the Holy Spirit are the marks of the true Christian. Without the personal experience, without the evidence of gifts, there is no conversion. Having made his personal confession of faith and having come to know Jesus, Robertson is about to be introduced to the power of the Holy Spirit, and the next chapters of his narrative chronicle this baptism in faith.

Perhaps the most effective sections of *Shout It from the Housetops* are those chapters that present Robertson's introduction to the evangelical community during the late 1950s. Robertson is well aware of the tension he had created in his family with his conversion, and as he describes his growing involvement with the evangelical community in and around New York, he contrasts his enthusiasm with the concerns of his wife, Dede, who, although supportive, was not yet a born-again Christian. Two examples illustrate the Robertson family struggle. First, shortly after his conversion, Robertson left his pregnant wife and son for a month-long retreat at Campus in the Woods, a summer camp in Canada. The day he arrived he received a letter from his wife asking him to return. Wondering whether God or Satan was telling him to go home, Robertson prayed and opened his Bible and found I Corinthians 7:32: "But I would have you without carefulness. He that is unmarried careth for the things that belong to the Lord, how he may please the Lord: But he that is married careth for the things of the world, how he may please his wife." He stayed. The second incident occurred just before Robertson's move to Virginia. Asking the Lord what he should do with his life, he heard a voice in his mind say "Luke 12:33": "Sell that ye have, and give alms; provide yourselves bags which wax not old, a treasure in the heavens that faileth not, where no thief approacheth, neither moth corrupteth." While his wife was in Columbus, Ohio, Robertson sold all his furniture and gave all his money away. When she returned, she was less than pleased with Robertson's enthusiasm.

Robertson's primary narrative thrust is not, however, on family, but rather on his own developing awareness of his place in the evangelical movement. In chapters with such titles as "A Quest for Power," "Drunk on New Wine," "Insight into a Miracle," and "Consulting the Oracles of God," Robertson describes how he first discovers and then experiences such Pentecostal phenomena as speaking in tongues, healing by faith, and prophesying. Although students of contemporary American Christianity are familiar with the signs of the evangelical/Pentecostal movement, fewer readers were in 1972, and fewer still in the late 1950s, when Robertson was undergoing these experiences. Robertson portrays himself as being led by the Lord throughout, first to the New York Theological Seminary, then to work in Brooklyn's Bedford-Stuyvesant ghetto, and finally to Portsmouth, Virginia, and his fateful purchase of a television station.

It is in these chapters that Robertson begins to establish a rhetorical stance that he uses throughout the rest of his autobiography. At first sparingly, but then more consistently, as he describes his struggles to develop his television ministry, Robertson sets the Lord and Satan in direct opposition; he depicts himself and his supporters advised by the Lord and those who oppose his plans tricked by Satan or, on some occasions, possessed by demons. Thus as Robertson describes how he established CBN, he sets himself and his work at the center of the eternal struggle for the soul of mankind.

Robertson begins his account of his television ministry with a terse statement of the spiritual state of the Tidewater area of Virginia.

For years it had been in the grip of demon power.... Satanic vibrations, which traverse space and time, are the communication channels to which sensitives and mediums must attune themselves, and Virginia Beach was renowned as the prime receiving station of the Universal Transmitter (Satan). (p. 104)

Faced with this opposition, Robertson writes that he received "prophetic longings" from God to buy a run-down UHF television station and an affiliated FM radio station and that God told him to pay $37,000 for them. In a chapter called "The Bank of Virginia vs. The Bank of Heaven," Robertson describes how the Lord miraculously provided the money for both the station and his own salary.

When Robertson describes the growth of his ministry and his television network, he not only uses the word "miracle" continually, but he also presents God as an active agent in day-to-day decisions; God told him what funds will be necessary and where to raise them, and the Holy Spirit was in charge of programming. In describing the establishment of the original 700 Club, an appeal for 700 persons to pledge ten dollars a month to CBN, Robertson writes that God gave him immediate answers to business questions and that Satan was attempting to infiltrate his organization. At every crisis in the development of the ministry, Robertson is attacked by Satan but preserved by the Lord.

In the final chapters of the narrative, Robertson presents CBN at the crossroads. Part of his organization wanted the network to become more professional in both programming and fund-raising, whereas others wanted to remain close to CBN's spiritual beginnings. Robertson, tempted by offers of support that turned out to be fraudulent, at first leaned toward professionalism but then opted for spirituality, saying to his staff: "The entire operation could go down the tubes tomorrow should the Lord choose to remove his grace. But now I'm beginning to believe that this is the way God intends it—all of us leaning on Jesus (p. 253). The ending of *Shout It from the Housetops* is somewhat ironic, given the direction of Robertson's television network and political career since the publication of the autobiography.

CRITICISM

Before the rise of the evangelical right, Pat Robertson received little critical attention in the secular press. As fundamentalist Christians began to become politically active in large numbers, Robertson and such other television ministers with political agendas as Jerry Falwell and James Robison became the targets of media scrutiny, and when Robertson became a candidate for the Republican nomination for president, many popular journals devoted a good deal of space to cover his candidacy. In addition, in the wake of the scandals involving televangelists Jimmy Swaggart and Jim Bakker, all television ministers were carefully examined by the press.

As would be expected, most of what has been written about Robertson are his political activities. Not only did the press find it unusual for an ordained minister to be a presidential candidate, since Robertson was a public figure because of his television ministry, but the press also was able to depict him as the representative figure for the evangelical political movement. This depiction was simplistic, as both Robertson and political evangelicals are more complex than the stereotypes that often appear. Nevertheless, candidate Robertson often was seen as a contemporary Elmer Gantry, leading public crusades for morality and attempting to lead the religious right to the promised land of electoral success.

Also mentioned with frequency are Robertson's success in television and Pentecostal beliefs. Typical is part of a short biographical entry in *Prime Time Preachers: The Rising Power of Television*, one of the better examinations of televangelism. The authors, Jeffrey Hadden and Charles Swann, introduced Robertson as

an evangelical preacher of the first rank, a faith healer, a speaker in tongues, and a hearer of direct revelation which he calls "Words of Knowledge" from God.

Robertson is the host of "The 700 Club" . . . he is president and chief executive officer of the Christian Broadcasting Network. (p. 35)

In addition to providing revelations about Pat Robertson's conversion and early television history, *Shout It from the Housetops* does suggest reasons for Robertson's success. Robertson's combination of evangelical Christianity and conservative politics appears to be a synthesis of the concerns of his political father and pious mother. His adaptation of evangelical Christianity and conservative politics to television is his own.

BIBLIOGRAPHY

Alter, J. "Pat Robertson: The Telepolitician." *Newsweek*, 22 February 1988, 18–19.
Anderson, D. E. "The Robertson Candidacy." *Christianity and Crisis*, 17 November 1986, 406–8.

Barlow, J. S. "Political Immersion." *Commonweal*, 11 July 1986, 392–94.

Donovan, John B. *Pat Robertson: The Authorized Biography*. New York: Macmillan, 1988.

"Eyes on Seventh Heaven." *The Economist*, 20 February 1988, 24–25.

"First Shall Be Last?" *The Economist*, 23 January 1988, 20.

Frost, D. "The Gospel According to Robertson." *US News & World Report*, 22 February 1988, 21–22.

Green, J. C., and J. L. Guth. "The Christian Right and the Republican Party: The Case of Pat Robertson's Supporters." *Journal of Politics*, 50 (1988): 150–65.

Hadden, Jeffrey, and Charles Swann. *Prime Time Preachers: The Rising Power of Televangelism*. Reading, Mass.: Addison-Wesley, 1981.

Harrell, David Edwin. *Pat Robertson: A Personal, Religious, and Political Portrait*. San Francisco: Harper & Row, 1987.

Hertzberg, H. "Robertson's Oedipus Complex." *The New Republic*, 28 March 1988, 15–19.

Moritz, Charles, ed. *Current Biography Yearbook, 1987*. New York: Wilson, 1987.

"Republican King-Makers? Evangelicals." *The Economist*, 5 December 1987, 28–29.

Robertson, Pat. *Shout It from the Housetops*. South Plainfield, N.J.: Bridge, 1972.

———. *My Prayer for You*. Old Tappan, N.J.: Fleming H. Revell, 1977.

———. *The Secret Kingdom*. Nashville: Thomas Nelson, 1982.

———. *Beyond Reason*. New York: William Morrow, 1984.

———. *Answer to 200 of Life's Most Probing Questions*. Virginia Beach, Va.: CBN University Press, 1985.

———*America's Date with Destiny*. Nashville: Thomas Nelson, 1986.

Straub, Gerard Thomas. *Salvation for Sale: An Insider's View of Pat Robertson's Ministry*. Buffalo: Prometheus Books, 1986.

Wroe, M. "God's Own Candidate." *New Statesman*, 19 February 1988, 22–23.

25 • MARY ROWLANDSON (C. 1635–1678 OR 1711)

The Soveraignty and Goodness of God, Together with the Faithfulness of His Promises Displayed; Being a Narrative of the Captivity and Restauration of Mrs. Mary Rowlandson

BIOGRAPHY

Mary White Rowlandson was born in England in or about 1635. Her parents, John and Joan White, emigrated to the Massachusetts Bay colony and settled in the frontier village of Lancaster. In 1656, she married the Reverend Joseph Rowlandson, the Puritan pastor of the Lancaster church. On February 10, 1676, a war party of Wampanoag Indians attacked Lancaster and after destroying the village and killing many of the villagers took Rowlandson, her three children, and twenty others captive. Rowlandson was ransomed and returned three months later. During her captivity, she was separated from her two oldest children and watched her youngest daughter, Sarah, who was wounded in the initial attack, die. In 1677, Joseph Rowlandson became pastor of the church in Wethersfield, Connecticut, and died there the next year. In 1678, the town of Wethersfield voted Mary Rowlandson a pension for "so long as she remained a widow among (them)." Most scholars cite 1678 as the year of her death, but David Greene, in "New Light on Mary Rowlandson" (*Early American Literature*, 20, 1 [1985]: 24–37), states that Rowlandson married Samuel Talcott in 1679 and lived in Wethersfield until 1711.

Rowlandson wrote a narrative of her captivity, *The Soveraignty and Goodness of God* (also known as *The Narrative of the Captivity and Restauration of Mrs. Mary Rowlandson*). Her narrative was the first published captivity narrative and is recognized by most scholars as the best. First published in 1682, the story of her captivity has appeared in more than thirty editions.

THE AUTOBIOGRAPHY

In his excellent study of American writing, *Regeneration Through Violence: The Mythology of the American Frontier*, 1600–1860, Richard Slotkin calls Rowlandson's autobiography "an archetype—that is, the initiator of a genre of narrative within American culture, the primary model of which all subsequent captivities are diminished copies, or types" (p. 102). The narrative of captivity is closely related to the narrative of conversion, and in composing her account of her captivity and restoration, and setting it within the ideological frame of reference of Christian experience, Rowlandson established a model not only for other writers of captivities, but also for all writers of religious experience in America.

Shortly after her return from captivity, Mary Rowlandson wrote her narrative, dedicating it to her children, who also had been captured, so that they could understand the spiritual significance she gained from her experience. Rowlandson, like many of the Puritan settlers living in New England, believed that the Indians often were instruments of God (sometimes, however, under the direction of the devil) and that God used them to test or punish his people. As Rowlandson describes the attack on Lancaster and her subsequent journey into the wilderness, she designs a moral narrative based on Hebrews 12:6: "For whom the Lord loveth he chasteneth, and scourgeth every son whom he receiveth."

Rowlandson begins her narrative with a flat declaration: "On the tenth of February, 1675, came the Indians in great numbers upon Lancaster" (p. 3). She then describes the attack, the killing and capture of the villagers, and the burning of the village. In her re-creation of the traumatic event, Rowlandson focuses on the disintegration of the community—families literally torn apart—and the resulting isolation of the survivors. She also begins to establish one of the basic structural patterns of her narrative, description and reflection, as she pauses while describing Indian bullets rattling against her house to observe, "The Lord hereby would make us the more to acknowledge his hand, and to see that our help is always in him" (p. 5). At the end of the first section of the narrative, Rowlandson observes that the Lord preserved twenty-four villagers from death. This preservation leads Rowlandson to comment on her narrative, and she writes that to "better declare what happened," she will organize her experience around "several Removes we had up and down the wilderness" (p. 9).

In describing the twenty removes that make up the rest of her narrative, Rowlandson is able to draw on scripture for both support and parallels of her own experience. Puritan theology had given her a way of looking at her experience as prefigured by Old and New Testament narratives. The

Puritans used this form of identification, or typology, to equate their own leaving of England for America with the Israelite's journey from Egypt to the Promised Land, for example. For Rowlandson, Exodus, with the narrative of the journey through the wilderness; Isaiah, with the narrative of Israel in exile and captive in Babylon; and Job, with the narrative of endurance under suffering, provide both comfort during her captivity and literary and theological parallels for the construction of her narrative.

Rowlandson's reconstruction of her ordeal demonstrates the Puritan habit of drawing moral lessons from experience. Through her captivity, she looks back on her earlier life to see where she has failed, and in a famous passage, she isolates one of her sins:

The next day was the Sabbath. I then remembered how careless I had been of God's holy time; how many Sabbaths I had lost and misspent, and how evilly I had walked in God's sight; which lay so close upon my spirit, that it was easy for me to see how righteous it was with God to cut off the thread of my life and cast me out of his presence forever. Yet the Lord still showed mercy to me, and upheld me; and as he wounded me with one hand, so he healed me with the other. (p. 14)

Although most modern readers would find the destruction of the village of Lancaster and captivity by Indians an extreme punishment for misspent sabbaths, Rowlandson is writing from within a Calvinistic context of total depravity that not only makes the preceding passage understandable, but also provides the ideological foundation for Jonathan Edwards' famous sermon, "Sinners in the Hands of an Angry God." Rowlandson writes that shortly after the realization of her sinfulness, the Lord showed her great mercy by delivering a Bible to her, and she opened it and discovered Psalm 27:14: "Wait on the Lord: be of good courage, and he shall strengthen thine heart; wait, I say, on the Lord" (p. 20).

Throughout the rest of her narrative, Rowlandson continues to draw instruction from her experiences. When her six-year-old child dies in her arms, the Psalms ease her pain. When she is separated from her remaining children, Jeremiah 31 provides her comfort with the promise of their return. And as she endures starvation, cold, and suffering through the twenty removes of her ordeal, Rowlandson begins to see her captivity as the evidence of divine providence; her captivity is a demonstration of the Lord's love.

As Rowlandson describes her ordeal at the hands of the Indians—cold, hunger, isolation, loss of family, threats of death—she never loses faith, and in fact asserts that this is the very affliction from God that she had yearned for before her captivity. She concludes her narrative by emphasizing this very point: "Affliction I wanted and affliction I had, full measure (I thought) pressed down and running over.... And I hope I can say in some measure, as David did, It is good for me to have been afflicted" (p. 79).

Although *The Sovereignty and Goodness of God* is a classic captivity narrative, it shares a number of features with narratives of conversion. In fact, the popularity of Rowlandson's work and others like it created the captivity narrative, the first popular genre in American literature. In her autobiography, Rowlandson describes her experience in a three-part structure: she is at ease as a member of a community, the community is broken and she finds herself alone and tested, and she eventually returns to her community stronger in her faith. Although she does not undergo a conversion as such, she emerges from her ordeal a much stronger Christian. The confirmation, or regeneration, of her faith is the same as a conversion, and as Richard Slotkin noted, Rowlandson uses the elements of quest and pilgrimage in her narrative and roots them in an actual historical and geographical reality and so makes the captivity experience relevant to the experience of conversion (p. 103). Captivity and conversion are seen as experiences that transform the normal into the extraordinary and test the individual. And many writers since Rowlandson use the metaphor of captivity to define their own ordeal of conversion.

CRITICISM

Mary Rowlandson and her autobiography have received a good deal of attention. Her narrative is considered one of the standard works of colonial American literature and the finest example of the captivity genre. In addition, it was not only the first written, aside from sixteenth-century Spanish accounts, but the first published in North America (*Dictionary of Literary Biography*). Among the many useful studies, David L. Greene's "New Light on Mary Rowlandson" is an excellent biographical examination that suggests that Rowlandson lived much longer than earlier scholars believed and contains a fine bibliography. Richard Slotkin's *Regeneration Through Violence* provides an excellent overview of captivity narratives and Puritan writing as well as insightful comments on Rowlandson and her work. Richard VanDerBeets' *The Indian Captivity Narrative; An American Genre* and Alden Vaughn and Edward Clark's *Puritans Among the Indians* also are useful.

BIBLIOGRAPHY

Dictionary of Literary Biography. Vol. 24: *American Colonial Writers, 1606–1734*. Detroit: Gale, 1984.

Greene, David. "New Light on Mary Rowlandson." *Early American Literature*, 20, (1985): 24–37.

Leach, Douglas. *Flintlock and Tomahawk: New England and King Philip's War*. New York: W. W. Norton, 1958.

Nourse, Henry. "Mrs. Mary Rowlandson's Removes." *Proceedings of the American Antiquarian Society*, 12 (1898): 401–9.

Rowlandson, Mary. *The Soveraignty and Goodness of God*. Boston: Houghton Mifflin, 1930.

Slotkin, Richard. *Regeneration Through Violence: The Mythology of the American Frontier, 1600–1860*. Middletown, Conn.: Wesleyan University Press, 1973.

VanDerBeets, Richard. *Held Captive by Indians: Selected Narratives, 1642–1836*. Knoxville: University of Tennessee Press, 1973.

———. *The Indian Captivity Narrative; An American Genre*. Washington, D.C.: University Press of America, 1983.

Vaughn, Alden, and Edward W. Clark, eds. *Puritans Among the Indians: Accounts of Captivity and Redemption*. Cambridge, Mass.: Harvard University Press, 1981.

26 • THOMAS SHEPARD (1605–1649)

The Autobiography of Thomas Shepard

BIOGRAPHY

Thomas Shepard was born on November 5, 1605, in Northamptonshire, England. His father was apprenticed to a grocer, and his mother was a grocer's daughter. His mother died when he was three, and his father died when Shepard was ten. In 1620, he entered Emmanuel College, Cambridge, where he received his B.A. and M.A. degrees. He was ordained in 1627. Shepard had been influenced by the Puritan movement at Cambridge, and sided with the Nonconformists, who refused to go along with Bishop William Laud's program to establish Anglican uniformity, and was barred from preaching. As a result, Shepard moved about England, primarily preaching in the private houses of Puritans. In 1635, Shepard joined the exodus of Puritans and sailed for New England.

In New England, Shepard became one of the leaders in the Puritan community. He was appointed pastor of the Congregational Church in Newtown (later Cambridge) and served as the unofficial chaplain to Harvard College. Shepard was one of the most influential of the first generation of American Puritans. He was known as an effective preacher, and many of his sermons were published during his lifetime. Shepard defended the Puritan system in New England against criticism in England, preached the election day sermon, and gave instruction to magistrates as well as guiding his congregation. He died at age forty-three, leaving a son who also became a famous Puritan minister.

THE AUTOBIOGRAPHY

In addition to his many published sermons, Thomas Shepard is best known for two works, his *Journal* and *Autobiography*. The *Journal* was first published in 1747 by the Reverend Thomas Prince in *Three Valuable Pieces* and was later reprinted in Scotland. The autobiography was published as *The Autobiography of Thomas Shepard, the Celebrated Minister of Cambridge, New England* by Nehehiah Adams in 1832. In 1972, the University of Massachusetts Press issued an excellent edition of the *Autobiography* and *Journal* titled *God's Plot: The Paradoxes of Puritan Piety*, edited by Michael McGiffert.

Thomas Shepard begins his autobiography with a conventional Puritan dedication:

To my dear son Thomas Shepard with whom I leave these records of God's great kindness to him, not knowing that I shall live to tell them myself with my own mouth, that so he may learn to know and love the great and most high God, the God of his father. (p. 33)

Two elements of the dedication are significant. First, despite Shepard's loss of both parents, death of a son, exile from his homeland and tribulations in a new and strange land, he recalls and records the events of his life from the perspective of "God's great kindness." His suffering is evidence of God's testing, and only in the testing is there triumph. Second, when Shepard writes that his purpose is to enable his son to "know and love the great and most high God," he places his work within the evangelistic tradition. His autobiography is for the edification of others, part of his ministry, in fact. Puritans wrote autobiographies for other reasons, of course. One of the primary purposes was to demonstrate a saving experience, or conversion, for admission to full church membership. Shepard writes as a pastor, and his early chronicle of the work of grace on his soul provides an excellent example of how the first-generation Puritans saw themselves and their errand into the wilderness.

After addressing his son and highlighting the Lord's mercies, Shepard begins the story of his life with his birth, remarking "and that very hour of the day wherein the Parliament should have been blown up by Popish priests, I was born" (p. 37). Shepard follows this reference to the Gunpowder Plot with a brief summary of his youth, noting that his mother died when he was three and his father when he was ten, leaving him an orphan living with his older brother John. These early parts of the narrative establish a pattern of loss and renewal that Shepard develops throughout his autobiography. This pattern carries through all three phases of the narrative: life in England, the voyage to the New World, and service in the colony. Throughout his life, Shepard experienced traumatic losses—parents, children, wife—and yet he constantly saw each loss as a lesson sent from God and managed to recover strengthened.

One of the most significant periods of Shepard's life was his time at Cambridge. In his autobiography, he devotes considerable attention to his years as a student, writing that he spent his first two years in studying but "much neglect of God and private prayer" (p. 40). He also notes that he "fell from God to loose and lewd company, to lust and pride and gaming and bowling and drinking" (pp. 40–41). Shepard writes that at this moment in his life, God sent Dr. John Preston, an influential Puritan preacher, to be master of the college, and under his direction, Shepard began serious prayer and meditation. He recalls that he found himself sinful and unworthy, and even contemplated suicide for a period of three-quarters of a year. This reflects the sense of unworthiness, one of the initial stages in the conversion process. He could find no consolation and thought only of his own damnation, but he observes that on one particular sabbath day evening,

> it came to my mind that I should do as Christ: when he was in agony he prayed earnestly. And so I fell down to prayer, and being in prayer I saw myself so unholy and God so holy that my spirits began to sink, yet the Lord recovered me and poured out a spirit of prayer upon me for free mercy and pity.... And the terrors of the Lord began to assuage sweetly. (pp. 43–44)

Shepard is careful not to isolate this particular moment as his conversion experience; rather, he presents his conversion as a process beginning with his sense of sin and extending long past the one sabbath evening, with periods of doubt and uncertainty alternating with periods of comfort. This ongoing conversion continued throughout his studies at Cambridge, reaching one climax when he felt that the Lord gave him peace and the call to preach.

Shepard writes that after this call, "the course I took in my preaching was (1) to show the people their misery; (2) the remedy, Christ Jesus: (3) how they should walk answerable to this mercy, being redeemed by Christ" (p. 48). His preaching followed standard Puritan practice and was an attempt to help others undergo a process similar to his own. As Shepard chronicles his work as a "nonconformable man," one who would not conform to the standards of the established church as set down by Archbishop Laud, he describes being forced to move about the country, preaching in private for fear of arrest. Like other nonconformists during this period, Shepard faced persecution for his beliefs.

After describing his ministry in England, Shepard gives his reasons for emigration. He lists eight reasons, some personal and some religious. They range from the inability to find peace and comfort for himself and his family in old England to a sense that the Lord was departing from England with the emigration of such notable Puritans as Reverend Hooker and Reverend

Cotton. He concludes his list of reasons with a frank statement of his position:

Though my ends were mixed and I looked much to my own quiet, yet the Lord let me see the glory of those liberties in New England, and made me purpose, if I ever should come over, to live among God's people as one come out from the dead. (p. 56)

The phrase "as one come out from the dead" is significant here, for it indicates the Puritan attitude toward the converted or regenerate. Before the experience of regeneration, there is only death and damnation, and Shepard here explicitly compares the physical voyage to spiritual regeneration.

Perhaps the most dramatic and most famous section of Shepard's narrative is his description of the passage from the old world to the new. As G. Thomas Couser observes in his excellent study *American Autobiography: The Prophetic Mode*, Shepard presents emigration as the equivalent to conversion, and in doing so provided a model for the personal narratives of other Puritans. The conversion experience itself involves fear, recognition of personal insignificance and the power of God, and, finally, a sense of peace, and Shepard describes his winter voyage using the same pattern.

Shepard begins his narrative of the crossing by announcing that "here the Lord's wonderful terror and mercy to us did appear" (p. 57). The terror appeared first. Shortly out of port, Shepard's ship ran into a storm and was forced back at the loss of the ship's mast. Shepard writes that from this wonder, he realized God's power and mercy in threatening the ship and then saving it. After this trial, Shepard soon faced another. Before the ship was ready to sail, his son became ill and died. Shepard writes that this, too, was a lesson from the Lord, teaching him his "weak faith, want of fear, pride, carnal content, immoderate love of creatures and of my child especially" (p. 61). Shepard and his wife buried their son and returned to London, where they hid, had a second son, and finally sailed to New England the next year.

Having at last crossed over, Shepard began his new life in New England facing more trials. These trials are communal rather than personal, however, Shepard describes the attacks of the Pequot Indians and the dissension caused by Anne Hutchinson. These two events provided the most serious trials for the first-generation Puritans, the Pequot attacks providing an external threat to the new community and Anne Hutchinson's antinomianism threatening the internal integrity of the new colony. The autobiography in fact becomes more communal as Shepard writes of his life in New England. The Thomas Shepard of the last part of the autobiography is no longer the outcast of the opening sections or the exile of the crossing; rather, he is a respected member of a religious community who is able to look back on his life and write, "The Lord therefore hath showed his tenderness to me and mine in carrying me to a land of peace" (p. 70).

CRITICISM

Thomas Shepard remains one of the most significant writers of the first generation of American Puritans. As Thomas P. Slaughter observes in the *Dictionary of Literary Biography*:

The lasting significance of Shepard's writing lies in its epitomization of the Puritan quest. He reveals as well as any writer in the Puritan genre the process of sainthood, the balancing of anxiety and self-assuredness of the most introspective saints. (p. 286)

This "epitomization of the Puritan quest" was one of the reasons for Shepard's ministerial success during his lifetime and his reputation after his death. Shepard managed to capture the emotional, intellectual, and religious strands of the first generation of American Puritans and weave them into a dramatic narrative. As Michael McGiffert observes in his introduction to *God's Plot: The Paradoxes of Puritan Piety Being the Autobiography and Journal of Thomas Shepard*:

The *Autobiography* dramatizes what Shepard called "God's great plot of reformation and redemption, making vivid the faith in divine design by which Puritans affirmed their sense of the moral order of existence in an age of revolutionary turmoil, defined their part in the play of God's purpose, and affirmed the cosmic dimension of their existence. (p. 3)

In his lifetime, Shepard succeeded in using the sermon form to order experience for his audiences. The *Autobiography* also is a successful ordering of experience. Short and dramatic, it presents a life that is both real and immediate and representative and communal. As such careful critics of American autobiography as Daniel Shea and G. Thomas Couser have noted, Shepard, in his careful shaping of experience, helps to create the image of the American Puritan that has survived to this day.

BIBLIOGRAPHY

Bercovitch, Sacvan. *The Puritan Origins of the American Self*. New Haven, Conn.: Yale University Press, 1975.

Couser, G. Thomas. *American Autobiography: The Prophetic Mode*. Amherst: University of Massachusetts Press, 1979.

Emerson, Everett H. *Puritanism in America, 1620–1750*. Boston: Twayne, 1977.

Miller, Perry. *The New England Mind: The Seventeenth Century*. New York: Macmillan, 1939.

———. *Errand into the Wilderness*. Cambridge, Mass.: Harvard University Press, 1956.

Moran, Susan Drinker, "Thomas Shepard and the Professor. Two Documents from the Early History of Harvard." *Early American Literature*, 17.1 (1982): 24–42.

Pettit, N. "Grace and Conversion at Cambridge." *New England Quarterly*, 55 (1982): 596–603.

Selement, George. "The Meeting of Elite and Popular Minds at Cambridge, New England, 1638–1645." *William and Mary Quarterly* series, 3:41 (1884): 32–61.

Shea, Daniel. *Spiritual Autobiography in Early America*. Princeton, N.J.: Princeton, University Press, 1968.

Shepard, Thomas. *The Autobiography of Thomas Shepard, the Celebrated Minister of Cambridge, N.E.* . . . Boston: Pierce & Parker, 1832.

———. *The Works of Thomas Shepard, First Pastor of the First Church, Cambridge, Mass.* . . . Boston: Doctrinal Tract and Book Society, 1853.

———. *God's Plot: The Paradoxes of Puritan Piety Being the Autobiography and Journal of Thomas Shepard*. Edited by Michael McGiffert. Amherst: University of Massachusetts Press, 1972.

Slaughter, Thomas P. "Thomas Shepard I." *Dictionary of Literary Biography*. Vol. 24: *American Colonial Writers, 1606–1734*. Edited by Emory Elliott. Detroit: Gale, 1984.

Tipson, Baird. "The Routinized Piety of Thomas Shepard's Diary." *Early American Literature*, 13.1 (1978): 64–80.

27 • PIRI THOMAS (1928–)

Down These Mean Streets

BIOGRAPHY

Piri Thomas is, without a doubt, the best-known Puerto Rican writer in the United States. His work has been reviewed in such mainstream periodicals as *Life*, *Atlantic*, *Newsweek*, *Time*, *Harper's*, and the *New Republic*, and his work in Spanish Harlem is the subject of a film, *Petey and Johnny*. Because of his stature in both the Puerto Rican and the Anglo communities, Thomas is an important figure in the Puerto Rican community in New York and a spokesman for Puerto Rican interests, both social and literary.

Thomas was born in New York City in 1928. He grew up in Spanish Harlem before his parents moved to Long Island during World War II. After less than two years, Thomas returned to Spanish Harlem, where he began to use drugs and commit crimes to support his habit. In 1950, he was convicted of attempted armed robbery of a Greenwich Village bar. He served six years in prison before returning to Spanish Harlem, where he worked in a rehabilitation center for drug addicts and became involved in the Pentecostal movement. Thomas' autobiography, *Down These Mean Streets*, appeared in 1967. He later wrote two additional autobiographical works, *Savior, Savior, Hold My Hand* and *Seven Long Times*. These three works chronicled Thomas' life in Spanish Harlem and prison from the late 1930s to the 1960s. Thomas continues to live and work in New York City.

THE AUTOBIOGRAPHY

Thomas' most famous book is *Down These Mean Streets*, which chronicles his life through his release from prison. *Savior, Savior, Hold My Hand* continues Thomas' life story, but emphasizes his work as a lay Pentecostal missionary in Spanish Harlem. *Seven Long Times* is a straightforward prison narrative, describing the Comstock prison riot of August 1955, that Thomas wrote in response to the Attica prison riots of 1971. Although each book is part of the overlapping narrative of the life of Piri Thomas, *Down These Mean Streets* is the most complete and comprehensive of his three autobiographical works.

Down These Mean Streets is a realistic description of ghetto life, a story of crime and punishment, a captivity narrative, and a conversion story. In it, Piri Thomas exhibits the concerns of many other ethnic-American writers. He dramatizes the problems of class, generational conflict, ethnic rivalry and hostility, poverty, identity, and religion. But for Thomas, the pervasive issue of race influences all the conflicts he faces. He creates an autobiographical self, a dark-skinned Puerto Rican, caught between two worlds, and in his search for identity within a divided culture, he raises serious issues about the multiethnic nature of American society.

Thomas calls the first section of his narrative simply "Harlem," and in it, he creates a vivid picture of the urban environment and begins to develop the conflicts he faces. Thomas depicts his father digging ditches for the Works Progress Administration while he roams the Upper East Side of Manhattan. The conflicts and hostility found in a changing ethnic community are a central part of Thomas' narrative.

Sometimes you don't fit in. Like you're a Puerto Rican on an Italian block. After my new baby brother, Ricardo, died of some kind of germs, Poppa moved us from 111th street to Italian turf on 114th Street between Second and Third avenues. I guess Poppa wanted to get Momma away from the hard memories of the old pad.

I sure missed 111th Street, where everybody acted, walked, and talked like me. But on the 114th Street everything went all right for a while. There were a few dirty looks from the spaghetti-an'-sauce cats, but no big sweat. Till that one day when I was on my way home from school and almost had reached my stoop when someone called: "Hey, you dirty, fuckin' spic." (p. 33)

To survive in the streets, Thomas has to prove that he has "heart" by fighting, and he soon becomes known as a young man with courage.

In 1944, Thomas' father began working in an airplane factory and soon moved his family out of the Barrio to Babylon, Long Island. It is there that Thomas' identity crisis came to a head. Thomas recalls that his family was accepted, but because he was the darkest member of the family, he became an outcast. At school, he was ignored or made the object of racial comments. His white classmates considered him black, and one day he overheard one of them say that he was only passing for Puerto Rican because he was too dark to pass for white.

Thomas discovers that the racism and hostility he encountered in the ghetto are deeply ingrained throughout American society, and that his ability to interact with people is determined not by his actions or character, but by the color of his skin. This lesson is reinforced when he leaves his family to return to the Barrio. There he and a friend apply for jobs as door-to-door salesmen. Thomas is not hired, but his "whiter" friend is. Thomas writes:

I didn't feel so much angry as I did sick, like throwing up sick. Later, when I told this story to my buddy, a colored cat, he said, "Hell, Piri, Ah know stuff like that can burn a cat up, but a Negro faces that all the time."

"I know that," I said, "but I wasn't a Negro then. I was still only Puerto Rican." (p. 107)

After these lessons, Thomas begins to identify with blacks, and to test this new identity, he signs on a merchant ship sailing out of New York. As in the narratives of many newcomers to America, the movement away from the city is depicted by Thomas as a necessary part of coming to terms with the totality of American society. Thomas deliberately depicts his journey as a voyage of discovery. He plans to travel to the South, in his mind the geographic heart of American prejudice, to try to learn the causes of prejudice and understand it better.

Thomas' southern voyage leaves him bitter and angry. On ship and ashore he discovers a pervasive racist system that labels him black and keeps him in the most menial jobs and out of the places he wants to visit. On his return to New York, Thomas becomes a drug addict.

Thomas' description of his drug addiction is one of the most powerful and graphic sections of his autobiography. The inevitable progress from snorting heroin to skin-popping to full-time addiction show Thomas losing both his self-respect and self-control. Dealing drugs to support his growing habit, Thomas eventually ends up without either money or drugs, and strung out and broke, he decides to kick his habit cold turkey. He writes about this experience in cold, bitter terms, emphasizing the pains of withdrawal.

After his recovery, Thomas gets a job washing dishes, but again confronts hostility and prejudice. He turns to crime and learns that this questions a man's heart, not his color. He joins a gang of thieves and is told by its leader, Danny, that the gang is a kind of league of nations: "Billy's a Polack, I'm Irish, Louis is a white Puerto Rican, and you, who the hell knows?" (p. 208). Thomas is skeptical, but when he proves his courage by robbing a cigar store and is accepted by the others, he believes that he finally has found a group that accepts him for what he can do and not for what he looks like. He remains with the gang for more than a year, robbing small bars throughout New York City, until police pressure forces the gang to disband.

After a one-year hiatus, the gang regroups for another job, and Thomas' account of the attempted armed robbery of a Greenwich Village bar in

February 1950 is a small masterpiece. He re-creates the sense of anticipation and the intensity, confusion, and horror of the action so effectively that the reader seems to be watching the robbery taking place. This particular job is the gang's one failure; the bar is too crowded, the patrons panic, and an off-duty policeman present shoots Thomas. He shoots back, wounding the policeman, and fails in his attempt to escape.

Thomas has structured the first part of his narrative as a literal descent into hell; he has descended through the levels of poverty, racial discrimination, drug addiction, and crime until he finally is stripped of everything, lying naked and wounded under guard in a hospital room. Out of the ashes of one life another is made.

The conventions of the conversion narrative demand a contrast built around the conversion experience, and like others who have written about their conversion experiences, Thomas sets his conversion at the emotional center of his narrative, using it to turn his autobiography into more than a naturalistic look at urban street life. He depicts prison as a hell, a place of physical and emotional punishment, but it also is a place of purgation and potential rebirth. Thomas describes his feelings in prison succinctly:

One of the worst feelings I can imagine is to be something or someplace and not be able to accept the fact. So it was with me—I was a con in jail, but nothing in the world could make me accept it. Not the grey clothes, not the green bars, not the bugle's measuring of the time, not all the blue-uniformed hacks, not the insipid food, not the new lines of my face—nothing. (p. 245)

Although Thomas' accounts of the physical experiences of prison are important, he places his emphasis in the prison sections of his narrative on the effects of solitude and time. Both are crucial to him, for they compel him to begin searching for self-discipline as a way to avoid insanity. Solitude and discipline teach Thomas lessons about himself and his life; they teach him the need for reflection, and like many other writers, Thomas uses his time and reflection to put his life in a new perspective, a perspective that becomes the beginning of his autobiography.

In prison, Thomas meets two men who provide direction for his transformation. The first is Kent, an educated white prisoner whose skillful use of language fascinates Thomas. Kent provides Thomas with more than an interest in words; he introduces him to the world of books and writing, lasting influences. The second person of influence is Muhammed, a Black Muslim minister who teaches him the need for pride and discipline.

Thomas converts; the dignity, stability, and discipline taught by the Nation of Islam provide him with the means of coping with life in prison. He learns, grows, and eventually reenters the culture, and although his religious conversion is only temporary, a real transformation has taken place in his life. Looking back on his decision to become a Black Muslim, Thomas writes:

I became curious about everything human. Though I didn't remain a Muslim after my eventual release from jail, I never forgot one thing that Muhammed said, for I believed it too: "No matter what a man's color or race he has a need of dignity and he'll go anywhere, become anything, do anything to get it—anything." (p. 283)

The final chapters of *Down These Mean Streets* show Thomas' return to the streets of Spanish Harlem and, after a temptation to return to drugs, his turning from the Nation of Islam to Christianity. Thomas' conversion from Muslim to evangelical Christian is described as the second stage of an ongoing process. The Christianity he discovered on his release provided him with the same support that the Nation of Islam did while he was in prison. The suggestion in this part of the narrative is not that evangelical Christianity is superior to the Nation of Islam, but rather that both provide meaning and direction for Thomas. Christianity, however, is depicted as part of Puerto Rican–American culture, and as Thomas moves in that culture in Spanish Harlem, he adapts the lessons he learned as a Muslin and finally adopts Christianity.

Down These Mean Streets is not a typical conversion narrative, although it does contain such traditional elements as the depiction of early transgression, enlightenment in confinement, and good works after the conversion. And although Thomas does describe two religious conversions, his emphasis is on his search for identity and his discovery of his own sense of dignity and self-worth. He depicts religion as a means, not an end.

CRITICISM

Piri Thomas is an important figure in Puerto Rican–American literature. Unlike such earlier Puerto Rican writes as Jesus Colon and Pedro Juan Labarthe, Thomas has no personal connection with Puerto Rico, and English is his native language. His work is the first of the mainland Puerto Ricans, or Nuyoricans. In addition, Thomas captures urban street life effectively. As Wayne Charles Miller notes in *A Gathering of Ghetto Writers*:

Thomas creates in the autobiographical *Down These Mean Streets* a narrative that includes nearly all the elements of ghetto existence: the early gang wars, the early introduction to sex (in this case both heterosexual and homosexual), the early experiments with alcohol and drugs, the terrors of drug addiction, the early encounters with police and the later choice of crime as a means of getting the all-consuming American objective—money. (p. 67)

Down These Mean Streets is a significant autobiography for a number of reasons. First, it is a compelling narrative of one man's struggle to overcome numerous social handicaps. Second, Thomas' autobiography details the impact of racial discrimination and describes the kind of response discrimination can bring forth. Third, Thomas writes eloquently as a representative spokesman for America's fastest-growing minority, Hispanic Americans, and his voice speaks of lessons that must be learned. Finally, the narrative of Thomas' ongoing conversion demonstrates how complex the process is, especially in the contemporary world.

BIBLIOGRAPHY

Cordasco, Francesco, Eugene Bucchioni, and Diego Castellanos. *Puerto Ricans on the United States Mainland: A Bibliography of Reports, Texts, Critical Studies, and Related Materials.* Totowa, N.J.: Rowan & Littlefield, 1972.

Holte, James C. "The Representative Voice: Autobiography and the Ethnic Experience." *MELUS*, 9, 2 (1983):25–46.

———. *The Ethnic I: A Sourcebook for Ethnic-American Autobiography.* New York: Greenwood, 1988.

Klau, Susan L. "The Use of Spanish and the Works of Piri Thomas." Dissertation, University of Puerto Rico, 1977.

Miller, Wayne Charles. *A Gathering of Ghetto Writers.* New York: New York University Press, 1972.

Mohr, Eugene V. "Fifty Years of Puerto Rican Literature in English—1923–1973: An Annotated Bibliography." *Revista/Review Interamerican*, 3, 3 (1973): 290–98.

———. *The Nuyorican Experience: Literature of the Puerto Rican Minority.* New York: Greenwood, 1982.

Thomas, Piri. *Down These Mean Streets.* New York: Alfred A. Knopf, 1967.

———. *Savior, Savior, Hold My Hand.* Garden City, N.Y.: Doubleday, 1972.

———. *Seven Long Times.* New York: Praeger, 1974.

———. *Stories from El Barrio.* New York: Alfred A. Knopf, 1978.

Wakefield, Dan. *Island in the City: The World of Spanish Harlem.* Boston: Houghton Mifflin, 1959.

28 • ALAN WATTS (1915–1973)

In My Own Way

BIOGRAPHY

Alan Watts was born on January 6, 1915, in Chislehurst, England. The son of middle-class parents, Watts was educated at boarding schools—St. Hugh's, 1923 to 1928, and King's at Canterbury, 1928 to 1932. While at school, Watts became interested in Eastern culture through his reading, and in 1930, he discovered a Buddhist organization in London and began attending meetings. At the same time, Watts developed an interest in Zen, Hindu philosophy, and yoga. After he left school in 1932, he worked for his father in London and continued to study Eastern philosophy and culture. In 1932, Watts published *An Outline of Zen Buddhism*, which was followed by *The Spirit of Zen* (1936) and *The Legacy of Asia and Western Man* (1937).

In 1938, Watts married Eleanor Everett, the daughter of a wealthy American Buddhist, and shortly thereafter moved to the United States. From 1941 to 1944, Watts studied at Seabury-Western Theological Seminary in Evanston, Illinois, and in 1945, he was ordained an Episcopal priest. In 1950, after becoming an American citizen and serving as an Episcopal chaplain at Northwestern University, Watts left the Episcopal Church, divorced his wife, and returned to his study of Eastern religion.

During the 1950s, Watts moved to California, taught comparative philosophy and psychology at the American Academy of Asian Studies in San Francisco, earned a doctor of divinity degree from the University of Vermont, and published a number of major works on Zen. Among his most influential works were *The Way of Liberation in Zen Buddhism* (1955), *The Way of Zen* (1957), *Nature, Man, and Woman* (1958), and *Beat Zen, Square Zen, and Zen* (1959). Watts' work was influential in introducing Americans to Zen Buddhism, and throughout the late 1950s and 1960s, Watts wrote and lectured about the subject. In addition to his work on Zen, Watts wrote and lectured about the relations among world religions, Freudian and Jungian psychology, and the potential spiritual benefits of drug use. Watts died in 1973.

THE AUTOBIOGRAPHY

In the prologue to his autobiography, Alan Watts states that he has no business writing an autobiography because he is a sedentary and contemplative character who cannot make up his mind whether he is confessing or boasting. In addition, he writes that he had no story to tell because he had "not fought in any wars, explored mountains and jungles, battled in politics, commanded great business corporations, or accumulated vast wealth" (p. xii). Watts is only half serious as he dismisses the kind of narratives that many autobiographers write. Watts' narrative, *In My Own Way*, written the year before his death, is a record of a spiritual and philosophical journey that took Watts from middle-class life in England to Zen contemplation in Big Sur. Many narratives of contemplative people are as dramatic as the narratives of adventurous ones, and Watts, who writes of spiritual and cultural transformations with both insight and humor, accepts the role of teacher despite his protestations.

Watts begins his narrative, after stating that he does not believe in the "chronological or historical illusion that events follow one another in a one way street, in series" (p. 3), by describing his place of birth as the first step in a chronological account of his life. Watts is deliberately inconsistent; as a Zen teacher, he recognizes that chronological order is only a convention, but as an autobiographer, he realizes that he must use that convention in telling the story of his life.

In the first part of *In My Own Way*, Watts describes growing up in England between world wars. This part of his narrative is dominated by three ideas: a love for Chislehurst, the impact of boarding schools, and the discovery of Eastern philosophy. Chislehurst for Watts was one of the special places he would discover in his life, and he writes that he felt a "sophisticated nostalgia" for the well-forested area southeast of London where he grew up. He describes in detail Rowan Tree Cottage, his family's home, and the woods and gardens of the neighborhood. Watts remembers that his parents decided that he "should be a Brahmin, an intellectual, directed towards priestly, legal, or literary professions" (p. 21), and that became one of the directions for his life. A different direction was movement, and Watts writes that his window at Rowan Cottage faced southwest, and his interests throughout his life, an "interior compass," directed him through the west to the east. Throughout his autobiography, Watts uses a journey westward, from London through New York, Chicago, and California to Japan, to illustrate his spiritual growth.

In the two chapters describing his life at boarding school, "Tantum Religio" and "On Being Half-Miseducated," Watts denounces the spiritual and intellectual poverty of British education. He summarizes his position with the assertion, "I was brought up in a culture that for more than a thousand years had been smothered in and diseased with religion" (p. 46). Watts writes that British education is a representative of British religion, both marked by "intense and solitary seriousness." Writing about his own experiences, Watts recalls that boarding school education taught him to study things but not enjoy them, taught him to eat bad food and live on an arbitrary schedule, and taught him the vocabulary of scatology and sexual behavior. The Anglican Church offered him similar lessons; for Watts the church provided "no joy, no comraderie or conviviality, no sense of being turned on" (p. 61). In response to the emptiness he found in British spirituality, Watts, at age fifteen, turned to the Buddha for refuge.

Watts recognizes that his rejection of Christianity and acceptance of Buddhism was the major turning point in his life, and in his narrative, he devotes an entire chapter to describe the process. Watts had been reading about Oriental culture since he was thirteen, and had been particularly attracted to Edmond Holmes' *The Creed of Buddha* and Lafcadio Hearn's *Gleanings of the Buddha-Fields*. In 1930, he discovered a Buddhist lodge in London and became a member. Watts writes that the Western concept of God that he had been taught—a paternalistic lawgiver with no charm and no delight in the world he had supposedly created—was absolutely alien to him, and when he discovered that millions of people outside of Europe and the Near East had a completely different notion of the ultimate reality—known variously as the Universal Mind, the Tao, the Braham, or Buddha-nature—he immediately felt at home. Watts became awakened. He writes that he had no use for the "Onward Christian Soldiers" approach to life, and that Buddhism, especially Zen, was the right path. He would pursue it, with various interesting side trips, the rest of his life.

Watts writes that "no literate, inquisitive and imaginative person needs to go to college unless in need of a union card, or degree, as a certified lawyer, physician, or teacher" (p. 106). In 1932, after failing to receive a scholarship to Oxford, Watts began to work for his father in London and designed a program for his own higher education. He read Oriental philosophy, psychology, theosophy, magic, astrology, Christian mysticism, occultism, and herbal gardening. In addition, Watts studied the work of D. T. Suzuki, who was translating Buddhist works into English, and Swami Vivekananda, the founder of the Vedanta Society. By 1935, Watts was one of the best-read Englishmen in the field of Oriental religion, and in 1936, he published *The Spirit of Zen*, a popularization of Suzuki's work.

A second transformation began in Watts' life in 1938, when he married Eleanor Everett, the daughter of a wealthy Buddhist, and moved to the United States. While living in New York and teaching at the First Zen Institute, Watts began to reexamine his attitude toward Christianity. He wrote *The Meaning of Happiness*, which examined Eastern philosophy in light of Christian traditions. In addition, he decided to join the Episcopal Church and moved to Evanston, Illinois, to study theology at Seabury-Western Theological Seminary. In 1945, he was ordained an Episcopal priest and became Chaplain at Northwestern University. In describing those years in his autobiography, Watts calls himself a "paradox priest," and although he asserts that the Christian and Buddhist traditions can be understood and appreciated from a common perspective and that an understanding of one can increase the appreciation of the other, he admits to making "mistakes." Watts writes that he was not himself in his role of a Christian priest, especially in a role that called him to pray and preach in an "atmosphere of preoccupation with sin and the niceties of doctrine and belief" (p. 185). Watts records that his reconversion ultimately did not work, and that in the attempt to be of two worlds, he ultimately was more a Zen shaman than a Christian priest.

In 1950, Watts underwent another transformation. He resigned from the priesthood, dissolved his marriage, and went into seclusion. Watts calls this time an interlude between two careers—priest at Northwestern University and teacher at the American Academy of Asian Studies in San Francisco. When he emerged from his retreat, Watts moved to California with a renewed sense of who he was. In writing about his mature rejection of Western Christianity and culture and acceptance of Zen Buddhism, Watts stresses the repressive nature of Western culture and the openness of the Eastern.

In two important chapters in his autobiography, "Journey to the Edge of the World" and "Beginning a Counterculture," Watts describes his life in the 1950s, when his work began to reach a wide American audience and he became a major figure in the development of the American interest in Zen. A sense of place was always important to Watts, and on the California coast between Los Angeles and San Francisco he found what he called "Gondwanaland, the remaining fringe of a lost country that is not part of the United States" (p. 241). For him, this land around Big Sur, Santa Barbara, and Los Gatos became an exotic, romantic, and exciting frontier where East met West. In the mountains along the coast, Watts discovered writers, hermits, philosophers, Christian mystics, and Buddhist monks, and his internal compass told him that this was his home. The descriptions of the California coast are some of the most lyrical passages in the autobiography.

In describing his work in the 1950s, Watts asserts that cultural renewal occurs when radically different cultures interact. Looking back at his writing and teaching at the Academy of Asian Studies in San Francisco, Watts portrays himself as one of the pioneers of the American counterculture. He writes that American interest in Oriental religion and philosophy must be seen in the context of American military and industrial involvement with Japan, Korea, and Vietnam. He describes himself as a successful popularizer of Zen, a teacher who studied and wrote about what interested him in the subject. Because of his studies in psychology, Christian mysticism, and philosophy, Watts was in the perfect position to translate Zen Buddhism for the many Americans who were coming to it for the first time. Watts taught and then served as dean of the American Academy of Asian Studies until 1957, when, already recognized as a master of the subject, he became a free-lance teacher, speaker, and writer. Looking back at his work after leaving the Academy, Watts calls the vocation of an independent philosopher-teacher a happy confusion of work, play, business, and pleasure. Working at home unless on the road giving lectures or seminars, he found both freedom and intellectual stimulation lacking in a more formal role. He also suggests that the major drawback to his work is that many people confuse the philosopher-teacher with the missionary preacher, a vocation Watts firmly rejected.

In the final sections of *In My Own Way*, Watts describes his interaction with two groups of the American counterculture, the Beats and the Hippies. Watts served as godfather for both, being the source for information and popularizer of the works of such artists as Jack Kerouac and Gary Snyder. In addition, in the early 1960s, Watts began to experiment with and later extol the use of LSD and such other psychedelic substances as mescaline, psilocybin, and hashish as means to achieve a kind of mystical state of consciousness. As a result, he became a supporter of the early work of Harvard professor Timothy Leary. Watts describes the Beat movement and the rise of the counterculture in the 1960s as signs of cultural health.

In the final chapter of his narrative, "The Sound of Rain," Watts attempts to define Zen Buddhism and its fascination for Westerners. He writes that unlike any other religion, Zen "has no dogma, requires no particular belief, and neither deals in abstractions nor harps on morality" (p. 360). Instead, Zen is an experience of the universe as it is, an experience in which the individual is completely set free from himself and his ideas. It is, he suggests, like listening to the sound of rain, an experience that needs no translation and that is about nothing but itself.

CRITICISM

Alan Watts wrote more than twenty books on a variety of subjects, including Zen, Christian mysticism, psychology, and myth. In addition, he lectured widely throughout his life and provided weekly radio lectures on radio and several series of television programs for the National Educational Television Network. During his lifetime, Watts was undoubtedly the most well-known writer on Zen and other Eastern subjects in the United States. Two recent biographies exist: Monica Furlong's *Zen Effects: The Life of Alan Watts* and David Stuart's *Alan Watts*.

Watts is perhaps best known as a popularizer of Zen Buddhism. In that role, he made that seemingly esoteric subject available and popular to a generation of Americans. His books, especially *Beat Zen, Square Zen, and Zen* and *The Way of Zen*, were well read and influential. In addition, he was an accessible personality who influenced a variety of people in the United States, including a number of famous American writers, artists, and musicians. His conversion from the Anglican church to Zen Buddhism provided a model for the conversions of many others, and his assertion that Zen and Christianity, at a fundamental level, were not incompatible pointed the direction for exploration in Eastern and Western cultures that is still productive. His autobiography, *In My Own Way*, is a well-written overview of his life and a good introduction to the subject of Zen.

BIBLIOGRAPHY

Acton, Jay, Alan Le Mond, and Parker Hodges. *Mug Shots: Who's Who in the New Earth*. New York: World, 1972, 230–31.
"Alan Wilson Watts." *Current Biography*, March 1962, 43–45.
"Alan Wilson Watts." *Who's Who in America*, 38th ed., 1974–75. Vol. 2. Chicago: Marquis Who's Who, 1975, 3228.
"Eager Exponent of Zen." *Life*, 21 April 1961, 88A–88B+.
Fields, Rick. *How the Swans Came to the Lake: A History of Buddhism in America*. Boulder, Colo.: Random House, 1981.
Furlong, Monica. *Zen Effects: The Life of Alan Watts*. Boston: Houghton Mifflin, 1986.
Gold, H. "Alan Watts." *New York Times Book Review*, 7 March 1976, 10+.
McLeod, Dan. "Alan Watts." In *Dictionary of Literary Biography*. Vol. 16. Detroit: Gale, 1983, 534–39.
Melton, J. Gordon. *Biographical Dictionary of American Cult and Sect Leaders*. New York: Garland, 1986, 302–3.
Moritz, Charles, ed. *Current Biography Yearbook 1962*. New York: Wilson, 1963, 450–52.
"Redbook Dialogue." *Redbook*, May 1966, 52–53+.
Ross, N. W. "In My Own Way." *New York Times Book Review*, 12 November 1972, 50+.
Stuart, David. *Alan Watts*. Radnor, Pa.: Chilton, 1976.
Wakeman, John, ed. *World Authors, 1950–1970*. New York: Wilson, 1975.
Watts, Alan. *An Outline of Zen Buddhism*. London: Golden Vista, 1932.
———. *The Spirit of Zen: A Way of Life, Work and Art in the Far East*. London: Murray, 1936.

————. *The Legacy of Asia and Western Man: A Study of the Middle Way*. London: Murray, 1937.

————. *The Meaning of Happiness: The Quest for Freedom of Spirit in Modern Psychology and the Wisdom of the East*. New York: Harper & Brothers, 1940.

————. *Beyond the Spirit: A Study in the Necessity of Mystical Religion*. New York: Pantheon, 1947.

————. *Zen Buddhism: A New Outline and Introduction*. London: Buddhist Society, 1947.

————. *Zen*. Stanford, Calif.: Delkin, 1948.

————. *Easter: Its Story and Meaning*. New York: Shuman, 1950.

————. *The Supreme Identity: An Essay on Oriental Metaphysic and the Christian Religion*. New York: Pantheon, 1950.

————. *The Wisdom of Insecurity*. New York: Pantheon, 1951.

————. *Myth and Ritual in Christianity*. New York: Vanguard, 1953.

————. *The Way of Liberation in Zen Buddhism*. San Francisco: American Academy of Asian Studies, 1955.

————. *The Way of Zen*. London: Thames & Hudson, 1957.

————. *Nature, Man, and Woman*. New York: Pantheon, 1958.

————. *Beat Zen, Square Zen, and Zen*. San Francisco: City Lights, 1959.

————. *This Is It, and Other Essays on Zen and Spiritual Experience*. London: Murray, 1960.

————. *Psychotherapy East and West*. New York: Pantheon, 1961.

————. *The Joyous Cosmology: Adventures in the Chemistry of Consciousness*. New York: Pantheon, 1962.

————. *Patterns of Myth*. New York: Braziller, 1963.

————. *Beyond Theology: The Art of Godmanship*. New York: Pantheon, 1964.

————. *The Book: On the Taboo Against Knowing Who You Are*. New York: Pantheon, 1966.

————. *Does It Matter? Essays on Man's Relation to Materiality*. New York: Pantheon, 1970.

————. *In My Own Way: An Autobiography, 1915–1965*. New York: Pantheon, 1965.

————. *Clouds Hidden, Whereabouts Unknown: A Mountain Journal*. New York: Pantheon, 1973.

"Wayward Mysticism of Alan Watts." *Philosophy East and West*, July 1980, 381–401.

29 • JOHN WOOLMAN (1720–1772)

The Journal of John Woolman

BIOGRAPHY

John Woolman was born in Burlington County, New Jersey, on October 19, 1720. Woolman's father was a relatively successful Quaker farmer who had friends among the leading Quaker businessmen in Philadelphia. Woolman, the fourth of thirteen children, had ten years of formal education and read widely from his family's library and the libraries of his family's friends. His family provided a thorough Quaker influence, and Woolman, after having some doubts and an emotional religious experience in adolescence, became a devoted and respected member of the Society of Friends (commonly known as the Quakers).

In 1741, Woolman moved to Mount Holly, New Jersey, where he worked for a shopkeeper and later became an apprentice to a tailor. In addition, he worked as a surveyor, drew up legal documents for his neighbors, and worked his farm. The Society of Friends had no ordained ministers; instead, individuals spoke at meetings when they felt moved by the Holy Spirit. Individuals who believed themselves especially called could become public ministers. They were responsible for providing their own support while they traveled to other Quaker communities. In 1742, Woolman began speaking at meetings, and in 1743, he made his first visits to other Quaker communities. Although Woolman traveled extensively along the Atlantic coast and made trips west to the frontier and to England, he usually was away from home less than one month per year.

In 1749, Woolman married Sarah Ellis; his father died the next year. For several years, Woolman had been concerned with the practice of some Quakers of keeping slaves. In 1754, he published *Some Considerations on the Keeping of Negroes*, which pointed out the ethical contradictions inherent in a member of the Society's keeping someone as a slave. In his public ministry, Woolman continually argued against the keeping of slaves. When he visited slave-owning Quakers in Maryland, Virginia, and North Carolina, he would try to persuade the owners to free their slaves. In 1758, Woolman was instrumental in having the Philadelphia Yearly Meeting adopt a resolution calling for the freeing of slaves held by Quakers. In 1761, Woolman decided to give up wearing dyed clothing, believing that such clothing was both an ostentation and a cause for the exploitation of workers, both slave and free.

In response to the call for taxes for the defense of the Pennsylvania frontier, Woolman called for peace missions to native Americans and a refusal to pay any taxes to support the military. In addition, he called for Quakers involved in the government of the colony to resign.

By 1770, Woolman was the leading antislavery advocate in the colonies. He also was a leading advocate of pacifism and better treatment for native Americans. He continued to write, make public journies, and speak at meetings of the Society. In 1771, he sailed to England to meet English Quakers and advocate support for the abolition of slavery and the return to the more radical beliefs of early members of the Society. While in England, he wrote five essays. He contracted smallpox in York and died there on October 7, 1772.

THE AUTOBIOGRAPHY

John Woolman may be the most famous American Quaker, and his *Journal* perhaps the most celebrated Quaker text produced on this continent. As Philips P. Moulton notes in his introduction to his edition of the *Journal* and major essays of Woolman, Woolman's autobiography was influential for Samuel Taylor Coleridge, Charles Lamb, Ralph Waldo Emerson, John Greenleaf Whittier, and Theodore Dreiser. Woolman's writings, especially *Considerations on Keeping Negroes*, *A Plea for the Poor*, and the *Journal*, have been influential since their time of composition. Woolman, writing at a time when American Friends were reaching accommodations with both business success and political power, called his readers back to the radical roots of the Society of Friends and urged them to live up to the ideals of George Fox, founder of the Quakers.

No understanding of Woolman and his writing is possible without a brief outline of the major beliefs of the Society of Friends. George Fox was part of the radical Protestant movement in England during the seventeenth century. A contemporary of John Bunyan, Oliver Cromwell, and John Milton, Fox went beyond most of the Puritan revolutionaries who overthrew King

Charles and established the Commonwealth by asserting that every man was his own teacher and that the Inner Light, sometimes referred to as the Holy Ghost, would lead men to a proper relationship with God and their fellow men. Fox urged his followers to be radical in their dealings with men: They were to swear no oaths, take no interest in worldly goods, avoid war, and follow the Inner Light in love and peace. Rather than rely on an ordained ministry and the close reading of scripture, as did the Puritans, Quakers trusted in the Inner Light, or personal revelation, to guide them. As a result, in most places, members of the Society of Friends were not members of the political and economic establishment. The colony of Pennsylvania, however, had been established by William Penn, a famous and prosperous Quaker. As a result, many Quakers immigrated to the colony, so by the middle decades of the eighteenth century, the Quakers found themselves in the awkward position of being called by faith to live outside the concerns of the world and being called by circumstances to govern a colony. Woolman's *Journal* records the life of a man who discovered that he could not live for both God and man.

Woolman begins his autobiography with the simple statement: "I have often felt a motion of love to leave some hints in writing of my experience of the goodness of God, and now, in the thirty-sixth year of my age, I begin this work" (p. 23). Woolman follows the pattern well established by earlier Christian autobiographers, including George Fox himself, by describing his early life, his experience of conversion, and his acts as a converted Christian. Woolman grew up in a community of faith and never had serious doubts, so his narrative, although including a spiritual conversion, stresses his evangelical work. In the first sections of his narrative, he does describe his early sinful ways. He writes that his parents gave him pious instruction when he fell among wicked children and that he once killed a robin with stones only to realize that the bird's children would die of starvation. He then climbed up in the tree and killed them, afterward being much troubled by the cruelties he committed but made wise about the effects of violence.

Between the ages of sixteen and twenty, Woolman experienced a series of emotional and religious trials. He writes:

Having attained the age of sixteen years, I began to love wanton company, and though I preserved from profane language or scandalous conduct, still I perceived a plant in me which produced much wild grapes. (p. 25)

In addition, he had a series of illnesses, which left him quite weak and doubting. Finally, Woolman records that he "prayed to the Lord for his help that I might be delivered from all those vanities which so ensnared me" (p. 27), and he was then drawn to the "pure Truth" and silently wondered at the change that had been brought on him. Woolman's conversion was neither dramatic nor sudden. Rather, in accordance with Quaker doctrine, it was an ongoing unfolding of truth that began when Woolman was young but continued throughout his life. A reading of the *Journal* that suggests everything after this experience is merely a recitation of the works of the converted Woolman unfairly simplifies the narrative. As he charts his growth in faith and action, Woolman is careful to describe how truth is constantly being revealed and how he must continually adapt his behavior to the demands of his inner light. For Woolman, revelation never ended.

Woolman records that after his conversion, he felt called to the public ministry, and soon after, he felt "drawn" to visit members of the Society who lived in Virginia and Carolina. On this visit, he discovered the basic contradiction that compelled him to confront the issue of slavery: How could one be a member of the Society of Friends and be a slave owner?

In 1746, Woolman began his first Southern journey, traveling for three months through Pennsylvania, Maryland, Virginia, and North Carolina. He records that many of his visits were successful. He found faithful members of the Society in many places, noting, for example, that on the Perquimans River in North Carolina, he held several successful large open meetings attended by young people. He writes that two concerns began to develop. First, whenever he would visit a homestead established by the labor of slaves, he felt uneasy. Second, he observed that the importation of slaves and their use on farms created a class of people drawn to leisure and the accumulation of wealth. Woolman records that these ideas frequently were in his thoughts, and then provides the following summary of his journey:

I saw in these southern provinces so many vices and corruptions increased by this trade and this way of life that it appeared to me as a dark gloominess hanging over the land; and though now many willingly run into it, yet in future the consequences will be grievous to posterity! (p. 38)

It is interesting to note that Woolman's first reflections against slavery arise from personal experience and observation and his awareness of his own ethical dilemma and the consequences of slavery on slave owners. Later, as Woolman continues to consider the question of slavery, he addresses other questions, including the morality of slavery itself.

Throughout the rest of his narrative, Woolman records the evolution of his thoughts on slavery. By 1754, he had come to the position that slave-owning or slave-trading was immoral, and urged the Society of Friends to take a public position on the issue. He argued for this Quarterly and Yearly Meetings as well as in his famous publication *Some Considerations on the Keeping of Negroes*. In 1757, he undertook a second southern journey. On his return, he argued that the Quakers should publicly advocate the abolition of slavery, the visitation of slaveholders, and the exclusion of anyone who buys or sells slaves from the business affairs of the church. In 1762, he published *Consideration on Keeping Negroes: Part Second*, in which he argued that both the Inner Light and scripture prohibit slavery and that neither slave nor slave owner benefits from the system.

Woolman's arguments against slavery are only one of the ethical threads running through the *Journal*. Once Woolman began to examine what the ethical demands on a Quaker were in regards to the keeping of slaves, he refused to compromise. He also refused to speculate without experience. Woolman's *Journal* is a record of his growing recognition of the ethical demands of his faith and his willingness to change the way he lived to conform to his beliefs. Woolman writes, for example, that through the mercy of God he became a successful businessman, buying and selling only things "really useful." However, "the increase in business became my burden, for though my natural inclination was toward merchandise, yet I believed Truth required me to live more free from outward cumbers" (p. 53). After prayer and consideration, Woolman gave up his store and worked only as a tailor and in his orchard. Later Woolman became convinced that much misery was caused by the pursuit of wealth to support such habits as wearing fancy clothing. Again, after prayer, he decided to wear nondyed clothes, but being a prudent man, he wore his old clothing until it wore out.

Perhaps the most dramatic example of Woolman's ethical honesty occurred in 1763. On the western frontier of the Pennsylvania colony, war had broken out with the Native Americans. Chief Pontiac was leading a confederation against white incursions, and the colonial government, including many influential members of the Society of Friends, were forced to raise taxes to support a military response. Quaker doctrine called for pacifism in response to violence, but for many in the Quaker community, that response appeared suicidal. Facing this dilemma, Woolman not only urged Quakers to remain true to their spiritual heritage, but also made a missionary journey to the Wyalusing Indians of Pennsylvania, hoping to prevent war and bring them his Christian faith. Although he was not successful in averting war, he writes that he was "made thankful to God, who thus led me about and instructed me that I might have a quick and lively feeling of the affliction of my fellow creatures whose situation in life is difficult" (p. 137).

Throughout the *Journal*, Woolman gives evidence to an ever-growing awareness of his ethical responsibility for his actions. He writes that if one were to live in true simplicity, one must avoid all exploitation and take no profit or ease from any situation that has been produced by the exploitation of man or beast. His description of his journey to England provides a number of examples of his growing ethical concerns. Woolman writes that his conscience troubled him when he boarded his ship and found his cabin large and covered with "sundry sorts of carved work and imagery" (p. 164). He saw the ornamentations as superfluities, designed to please the minds of those who conformed to the world. Desiring to have no part in conformity or dwell in luxury, he changed his cabin for steerage, where the Lord permitted him to discover the terrible conditions endured by sailors. This leads

Woolman to plead to shipowners to follow the "perfect law" and treat sailors better.

In the final pages of his autobiography, Woolman records a dream he had several years before. He writes that during an attack of pleurisy, he fell into a deep sleep in which he heard the voice of an angel saying, "John Woolman is dead." He then writes:

I was then carried in spirit to the mines, where poor oppressed people were digging rich treasures for those called Christians and heard them blaspheme the name of Christ, at which I was grieved, for his name to me was precious. Then I was informed that these heathens were told that those who oppressed them were the followers of Christ, and that they said among themselves: "If Christ directed them to use us in this sort, then Christ is a cruel tyrant." (p. 186)

Woolman's dream is a summary of his life and ethical system. For Woolman, treasures were meaningless, and only through the works of men could the Inner Light or true nature of Christ be made known. The depiction of the exploitation of the miners, or capitalism without conscience, appeared to Woolman another form of slavery, and it was his duty, and the duty of all true Christians, to oppose such exploitation. Woolman died within a month of recording his dream.

CRITICISM

John Woolman's *Journal* is one of the major works of American autobiography. Two excellent scholars of American autobiography, Thomas Couser, in *American Autobiography: The Prophetic Mode*, and Daniel Shea, in *Spiritual Autobiography in Early America*, note the central place Woolman's work has in American literature. Couser observes that Woolman captures the Quaker ideal and that his *Journal* is as central to the understanding of Quakerism as the work of Jonathan Edwards is to an understanding of Puritanism. In addition, he writes that Woolman challenges his readers by pointing out the contradictions between what Americans professed and how they actually lived. Shea provides a careful reading of the autobiography, noting how carefully crafted a work it is. One of Shea's major observations is how crucial to Woolman is the connection between what a man knows and how he should act. Shea believes that the form and substance of the *Journal* are one:

The central idea of Woolman's *Journal*, then fully informs its style: the self must recede, must be denied, so that Light may enter and Truth be affirmed over personality and individual inclination. (p. 83)

And in his introduction to the *Journal*, Philips P. Moulton lists Woolman's narrative along with Franklin's *Autobiography*, Thoreau's *Walden*, and

Whitman's *Democratic Vistas* as major works of the American autobiography. In addition, he argues that Woolman's work has more than literary value because its insights, especially its ethical convictions, remain relevant to this day.

Other writers have pointed out that Woolman's influence has been more than literary. He has become known as an "American saint," and his arguments against slavery, for the just treatment of native Americans, and against war have made him an influential figure for the abolitionists in the nineteenth century and the antiwar movement in the twentieth.

The *Journal* of John Woolman is a significant narrative for a variety of reasons. First, it is one of the most accessible early American autobiographies. Second, it provides a clear and understandable depiction of American Quakerism in the eighteenth century as well as a vivid picture of the growing ethical conscience of John Woolman. Finally, it is a significant work because the concerns addressed by Woolman remain, to a large extent, the concerns faced by Americans today.

BIBLIOGRAPHY

Altman, Walter F. "John Woolman's Reading of the Mystics." *Bulletin of Friends' Historical Association*, 48 (1959): 103–5.

Cady, Edwin. *John Woolman: The Mind of the Quaker Saint*. New York: Washington Square, 1966.

Carroll, K. L. "Influence of John Woolman on Joseph Nichols and Nicholites." In *Then and Now*. Edited by Anna Brinton. Philadelphia: University of Pennsylvania Press, 1960, 168–79.

Christian, William A. "Inwardness and Outward Concerns: A Study of John Woolman's Thought." *Quaker History*, 67 (1978): 88–104.

Cope, Jackson I. "Seventeenth-Century Quaker Style." *PMLA*, 71 (1956): 725–54.

Couser, Thomas. *American Autobiography: The Prophetic Mode*. Amherst: University of Massachusetts Press, 1979.

Drake, Thomas E. *Quakers and Slavery in America*. New Haven, Conn.: Yale University Press, 1950.

Friedrich, Gerhard. "Theodore Dreiser's Debt to Woolman's *Journal*." *American Quarterly*, 7 (1955): 385–92.

Hintz, Howard W. *The Quaker Influence in American Literature*. New York: Revell, 1940.

Jones, Rufus. "Evidence of the Influence of Quitism on John Woolman." *Friends Intelligencer*, 105 (1948).

———. *The Quakers in the American Colonies*. New York: Russell & Russell, 1962.

Moulton, Philips P. "The Influence of the Writings of John Woolman." *Quaker History*, 60 (1971): 3–13.

———. "John Woolman (1720–1772): Exemplar of Ethics." *The Christian Century*, 4 October 1972, 984–86.

———. *Living Witness of John Woolman*. Wallingford, Pa.: Pendle Hill, 1973.

Peare, Catherine. *John Woolman: Child of Light*. New York: Vanguard, 1954.

Rosenblatt, Paul. *John Woolman*. New York: Twayne, 1969.

Shea, Daniel. *Spiritual Autobiography in Early America*. Princeton, N.J.: Princeton University Press, 1968.

Tolles, Frederick B. *Meeting House and Counting House: The Quaker Merchants of Colonial Philadelphia, 1682–1763*. Chapel Hill: University of North Carolina Press, 1948.

Werge, Thomas. "John Woolman." *Dictionary of Literary Biography*. Vol. 31: *American Colonial Writers, 1735–1781*. Edited by Emory Elliott. Detroit: Gale, 1984, 274–90.

Whitney, Janet. *John Woolman. American Quaker*. Boston: Little, Brown, 1942.

Whittier, John Greenleaf. Introduction to *The Journal of John Woolman*. Boston: Osgood, 1871.

Woolman, John. *Some Considerations on the Keeping of Negroes. Recommended to the Professors of Christianity of Every Denomination*. Philadelphia: James Chattin, 1754.

———. *Consideration on Keeping Negroes; Recommended to the Professors of Christianity, of Every Denomination. Part Second*. Philadelphia: B. Franklin & D. Hall, 1762.

———. *Considerations on Pure Wisdom and Human Policy*. Philadelphia: D. Hall & W. Sellers, 1768.

———. *Considerations on the True Harmony of Mankind: And How It Is to Be Maintained*. Philadelphia: Joseph Crukshank, 1770.

———. *An Epistle to the Quarterly and Monthly Meetings of Friends*. Burlington, N.J.: Isaac Collins, 1772.

———. *Some Considerations on Various Subjects of Importance*. London: Mary Hindle, 1773.

———. *The Works of John Woolman. In Two Parts*. Philadelphia: Joseph Crukshank, 1774.

———. *A Plea for the Poor or a Word of Remembrance and Caution to the Rich*. Dublin: Jackson, 1793.

———. *A Journal of the Life, Gospel Labors, and Christian Experiences of That Faithful Minister of Jesus Christ, John Woolman*. Edited by John Comly. Philadelphia: Chapman, 1837.

———. *The Journal and Essays of John Woolman*. Edited by Amelia Gummere. New York: Macmillan, 1952.

———. *The Journal and Major Essays of John Woolman*. Edited by Philips P. Moulton. New York: Oxford University Press, 1971.

30 • Ann Eliza Young (1844–1930?)

Life in Mormon Bondage: A Complete Exposé of Its False Prophets, Murderous Danites, Despotic Rulers, and Hypnotized Deluded Subjects

BIOGRAPHY

Ann Eliza Webb Young was born in Nauvoo, Illinois, on September 13, 1844. Both her parents were devout Mormons and among the first group of converts to the Church of Jesus Christ of the Latter-Day Saints. Her father, Chauncey G. Webb, was converted by Joseph Smith in 1833, and her mother, Eliza C. Webb, also was converted and became a close friend of Brigham Young. The Webbs moved with the Mormons to Ohio, Missouri, Illinois, and eventually Utah. Chauncey Webb, a wheelwright, was a prosperous member of the Mormon community. He built many of the wagons used by the pioneers on their pilgrimage to Utah in 1847, and he followed with his family in 1848.

Ann Young grew up on the frontier. Her parents had accepted the decrees on plural marriages, and she lived in a polygamous household, although neither she nor her mother were satisfied with the arrangement. In 1863, after working as an actress in the Salt Lake City Theater, she married James D. Lee. The marriage was not successful. The couple lived with Young's parents, and Lee beat his wife. Young divorced Lee in 1865.

Shortly after her divorce, Brigham Young began to seek her out and eventually proposed to her. After initially rejecting his offer to become his nineteenth wife, she accepted, and she and Brigham Young were married on April 7, 1869. For four years, she remained one of Brigham Young's wives, but she left Salt Lake City in 1873 and secured a divorce from him. After her divorce, she converted to Methodism and began a lecture career denouncing polygamy and Mormonism. In 1875, she published the first version of her autobiography, *Wife No. 19, or the Story of a Life in Bondage, Being a Complete Exposé of Mormonism, and Revealing the Sorrows, Sacrifices, and Sufferings of Women in Polygamy, by Anna Young, Brigham Young's Apostate Wife*. In 1908, the second version was published.

THE AUTOBIOGRAPHY

Life in Mormon Bondage is a bitter attack on the Church of Jesus Christ of the Latter-Day Saints and the practice of polygamy. It also is a statement on women's rights and a critique of patriarchal authority. Ann Eliza Young broke with Mormonism and became a Methodist after 1873, and in describing her life, she decided to emphasize the evils she lived with before her conversion. In the title of the first edition of her autobiography, she calls herself an apostate, and the apostate's story, the narrative of one who has given up a particular faith, usually looks backward to the old faith rather than forward to the new. In addition, Young drew on her notoriety as one of Brigham Young's wives to make her critique of Mormon doctrine and practice more effective. She establishes the persona of one who was at the center of the faith and knew its secrets. She knew that revelations have always made for interesting autobiographies.

Because Young intended *Life in Mormon Bondage* to be an exposé of Mormonism and polygamy, she begins her autobiography not with her birth, but with the birth of the Church of Jesus Christ of the Latter-Day Saints. The first six chapters of the text in fact provide an overview of the developing faith from Joseph Smith's early visions to his death and the election of Brigham Young as Prophet. She establishes her attitude toward her old faith in the second paragraph of her narrative:

In this land of boasted light and liberty I was born a spiritual slave, and was trained by fond but deluded parents to hug the chains of that slavery. Knowing no better, I willingly embraced the false creed and grovelling superstition of Mormonism. I yielded submission to its dreadful doctrines and practices. But after many years of patient suffering and mental torment I was providentially rescued from this intolerable bondage and granted the precious blessing of a new life. (p. 17)

This passage provides both an outline of Young's autobiography and a summary of her basic argument. In her narrative, she documents the "false creed and grovelling superstitions" as well as the "dreadful doctrines and practices" of Mormonism, and she does so with language borrowed from slave narratives and Christian conversion stories. In looking back on her life to write her narrative, Young saw a progression from bondage, chains, and slavery to the blessing of a new life.

Young's account of the establishment of the Mormon Church is, as might be expected, different from the orthodox version. Her account of the Angel Moroni's visit to Joseph Smith and Smith's reception of the golden *Book of Mormon* and the silver spectacles with the two transparent stones, Urim and Thummim, emphasizes the fantastic, and her comments on the *Book of Mormon*, which tells the story of Christ's alleged postresurrection appearance and preaching in America to the Native Americans, or lost tribes of Israel, suggest that the entire story was first written as a popular romance. Although discounting Smith's angelic vision and the authoritative nature and even the existence of the famous golden plates, Young does provide a detailed record of early Mormon Church organization, teachings, and movement from western New York to Ohio, Missouri, and Illinois.

In describing the history of the church before the journey to Utah, Young begins to develop two major themes of her autobiography: the development of the doctrine of plural marriage, or polygamy, and the exclusivity of the Mormon community. She writes that although the Revelation on Celestial Marriage was proclaimed by Brigham Young in Utah in 1852, Joseph Smith himself preached and practiced the doctrine, which called for the reestablishment of the biblical patriarchy and the taking of plural wives in order to multiply and replenish the earth with believers, as early as 1840, and this, as well as the business failures of the church, caused hostility among Mormon neighbors and the need for continual removal west.

Young's chronicle of the Mormon experience in Missouri and Illinois provides an important background for the hostility the new church faced and the ultimate decision to transport the entire community to Utah. She writes that in Missouri, Joseph Smith declared that the Lord had given the church control of the state and it was to establish a theocratic government. The gentiles, or non-Mormons, living in Missouri at the time were violently opposed, and soon a full-blown religious war broke out, with atrocities committed by both sides. The Mormons eventually were driven out of Missouri and established a community in Illinois, at Nauvoo, which translated as "The Beautiful" in the "Reformed Egyptian," the language of the *Book of Mormon* and the early revelations of Joseph Smith.

At Nauvoo, Joseph Smith began to establish the pattern of community life that the Mormons would develop in Utah. He built a temple, organized religious and social activities, and began an aggressive missionary program. Mormon missionaries soon had success in England, Denmark, Norway, Sweden, Germany, and Switzerland; and financial support and immigrants soon began to arrive. Because of the success of the Mormon community and its influence in the state, opposition, especially to Smith's Nauvoo Legion, a private military, arose. Young writes that the division between the saints and the gentiles was enhanced by the ignorance each community had of the other. Each side, she writes, was convinced that it was being persecuted for righteous sake, and when rumors of polygamy began to spread, Joseph Smith was arrested, and on July 27, 1844, he and his brother Hyrum were assassinated while in jail in Carthage, Illinois.

Before describing the trek west, Young begins to develop the main theme of her narrative, the impact of polygamy on the Mormon community, and especially the women in the community. She writes that while at Nauvoo, Joseph Smith began preaching the doctrine of celestial marriage to an inner group of saints, including Young's parents. She writes that at first, they were opposed to the doctrine, but that her father was commanded by Smith to "live up to his privileges" (p. 83). Young's mother was opposed, but as a faithful member of the church, she eventually agreed, and her father married Elizabeth Taft. Young writes that from this moment, unhappiness and bitterness entered the family. She observes that

as is the custom with men in polygamy, my father fell more easily into the new arrangement, and even found a certain comfort in it, and he wondered very much that my mother could not be happy as well. Indeed, he became impatient, after a while, that she would not say she was content and satisfied in the new relation. (p. 87)

Throughout her narrative, Young argues that the institution of polygamy destroys all family relations. She contends that before her father's decision to take a second wife, the family was content, but afterward, although her mother remained a faithful wife and a faithful member of the church, family life was a trial. In addition, Young begins to develop her argument that polygamy was part of a conscious program to keep all power and authority in the hands of men and to disenfranchise women, even from the base of their traditional authority, the home. Throughout her narrative she uses the example of her own family, with a good, hardworking father and a strong, kind, and loving mother, as the example of the negative impact of polygamy.

In the central chapters of her narrative, Young tells the familiar story of the Mormon's pilgrimage to the promised land in Utah. Young presents the major events of the exodus: the struggle for leadership after the death of Joseph Smith, the election of Brigham Young as president and prophet, Mormon banishment from Illinois, building the wagon train, the actual journey west, and the establishment of Deseret at the Salt Lake. Because this is an apostate's narrative, Young does not present the standard heroic version of the journey; instead, she uses the major events to continue her criticism of the patriarchial leadership of the Mormon Church. In describing the establishment of the community in Utah, for example, she emphasizes the contradiction between the Mormon practice of polygamy in Deseret and the missionary preaching in the East and Europe that denied the practice. She records the battles between the Mormons and the gentile pioneers who passed through Mormon territory. Her most dramatic example of the hostility of the leaders of the church to the outside world is her account of the Mountain Meadows Massacre, during which a Mormon group led by John Lee attacked a party of Arkansas pioneers heading to California and killed 133 men, women, and children. Lee eventually was captured by federal officers and executed in March 1877 for his part in the assault. Young depicts this event not as an isolated incident, but as a natural outgrowth of the authoritarian control, secrecy, and duplicity of the church leaders. She writes of the period:

The most revolting and blasphemous doctrines were taught, and between Blood-Atonement [the doctrine that it was the duty to kill those who attacked the church], massacres of the Gentiles, and the worst phases of polygamous marriage, there was nothing good in the entire Territory. It was utterly corrupt, a modern Sodom. (p. 238)

Having established the state of the Mormon community in Utah, Young returns to the account of her own family. She describes her father's taking third, fourth, and fifth wives, her mother's suffering, and her own sense of alienation. She asserts that women were forced into plural marriages, men married sisters, and daughters became rivals to their mothers. In her attack on polygamy, Young depicts the Deseret community as a sexual and familial anarchy led by an "absolute monarch," who preached, among other doctrines, that "Jesus Christ was a practical polygamist; Mary and Martha, the sisters of Lazarus, were his plural wives, and Mary Magdalene was another" (p. 238).

In the chapters that follow, Young recounts her own married life, first to James D. Lee and later to Brigham Young. Young and Lee were married in 1863 and lived in her mother's house. Young writes that Lee beat her, and when her parents discovered his conduct, they helped her get a divorce. She also writes that the violence she discovered in her marriage was a direct result of the Mormon attitude toward women. After her divorce, Brigham Young became interested in her, and proposed that she become his nineteenth wife. Although she refused several times, she eventually agreed to help her parents, who were being coerced by Brigham Young to support the marriage.

Anna Young's description of her life as one of Brigham Young's wives is the most personal and most dramatic part of her narrative. She provides domestic portraits of Brigham Young and a number of his wives. Brigham Young's portrait is not flattering. She describes him as a selfish and arbitrary authoritarian who lived in splendor while he forced his wives to work for their keep and take in boarders to pay for the rents of their houses. Her portrait of the wives is far more sympathetic; she sees them as victims of a system of repression in which they have no power or autonomy.

Young recalls that the turning point in her life occurred when she met the Reverend Stratton, pastor of the Methodist Church in Salt Lake. He was the first representative of a religion outside the Mormon belief that she had ever met. She told them the story of her unhappy domestic life and the life of her parents and friends under polygamy, and they, in turn, told her of their views on marriage, "which regarded woman as an independent soul, with a free will, and capable of judgment" (p. 415). This idea of equality seemed like a revelation to her, and after Brigham Young refused to purchase a cooking stove for her, she began divorce proceedings against him. She writes that she was forced to sell her furniture and sneak out of town for fear of reprisals. When news of her flight became known, the case attracted national interest. The trial judge eventually fined Brigham Young for contempt of court and ruled that the polygamous marriage was void.

Young writes that during negotiations before the actual trial, Brigham Young had offered her support if she would drop the case, but she notes that she felt it her duty to expose the system of polygamy and help other women who were forced to live in circumstances similar to hers. She began a lecture series that took her around the country, and while lecturing in Boston, she began to receive instruction in Christianity. Of her decision to convert she writes simply: "This is what I want—this religion of love" (p. 438).

After her conversion, Young continued to lecture against Mormonism and for women's rights. She returned to Utah and helped to convince her parents to convert. In the final chapters of her autobiography, she records the death of Brigham Young and the publication of his will, naming nineteenth wives and forty-six children. She also continues her argument against the church, asserting that despite a public renunciation of polygamy by the leaders of the church and statehood for Utah, Mormonism is a "fundamental treason." She ends her autobiography with a call for Americans to "guard their homes" against it.

CRITICISM

Life in Mormon Bondage was a popular tract among those criticizing the Mormon Church at the time of its publication, and Young used much of the material in her narrative during her lectures. The response by Mormons was to discredit Young by calling her an apostate and her claims lies. One of the few critics who deals with Young is Hugh Nibley, and in his book, *Sounding Brass; Informal Studies of the Lucrative Art of Telling Stories About Brigham Young and the Mormons*, Young is placed within the context of those who drew on early Mormon experiences for personal gain and notoriety.

Young's autobiography is part of another tradition, however. Throughout the nineteenth century, American women used the conversion narrative as a vehicle to record their dissatisfaction with authoritarian, male-dominated institutions. Such diverse writers as Rebecca Cox Jackson and Carry Nation

experienced and wrote about religious conversions as reactions to patriarchial dominance and violence. Anna Young's autobiography, although a
deliberate attack on Mormon practice and doctrine, also is the story of one
woman's search for equality.

BIBLIOGRAPHY

Bitton, Davis. *Guide to Mormon Diaries and Autobiographies*. Provo: Brigham
    Young University Press, 1977.
Nibley, Hugh. *Sounding Brass: Informal Studies of the Lucrative Art of Telling
    Stories About Brigham Young and the Mormons*. Salt Lake City: Bookcraft,
    1963.
Young, Ann Eliza. *Life in Mormon Bondage: A Complete Exposé of Its False
    Prophets, Murderous Danites, Despotic Rulers, and Hypnotized Deluded
    Subjects*. 1875. Reprint. Philadelphia: Aldine, 1908.

Bibliographic Essay

Both conversions and autobiographies pose problems. In autobiographies, all events are filtered through the recollections of the autobiographer, and as a result, what is remembered and recorded is always influenced by such factors as memory and intention. Autobiographies are always subjective. Similarly, conversions are always subjective. In the conversion experience, beliefs, attitudes, and behaviors are changed, and as a result, what is recalled about a conversion is always influenced by similar factors. Any study of autobiography or conversion must confront these problems.

Contemporary students of conversion narratives have a number of excellent guides to assist them. Although few works were available for the study of either conversion or autobiography only a generation ago, recent scholarship has produced a body of work that provides students with invaluable help in confronting the complexities of the difficult subject.

Although almost neglected only thirty years ago, the study of the autobiography has become one of the more popular areas of literary study. Among the more significant general studies of the genre are: Mutlu Konuk Blasing's *The Art of Life: Studies in American Autobiographical Literature* (Austin: University of Texas Press, 1977); Thomas Couser's *American Autobiography: The Prophetic Mode* (Amherst: University of Massachusetts Press, 1979); Paul J. Eakin's *Fictions in Autobiography: Studies in the Art of Self-Invention* (Princeton, N.J.: Princeton University Press, 1985); Louis Kaplin's *A Bibliography of American Autobiographies* (Madison: University of Wisconsin Press, 1961); Phillipe Lejeune's *On Autobiography* (Minneapolis: University of Minnesota Press, 1988); Richard Lillard's *American*

Life in Autobiography (Stanford: Stanford University Press, 1956); James Olney's *Metaphors of Self: The Meaning of Autobiography* (Princeton, N.J.: Princeton University Press, 1972) and *Autobiography: Essays Theoretical and Critical* (Princeton, N.J.: Princeton University Press, 1980); Roy Pascal's *Design and Truth in Autobiography* (Cambridge, Mass.: Harvard University Press, 1960); William Spengeman's *The Forms of Autobiography: Episodes in the History of a Literary Genre* (New Haven, Conn.: Yale University Press, 1980); Albert Stone's *The American Autobiography: A Collection of Essays* (Englewood Cliffs, N.J.: Prentice-Hall, 1981); and Karl Weintraub's *The Value of the Individual Self and Circumstance in Autobiography* (Chicago: University of Chicago Press, 1978).

Among the many useful studies examining specific aspects of the autobiography are Patricia K. Addis' *Her Story: An Annotated Bibliography of Autobiographical Writings by Women* (Metuchen, N.J.: Scarecrow, 1991); Davis Bitton's *Guide to Mormon Diaries and Autobiographies* (Provo, Utah: Brigham Young University Press, 1977); Margaret Bottrall's *Every Man a Phoenix: Studies in Seventeenth Century Autobiography* (London: J. Murray, 1958); Russell C. Brignano's *Black Americans in Autobiography: An Annotated Bibliography of Autobiographies and Autobiographical Books Written Since the Civil War* (Durham, N.C.: Duke University Press, 1974); Stephen Butterfield's *Black Autobiography in America* (Amherst: University of Massachusetts Press, 1974); Thomas Colley's *Educated Lives: The Rise of Modern Autobiography in America* (Columbus: Ohio State University Press, 1976); Susanna Eagan's *Patterns of Experience in Autobiography* (Chapel Hill: University of North Carolina Press, 1984); James Craig Holte's *The Ethnic I: A Sourcebook for Ethnic-American Autobiography* (New York: Greenwood, 1988); Estelle C. Jelinek's *Women's Autobiography: Essays in Criticism* (Bloomington: Indiana University Press, 1980); Mary Grimley Mason and Carol Hurd Green's *Journeys; Autobiographical Writings by Women* (Boston: G. K. Hall, 1979); Georg Misch's *The History of Autobiography in Antiquity* (Cambridge, Mass.: Harvard University Press, 1951); Robert F. Sayre's *The Examined Self: Benjamin Franklin, Henry Adams, and Henry James* (Princeton, N.J.: Princeton University Press, 1964); Daniel Shea's *Spiritual Autobiography in Early America* (Princeton, N.J.: Princeton University Press, 1968); Wayne Shumaker's *English Autobiography: Its Emergence, Materials, and Forms* (Berkeley: University of California Press, 1954); Sidone Smith's *Where I'm Bound: Patterns of Slavery and Freedom in Black American Autobiography* (New York: Greenwood, 1974); and Robert B. Stepto's *From Behind the Veil: A Study of Afro-American Narrative* (Urbana: University of Illinois Press, 1979).

An equally significant body of work has begun to appear on the process of conversion. William James' 1902 classic work, *The Varieties of Religious Experience* (New York: New American Library, 1958), remains invaluable. In addition, among the numerous significant works available to students of conversion are Joe Edward Barnhart and Mary Ann Barnhart's *The New Birth: A Naturalistic View of Religious Conversion* (Macon, Ga.: Mercer University Press, 1981); David Bromley and Anson D. Shupe's *The New Vigilantes: Deprogrammers, Anti-cultists, and the New Religions* (Beverly Hill: Sage, 1980) and *Strange Gods: The Great American Cult Scene* (Boston: Beacon, 1982); Joseph Campbell's *Myths, Dreams, and Religion* (New York: Dutton, 1970); Bernhard Citron's *The Study of the Evangelical Doctrine of Conversion in the Protestant Fathers* (Edinburgh: University Press, Clarke, Irwin, 1951); Walter Conn's *Christian Conversion: A Developmental Interpretation of Autonomy and Surrender* (New York: Paulist, 1986) and *Perspectives on Personal and Social Transformations* (New York: Alba House, 1978); Ronald Enroth's *Youth, Brainwashing, and the Extremist Cults* (Grand Rapids, Mich.: Zondervan, 1977); Billy Graham's *How to Be Born Again* (Waco, Tex.: Word, 1977); Julian Jaynes' *The Origin of Consciousness in the Breakdown of the Bicameral Mind* (Boston: Houghton Mifflin, 1977); Cedric Johnson and H. Newton Malony's *Christian Conversion: Biblical and Psychological Perspectives* (Grand Rapids, Mich.: Zondervan, 1982); William Johnston's *The Inner Eye of Love: Mysticism and Religion* (San Francisco: Harper & Row, 1978); Hugh T. Kerr and John M. Mulder's *Conversions: The Christian Experience* (Grand Rapids, Mich.: Eerdmans, 1983); Weston LaBarre's *The Ghost Dance: Origins of Religion* (New York: Dell, 1970); John Lofland's *Doomsday Cult: A Study of Conversion, Proselytization, and Maintenance of Faith* (New York: Irvington, 1977); A. D. Nock's *Conversion: The Old and the New in Religion from Alexander the Great to Augustine of Hippo* (London: Oxford, 1933); Norman Pettit's *The Heart Prepared: Grace and Conversion in Puritan Spiritual Life* (New Haven, Conn.: Yale University Press, 1966); James T. Richardson's *Conversion Careers: In and Out of the New Religions* (Beverly Hills: Sage, 1978); Steven Tipton's *Getting Saved from the Sixties: Moral Meaning in Conversion and Cultural Change* (Berkeley: University of California Press, 1981); and Chana Ullman's *The Transformed Self: The Psychology of Religious Conversion* (New York: Plenum, 1989).

There are numerous excellent studies of the history of religion in the United States. Among the most useful are Sydney E. Ahlstrom's two volume *A Religious History of the American People* (New Haven, Conn.: Yale University Press, 1972); Joseph Blau's *Judaism in America* (Chicago: University of Chicago Press, 1976); Nelson R. Burr's *Religion in American Life* (New York: Appleton, Century, Crofts, 1971); William A. Clebsch's *From Sacred to Profane in America: The Role of Religion in American History* (New York: Harper & Row, 1968); John Cogley's *Catholic America* (New York: Dial, 1973); E. Franklin Frazier and C. Eric Lincoln's *The Negro Church/The Black Church Since Frazier* (New York: Schocken, 1974); Nathan Glazer's *American Judaism* (2d ed.; Chicago: University of Chicago Press, 1972); Edwin S. Gausted's *American Religious History* (Washington,

D.C.: Service Center for Teachers of History, 1966) and *Religion in America: History and Historiography* (Washington, D.C.: American Historical Association, 1973); Andrew M. Greeley's *The American Catholic: A Social Portrait* (New York: Basic, 1972) and *The Catholic Myth: The Behavior and Beliefs of American Catholics* (New York: Charles Scribner's Sons, 1990); Winthrop S. Hudson's *American Protestantism* (Chicago: University of Chicago Press, 1961); Martin E. Marty's *Righteous Empire: The Protestant Experience in America* (New York: Dial, 1970) and *A Nation of Believers* (Chicago: University of Chicago Press, 1976); Sidney Mead's *The Nation with the Soul of a Church* (New York: Harper & Row, 1975); Richard Niebuhr's *The Kingdom of God in America* (Chicago: Willett, Clark, 1937); Clifton E. Olmstead's *Religion in America: Past and Present* (Englewood Cliffs, N.J.: Prentice-Hall, 1961); James W. Smith and Albert Leland Jamison's *Religion in American Life* (Princeton, N.J.: Princeton University Press, 1961); and Ernest Lee Tuveson's *Redeemer Nation* (Chicago: University of Chicago Press, 1978).

Index

Page numbers in bold refer to the main entries.

About the Author

JAMES CRAIG HOLTE is Associate Professor of English at East Carolina University. His most recent book is *The Ethnic I: A Sourcebook for the Study of Ethnic American Autobiography* (Greenwood Press, 1988).

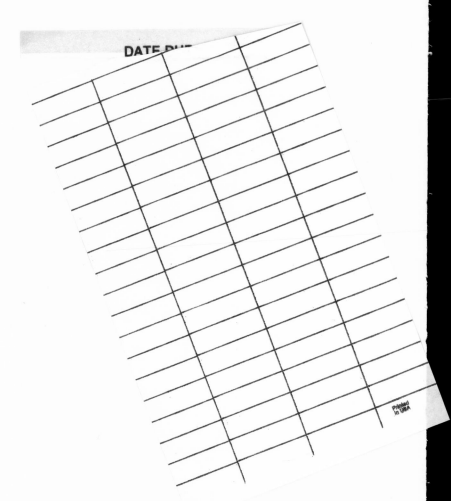

DATE DUE

Printed
in USA